PRAISE FOR

"I cannot imagine a better book on homeschooling well at the high school level than this third book by Leigh Bortins, the doyenne of classical education for homeschooling. Her exhortations to parents to take their responsibilities seriously but without being discouraged, her answers to the hard questions about why we should do it and what to hope for in the end, and the hard-won experience she and her husband share to encourage and illustrate are alone worth the price. But the clear, practical, accessible, copiously illustrated explanations of exactly how to do it—apply the principles of rhetoric to every subject—which occupy the bulk of the book put this at the very apex of the list of homeschooling parents' must-reads."

—**Wes Callihan, Schola Classical Tutorials**

"Having invented a curriculum for the grammar stage in *The Core* and the dialectic stage in *The Question*, here Leigh Bortins invents one for the rhetoric stage in *The Conversation*. Using the five canons of classical rhetoric—invention, organization, style, memory, and delivery—she provides a fine course of study for the high school curriculum, a course animated throughout by her desire to help parents teach their children how to prepare, not for just any life, but for the good life properly understood. Her understanding of the art of rhetoric is clear, informed, and inventive, and her application of that art to the last stage of the classical, Christian homeschool curriculum is fresh, honest, and prudent. As a professor at a university, I would appreciate teaching students formed by the pedagogy here; as a father, I would have greatly profited from it before our own son was grown. Leigh Bortins is a wonderful parent and teacher, and her trilogy, now fulfilled in *The Conversation*, can teach others to practice the calling of the home school—to give young people a liberal education, the one that will free them for a flourishing adulthood, during which they may practice the art of rhetoric—in her ample definition, 'the use of knowledge and understanding to perceive wisdom, pursue virtue, and proclaim truth.' The educational, familial, and civic benefits of *The Conversation* will be great."

—**Scott F. Crider, Professor of English at the University of Dallas, author of *The Office of Assertion*, *With What Persuasion*, and *Aristotle's Rhetoric for Everybody***

"Leigh Bortins has dedicated her career to cultivating a new generation of classical parents, and her years of experience shine throughout the pages of *The Conversation*. If you want to know what rhetoric is, and how and why you should teach it, *The Conversation* is your answer."

—**Janice Campbell**, author of *Transcripts Made Easy* and *Excellence in Literature*

"In *The Conversation*, Leigh Bortins urges families to teach science by sending their students outside and asking questions about their observations. This is right in line with Apologia's educational philosophy known as *Exploring Creation*. Who knows, you might be teaching the next Magellan who will discover new worlds."

—**Davis Carman, President of Apologia Educational Ministries**

"For those armed with truth and understanding, Leigh persuasively argues that the art and science of conversation (or rhetoric) is a powerful and necessary tool for education, for life. Through live conversations, conversations with books, and conversations with themselves, students can discover the interconnectedness of all subjects. These are conversations that can change their lives and the lives of those who enter into their worlds."

—**Chuck Hurst, Home School Legal Defense Association**

Also by Leigh A. Bortins:

"*The Core* provides an altogether practical curriculum, a handy reference work for busy parents who want their children to enter adulthood fully equipped with the knowledge and skills possessed by responsible citizens, discerning consumers, and ethical selves."

—**Mark Bauerlein, author of *The Dumbest Generation***

"Leigh Bortins has spent over a decade breaking new ground in classical education. With this new book, she explores new territories from which every classical educator will benefit. Leigh challenges, beckons, and encourages us to rediscover this inexhaustible treasure."

—**Andrew Kern, founder and president of the CiRCE Institute, author of *The Lost Tools of Writing***

Available from
CLASSICALCONVERSATIONSBOOKS.COM

THE CONVERSATION

Challenging Your Student with a Classical Education

LEIGH A. BORTINS

©2015 Classical Conversations® MultiMedia

THE CONVERSATION
©2015 Classical Conversations® MultiMedia

All rights reserved. No part of this publication may be reproduced, stored in a retrieval system or transmitted in any form by any means, electronic, mechanical, photocopy, recording, or otherwise, without the prior permission of the publisher, except as provided by USA copyright law.

All Scripture quotations, unless otherwise indicated, are taken from the King James Version of the Bible.

Printed in the United States of America

ISBN: 978-0-9904720-2-5

To William, my conversant son.

CONTENTS

Acknowledgments — xi
Preface — xiii
Foreword — xvii

Heather Shirley, *wife and mother of two homeschooled graduates, with one more to follow, seeking a better education while seeking first His kingdom. Founder of Sanctified Woman Ministries (SanctifiedWoman.com).*

Introduction — 1

PART ONE
High School at Home

| Chapter One | Confident Parents | 9 |
| Chapter Two | Rhetoric Defined | 33 |

PART TWO
The Rhetorical Arts

Chapter Three	Reading	53
Chapter Four	Speech and Debate	73
Chapter Five	Writing	91
Chapter Six	Science	109
Chapter Seven	Math	127
Chapter Eight	Government and Economics	145
Chapter Nine	History	159
Chapter Ten	Latin and Foreign Languages	173
Chapter Eleven	Fine Arts	189
Chapter Twelve	A Graduation Conversation	207
Epilogue	Looking Back, Looking Ahead	217

PART THREE
Appendices

Appendix One	Conversation Games	227
Appendix Two	Common Rhetorical Devices	235
Appendix Three	Resources	241
Appendix Four	Real Parents Respond	251
Index		255

ACKNOWLEDGMENTS

Once again, I have the joy of spending a week contemplating ideas with the Classical Conversations MultiMedia writing team as we develop *The Conversation*. Our first day is filled with conversations, the favorites always being the rabbit trails. Is Nicholas Sparks an emotional manipulator? How do you determine if Dickens uses *pathos* correctly? We know when alliteration is overused, but how do you define overuse? How does Milton's definition of rhetoric compare to Aristotle's?

We revisit favorites like Harriet Beecher Stowe, Elizabeth Gaskell, and C. S. Lewis. We remember student stories, children's insights, and modern authors' observations while discussing the chapter outlines. We move from the whiteboard to the lakeside to the dining table to the couch. We talk to employees we supervise, encourage the cook, and check e-mail from family members. Thinking and doing, conversations and silence all mark the first day.

Jennifer Greenholt kindly keeps us on task as the lead editor, knowing she will probably have to write more than the rest of us. Jennifer Courtney reminds us of the literature we've shared, demonstrating copious ideas. Courtney Sanford makes us laugh and laugh and laugh. She is our personal-observation comedian. Kate Deddens, classical to the bone, makes big words and heavy ideas accessible to the rest of us. Matt Bianco reminds us of inconsistencies and gives us permission to redefine old pagan terms into God-honoring ideas. Rather than destroy forests, we choose to water deserts. We choose to redeem rather than reject. Our writing team desires to bring all things into subjection to Christ's thoughts. Praise God for the conversations that bind this team together.

—LAB

PREFACE

Most of us think of rhetoric as a collection of sound bites or as tools of manipulation rather than edification. In order to teach students how to share their knowledge with the world and to be wise leaders, it matters that we reclaim the art of rhetoric as a means to seek truth for ourselves and to point others toward truth. We must engage in conversations about things that matter: God, truth, goodness, love, beauty, virtue, and grace.

Despite its negative connotations, rhetoric is, at its root, a truth-seeking art. We must return to those roots. *The Conversation* explains the five canons of rhetoric in light of real assignments completed by students pursuing classical education and real conversations that have taken place between parents, tutors, and students.

Conversations are the best way to fall in love with a person or an idea. I am fortunate to have people who value conversation in my home often. Most of them also like children and have lots of them. They agree with Canadian author Michael O'Brien who said in *The Island of the World* that a child is a "living icon, a strong and delicious word never before seen, never to be repeated." We converse with our families because we live. We have favorite words and favorite topics like feasting, incarnation, and imagination. We want our children to feast on math problems, incarnate truth and love, and imagine their legacy and their eternal inheritance.

A young woman who recently graduated showed me her 20,000-word booklet on classical music and art. She was appalled by her writing skills from two years earlier, and I applauded her for her improvement over two years.

Her faithfulness to communication prepared her to later earn income from it. Some students write as though no one will read their writing. My young author has now learned differently. Her effort has been rewarded. These kinds of conversations with teenagers speckle my daily life and explain my passion for homeschooling classically through high school.

I wrote *The Core* to encourage parents to provide a basic, thorough education for their young children. Then my team and I wrote *The Question* to call adults to cease lecturing and instead to lead students through difficult and important material by asking questions. Now we offer *The Conversation*. We want young adults to think and to challenge and to engage their elders and one another in conversation. Formal education tends to remove the natural inclination to ask questions that lead to interesting conversations. Conversations don't seem like academic skills, because their very nature implies multiple answers, not a single right answer to mark on a bubble sheet. The purpose of this book is to bring civil discourse back into our family culture.

Section 1 (chapters 1 and 2) provides an overview of rhetoric while encouraging parents to guide their young adult's education through high school. Section 2 (chapters 3 through 12) models a rhetorical education in the major subject areas your student is likely to cover in high school, providing real-world examples of the conversations and projects that will allow your family together to recover the lost tools of rhetoric. In the epilogue, I ponder the results of classical, Christian, community-based education now that the last of our four sons is nearing graduation.

FOREWORD

There are some conversations you never forget. They stay with you. They change you. One of my first conversations with Leigh Bortins changed me. With my three young children gathered around my knees, I met this woman who had started something called "Classical Conversations," and it had something to do with something called "classical education." As we conversed, she introduced me to a whole new language and set of ideas that would forever change how I viewed learning and education.

Through my conversation with Leigh and the encouragement of my dear friend Sheila, I joined the local Classical Conversations community of homeschoolers. There I began to learn again alongside my children. Throughout the elementary years, we memorized facts, events, Latin endings, poems, songs, and speeches, and we explored the natural world, artists, and composers. Our young family learned together.

As my children grew into the middle school years, our conversations grew through good questions. The questions I asked changed as well. I stopped limiting our questions to those about SAT scoring or about how what we were learning was immediately useful. Our questions expanded as we considered truth, goodness, and beauty. We began to evaluate what is permanent or eternal and what is merely temporal. With questions like these fueling our studies and conversations, we often enjoyed summers sitting near a body of water with good friends, learning language structure, diagramming sentences, reading books, learning mathematics, and enjoying science. We did the hard work of learning so we could traverse the challenging terrain of educating our children at home.

As my children moved through the high school years and then graduated from our home school, we enjoyed more conversations with Leigh, with new friends, with old friends, and with one another. Our children talked with their friends about things that are true, good, and beautiful. We read great books together, we worked translations together, and we worked geometry problems together. We discussed and debated ideas of justice, good, evil, love, sacrifice, grace, truth, life, and death together. We increasingly saw order and harmony in creation and created things. With each conversation, we learned more, saw more, and helped each other to see more. That's the power of conversations—they bring sight.

What you hold in your hand is a small artifact of a much larger vision for education, both for you and your children. This book is sure to spur you to begin new conversations and to join old ones. I pray it ignites and fuels more great conversations in your home, in your community, and in all the places you find yourself. You never know who is ready and waiting for the next unforgettable conversation.

Heather Shirley, *wife and mother of two homeschooled graduates, with one more to follow, seeking a better education while seeking first His kingdom. Founder of Sanctified Woman Ministries (SanctifiedWoman.com).*

INTRODUCTION

As my eighteen-year-old son, William, plopped into the chair with a plate of food, I asked, "What'd you do today?" He prayed for his food and then responded, "I tore up a deck with John, and then I studied wealth transition. I learned about the rule of 72. I think I do want to be an apprentice to that finance guy when we get back from Australia."

This kind of conversation is a normal part of our family's life. The breadth of conversation with my children and their friends stuns me as they learn about the things they love. The same way a converging lens focuses a beam of light, classical education allows me to focus on teaching my children the foundations and essentials of knowledge so they are equipped for the challenges of life. Now that they have worked through the core knowledge and the questions that comprise a classical education, it is time for the fruit: conversations.

My husband, Rob, and I have four sons, homeschooled through high school with at least some semblance of a classical education. We didn't start educating classically until the older two, Robert and John, were in middle school, but both of them have caught a lot of what we taught their younger brothers William and David. As I write this book on teaching in the rhetoric stage of high school, our last two sons are completing their home education. At least that's the way it may look to the rest of the world. To us, education is never finished. Our eldest sons are about thirty years old, and they are still learning. After earning college degrees, they moved back to our neighborhood to build the family businesses and raise their own families. The dynamic nature of life inspires them to learn constantly. Our next two sons are investigating their options for adult education.

Like parents of most young adults, we have conversations about college and career, service and mission, purpose and production, as William's comment about the apprenticeship shows. He could easily go to college, but his high school years have been so rich with teaching opportunities that he wants to live with men he can learn from and serve at the same time. He is already pondering living with a classical educator on the west coast after training with the finance guy in the South. Last year, he lived with a family in Alaska so he could hunt and fly planes. This year he's living in Australia. While his brother David plays rugby, William is producing math resources with a team of other young people. He has a lot to talk about, like other young adults do when they reach the rhetoric stage of education.

While sitting on the deck, completely exhausted from eleven hours of hard labor, he shared his plans to study finance, reminded us to bring his needed data so he can work on college applications, and applied the economic ideas he had studied to the family businesses. No one told him he had to work this week, but he would rather work than spend his time with technology. No one told him to study finance in the evenings. His school year has officially ended, but he has big decisions to make about his future and he wants to be sure he can afford them. Young adults have active minds and bodies, so they need to be busy. In the rhetoric stage, the classical model teaches them to be productive and to include others while pursuing the things they love.

William also recently performed both vocally and instrumentally before an audience of two hundred, even though he is new to these studies. He spent an intensive year studying performance, voice, and music theory while continuing his classical studies in history and philosophy, astronomy and physics, and working part-time. Yet he managed on a weekly basis to play rugby, attend church, help clean warehouses, and watch many movies. As a senior in high school he may miss the prom, but he goes swing dancing occasionally with his friends. He does these things because he loves life, not in order to earn a degree.

Our youngest son, David, is the fourth classically educated son in our family, so he grew up around all kinds of stories from different subjects. David hangs out with both theater types, who speak with good diction and memorize long passages of Shakespeare, and rugby players, who use foul language and seem to have a limited vocabulary. He likes to learn big words from the one crowd and share them with the other crowd. He uses a "Word of the Day" app in case he doesn't hear a good word to use from his daily conversations. I found out about this in a typically "David" way. He was demanding from a friend a very clear definition of a word. I asked him why he was so adamant about understanding the proper use of the word, and he explained, "The guys on the team think I am smart, and I don't want to let them down."

David is also committed to athletics. He does cardio, weightlifting, speed training, agility training, and rugby practice on a daily basis. One of the reasons we homeschool during high school is so that our boys have time to work hard at the things they love. David has used this freedom to his advantage athletically. He would love to play rugby in college and even in the 2020 Olympics. Our current conversations deal with kinesiology, nutrition, fitness, college in England, rugby academies in Scotland and New Zealand, and how to keep him free from injury. More important, we discuss parameters on attitude and responsibility so rugby does not become an idol. David happily completes his school assignments because he can't practice until he's finished all of his other tasks.

One of David's friends is another classically educated student who has worked in his father's sales business since he was a small boy. This young man loves telling stories about doing his school work and also learning his father's business while in the office. In sales, he has learned to help people, even if they are upset. Whenever I see him, he yells, "Happy Tuesday, Mrs. B. Isn't it a great day? Can I do anything for you?" He has taught us all to say, "If you act enthusiastic, you'll be enthusiastic!" Like William, these boys love life and learning.

Do William and David and their friends have exceptional lives? I hope all of my children do and that yours do too. But their lives are comparable to the other classically trained, homeschooled students in my community and in communities around the world. They dance, sing, travel, play instruments, study rigorous subjects, work with their parents, and serve in the community. They love Latin, physics, and literature. They take SATs, APs, and apply to colleges. They quote Aristotle, Augustine, and Aquinas as well as Sherlock Holmes, Bilbo, and Adele. They paint houses, plant gardens, and play Ultimate Frisbee. They do the same things as other high school students but with a subtle twist: they know the names of the giants of history on whose backs we all stand.

We all benefit from the hard work and sacrifice of those before us, but these students not only recognize the names "Einstein," "Kepler," "Washington," and "Lincoln" but also recognize the men's influence on modern times. They don't measure their thoughts by their own opinions but by those of individuals who are older and wiser. They seek answers in light of truth, goodness, and beauty, rather than personal preference or modern trends.

Does this description sound unrealistic? It is not. I am privileged to work with dozens of students who have been classically trained by their parents, and their maturity is remarkable. They have conversed with adults most of their lives rather than primarily with groups of other children. When you add quality content to this early maturation, it is not surprising that these students do well with academics and with life. Even more impressive is that their parents were not classically educated. Instead, these parents have entered classical education from many different backgrounds, unified by a hunger to access the great classical conversations of history and to realize great opportunities in the future.

Opportunities abound for students with a profound love of life and learning. The business community seeks to hire our children, the service community mentors our children, the church community disciples our children, and the academic community welcomes our children. These wider communities enhance our students' conversations. Students who have been educated at home and in community don't think of young children as bothersome or older adults as irrelevant; instead, they treat them as extensions of their families and are therefore comfortable entering into relationships with people of all ages.

These student experiences used to be more common. Mark Bauerlein explains in *The Dumbest Generation: How the Digital Age Stupefies Young Americans and Jeopardizes Our Future*:

> Many generations ago, adolescent years meant preparation for something beyond adolescence, not authentic selfhood but serious

work, civic duty, and family responsibility, with parents, teachers, ministers, and employers training teens in grown-up conduct. (168)

Young adults succeeded in making the transition because wise and loving mentors trained them for adulthood.

Today, our society has different expectations. Instead of expecting adolescents to run the family farm competently for a week in their parents' absence, society often extends adolescence well into the twenties. Instead of spending time with them, training them in job skills and life skills, we have created school environments in which they are limited to interaction with same-age peers. Peers, instead of adults, have become their counselors and mentors. Teachers struggle to mentor them because each teacher sees them for only 55 minutes per day. Parents struggle to mentor them because children are rarely home. When they are ready to practice the responsibilities of adulthood, we hold them back. Long school days make apprenticeships, meaningful work, and community life almost impossible. Our limited expectations for young adults have created the stereotypical teenager—irresponsible, disrespectful, and difficult.

Homeschooling is not perfect, but it does provide opportunities to transition young people into adulthood. Older children can be given the responsibility for younger siblings; many older siblings have even taught younger siblings to read and write and have tutored them in math. Centering education at home naturally affords more time for chores and home improvement projects. Our boys have laid tile, painted rooms, and helped build an addition to our house. Because our boys are not tied to a classroom, they have also worked in our family businesses. In all of these activities, we have been blessed by other interested, loving adults who have mentored our boys.

As a society, parents must reclaim the wise, loving guidance of their young people. Business owners should offer apprenticeships. Pastors should walk alongside children and answer their questions. When Rob and I first began homeschooling, we hadn't decided to homeschool through high school. However, by the time the boys reached that age, we knew we wanted to continue. We had grown to love being with our boys and to love the home-centered life we had created. We loved the freedom of reading books together, studying with other families, and exploring new activities like camping, scuba diving, and flying lessons. We loved running our business together, sharing great books together, and engaging in long hours of great conversations together. We didn't set out with a list of reasons we would homeschool in high school; rather, we pursued a life we loved. It has been a joy for a few main reasons:

A big classroom. My boys weren't confined to a school for the best hours of their day. Instead, we were able to explore life. We could learn on family vacations, take advantage of classes with traveling experts, and minister to our neighbors.

Great conversations. I loved rocking our babies, but there is something really special about the conversations I have with our children as they mature. They begin to ask really good questions about life. We walk alongside them and witness the opening of their minds as they begin to make sense of suffering, injustice, hardship, and heroism.

Real-life opportunities. It is curious that people consider school to be preparation for real life. At no other time in life are we segregated by age or moved in response to a bell. It is no wonder that students ask, "When will I use this in real life?" School doesn't show them real life. I am grateful that my boys have been able to study great books, to work, and to explore interests like rugby. Real life seldom happens in a man-made classroom; it happens all around God's classroom.

PART ONE

HIGH SCHOOL AT HOME

CHAPTER ONE

CONFIDENT PARENTS

> "Far better it is to dare mighty things, to win glorious triumphs, even though checkered by failure, than to take rank with those poor spirits who neither enjoy much nor suffer much, because they live in the gray twilight that knows not victory nor defeat."
> —Theodore Roosevelt, *Strenuous Life*

Over the last two decades, homeschooling has grown by leaps and bounds. Even so, a large number of children end up going to traditional schools for middle school, and an even larger number transition in high school. Why do parents who are committed to homeschooling their younger children switch their older children into institutions? What shakes their confidence in themselves or in the successes of homeschooling?

Over the years, I have learned one thing: parents love their children and want the best for them. Yet, it is hard to escape our past. We revert to cultural conformity when our confidence is shaken. Cultural constructs pre-form our choices and often prevent us from seizing unusual opportunities if we have doubts. Many parents doubt their ability to replicate the resources of a large high school. In addition, the course material may seem daunting. We are more comfortable duplicating our childhood school experience, instead of going with our initial instinct that institutional education is not the best method. Over the three decades I have spent homeschooling and working with homeschooling families, I have recognized the power of a confident parent. Before I describe classical education in high school, I will address the most common concerns parents have. I hope this chapter will grow parental confidence before the rest of the book enlarges the cultural vision for high school education. Let's look at the role of a homeschooling parent.

Homeschooling is a team sport. Our goal is not to launch our children as individuals, but to unify a family that can face the challenges and rewards of life as a team. Just like any other team, we have coaches, practices, and rules of the game. Coaches help players do things they neither wanted to do nor thought they could do as they lead. Coaches earn the respect of their players and have more knowledge than they do. On days when the players are sick of drilling the fundamentals, the coach doesn't lose sight of the team's goals. When the players feel unmotivated or defeated, the coach looks for ways to rejuvenate and refresh the daily practice while sticking to the team development plan. A beloved coach has the authority to lead her team and develop good fundamentals through daily practice habits. The coach doesn't do all of the physical labor—that is the players' responsibility. Rather, the coach ensures the players do the work. The coach demands excellence, offers advice and encouragement, slows down to teach details, and celebrates victories small and great. These attributes of a coach are true for any team sport.

As a homeschool parent, you are the coach, and your high school students are the players. The parent sees the end goal better than her student and counts on the student's respect for her authority when the child doesn't see why he has to drill or study a boring fundamental. The parent also recognizes that drilling the fundamentals develops good habits that strengthen a multitude of weaknesses. The parent can trust good habits to support the student when she is occupied elsewhere. Trusting the parent's authority and relying on good study habits allows a young adult to learn anything, just like good coaching fundamentals apply to learning how to play any game.

In summary, parents, like coaches, contribute to their children's education in three ways: authority, habits, and content.

- **Authority** doesn't mean "my way or the highway." It means that a high school student is mature enough to honor his parent's wishes.

Respecting authority is not the same as obeying authority. Honest respect comes from living together in a way that develops trust between the generations.
- **Habits** supply the daily structure of life. As adults, we know that the little habits make life work. My main job as a homeschooling mother of young men is to help them own the habits I taught them as children.
- **Content** is not the most daunting aspect of learning. When students trust their parents' authority and have developed good study habits, learning difficult content becomes manageable. Rather than delivering much of the content, the parent becomes a trusted advisor, facilitator, and tutor. Books, mentors, experiences, activities, and organizations contribute to the content.

Each of these three provisions counters some common fears and concerns parents often face. In the next section, I'll explain how.

Throughout this book, I hope to serve as a coach. Sometimes I will give advice, tips, and tricks; sometimes I will give a stern warning; sometimes I will explain specifics; and sometimes I will provide encouragement to do hard things because I see the goal. I have lived through it myself four times and have walked alongside others. When I seem especially emphatic, it is because I failed at that idea and now I see its importance. I want to spare you that experience.

AUTHORITY

I use the word "authority" rather than "responsibility" because it represents more accurately the parent's side of the relationship. A leader has the authority to teach others their duties. Older students should be responsible for the majority of their decisions, but they should honor the adult's authority when a course correction is necessary. For example, David wanted to study health and nutrition instead of general biology. I allowed him to make that deviation from the curriculum as long as he took his weekly biology lab seriously, including studying the biology text. I also increased his Latin load to make up for the easier course work. We were both satisfied because I could trust David to do the extra work and he could trust me to balance his educational experience. Many homeschooling parents let their young adults choose to go to school. That is not a burden we would place on our children. We do not expect students to be able to work out the machinations of the educational bureaucracy with wisdom.

Children are natural meters for hypocrisy.

If our growing children don't respect our decisions, we must determine why. Honor is given to the parent who models the same kind of living that is expected of their children. Children are natural meters for hypocrisy. Learning to obey does not guarantee trust and respect. My adult children are the best mirror of my failings. Sometimes I want to send them away to another teacher because the reflection is ugly. We all fail at parenting, but as Christians we know the power of forgiveness—God's mercies are new every morning. I will fail daily, but I will not give up.

How does authority affect socialization?

The beauty of homeschooling is that its flexible schedule allows time for reading, writing, and arithmetic in addition to employment, athletics, church attendance, fine arts, and service work. Balancing extracurricular activities is one way the homeschooling parent can gain the respect that should go along with her authority.

Look for a blend of activities that match your children's passions, your family's limitations, and your academic goals. Homeschooling may lack the convenience of giving your fifteen-year-old classes, debate club, and sports all in one location; however, including your children as you plan time commitments and the family's budget will help them understand why the family has to work together to make the best decisions for everyone. They will see the difficulty of being in two places at once and value the compromises the parents make to work out the best for everyone. They will grow up noticing that mom and dad think carefully and sacrifice often for the family. They will experience disappointments as young adults, but they will understand the reasons for them.

If socialization means peer-based activities, don't worry. Most communities around the country offer so many opportunities for homeschoolers that it can be difficult to stay home at all. Dedicated homeschooling families around the country have organized homeschool bands and choirs, high school sports leagues, PE classes, art classes, and much more. Parent-run homeschool co-ops and communities allow students to discuss literature and complete science labs together as well as to make oral presentations in front of their peers. Studies of social aspects of students from all kinds of schools place homeschooled students at or above the national average. For statistics on homeschool alumni, see Brian Ray's book, *Home Educated and Now Adults* (NHERI Publications, 2004). Our sons have participated in sports, bands, proms, dances, and field trips. Interested parents and creative business people provide a myriad of social opportunities for homeschooling families. I have learned to know our community members better as I look for those opportunities.

Here is a typical week for one of our sons in high school:

Sunday—church, lunch with friends, movie night

Monday—schoolwork, prepare for seminars

Tuesday—seminars with Classical Conversations students (Shakespeare reading, chemistry lab, algebra discussion, logic practice, writing analysis, Latin translations), rugby practice, dinner at older brothers' house

Wednesday—schoolwork, flying lessons, music practice

Thursday—schoolwork, construction work, rugby practice, dinner with study group

Friday—schoolwork, construction work, dinner and dancing with friends

Saturday—travel for rugby tournament

Meals with the family, dancing and Shakespeare with friends, rugby with other friends: this is an average week. Camps, travel, special course work, political events, online activities, and household chores are also part of an average week. If a school club exists, homeschooling parents and students will create the same opportunity. When another son, David, applied to play rugby in Australia, "homeschool" was a choice on the application, signifying how common homeschooling has become. Socializing through activities is not a problem.

Parents may be concerned that their older children won't have many friends. When we think of our own high school experience, many of us remember having only a few good friends even in a large school. It's hard to be friends with too many people in spite of the promises of social media. Your job is to make sure your child has plenty of time with one or two true friends.

When people curious about homeschooling ask about socialization, they should also include negative socialization. Does it automatically follow that we make more friends in large groups? Bullying and negative peer-pressure are equally likely to occur. Some students will feel left out whether they are at home or in an institutional school, while others simply prefer spending time alone. If you are making decisions based on the question of socialization, be sure your assumptions are realistic.

Our sons' best friends tend to be their homeschooled friends and their fathers since most of the young men they know are close to their fathers too. Discussing theology with church elders, shooting guns with their older brothers, watching sports with their father, and doing dishes for their friends' mothers are additional times for socializing in the context of authority that they can trust. Because we value wisdom as well as fun and work, we make sure our sons hang out with grown men as well.

Consider what kind of "normal" you desire for your children. When my friend's college-aged daughter commented that homeschoolers were weird, she replied, "Is that because they make eye contact when adults speak to them?" Being weird can be a good thing. Businesses, colleges, and parents seek out homeschooled high school students to work, recruit, and babysit.

If homeschooling means your kids stay home all day with no chance to pursue interests, then they will be miserable. If homeschooling means the whole world is the classroom, then what young adult would choose to stay in the same building all day? The parents who demonstrate that the world is a resource will raise children who respect their authority. If I want our boys to do hard things, I must do hard things. If I say the world is our classroom, I better get out there and show it to them!

The heart of socialization is communication. We want our students to express themselves well so that they may transfer information clearly to associates. We want our children to express their thoughts precisely, appropriately, and kindly. This is the definition of successful socialization.

The heart of socialization is communication.

How can I spend so much time at home?

In other words, what about socialization for parents who choose not to work or to work from home so they can homeschool their children?

Re-evaluating authority takes an interesting turn for the homeschooling parent. Making your own schedule and friends takes initiative, an important skill to teach your children. The loneliest times in my life have been at points of transition: entering high school, entering college, and leaving work to stay home with my young children. In high school, I had trouble finding like-minded peers, so I went to work and spent time with adults. In college, I was failing academically, so I made friends with self-described geeks who taught me how to learn. As a stay-at-home mom, I went through a year of depression. I had no schedule and no friends, so I befriended those unusual women called homeschool moms. I haven't been lonely since!

My friends are other homeschooling parents who are as committed as I am to the classical model of education. I have recently gained a new appreciation for my homeschooling friends now that we are completing this glorious journey. The same friends who took our children camping or lent us math books or joined us in book discussions are now available to continue the conversation with my husband and me and with our grown children. These friends provide caution to our children transitioning to full independence, encouragement to us as we train for post-homeschooling careers, and empathy over trials with grandchildren. We share the joys of having grown children competent beyond our abilities and pray together as they face adult struggles. Remember that life will be more fruitful if you cultivate your own friendships with supportive families. Thankfully, homeschooling today offers many opportunities for parents to gather and support one another. That's one of the benefits of Classical Conversations.

Besides facing the fear of loneliness, considering homeschooling requires making careful career decisions. It is daunting to think about becoming a single-income family, giving up professional relationships, or relinquishing a mission or cause. When Rob and I first decided to homeschool our children, it seemed impossible to live on one income; however, we decided that my ability to make my own schedule with our children outweighed any monetary resource. Eating peanut butter sandwiches at home with our sons replaced eating lunch with professional colleagues. Guiding the boys gently through their school frustrations rather than helping a colleague with her workload and celebrating their childhood joys rather than a co-workers' promotion began to provide a better return on my time. My need for personal space lessened as I enjoyed sharing a life with my husband, my children, and the families in our community. Taking charge of my time and cultivating deep friendships was a process I enjoyed sharing with our children.

As it turned out, staying home with my sons did not preclude other opportunities for entrepreneurship. The workforce is changing. Many homeschooling parents run successful businesses from their own homes. Nothing is guaranteed, but you may be surprised at the opportunities that emerge when you step out in faith.

What do I do if I don't get along with my student?

In all honesty, there are days when I want to abandon my children. I get tired and need a break just like anyone else. I have things I want to do. I tell our sons that I have to get just one more report finished, or travel just one more time this month, or get through one more conference call, and then I will be available. Thankfully, the Lord reminds me of the long-term game plan and renews my energy and desire.

One evening I was tired and watching a movie. I could hear our youngest son watching the NFL draft picks. I have no interest in the NFL, but I could hear him shouting, "Yes! Yes!" or "Aww!" as I watched a movie that wasn't engaging. Even though I was cozy and didn't want to move, because I love David, I joined him and watched the NFL draft picks. We held hands, prayed, and held our breath as we waited for the all-important thirteenth pick allotted to the Panthers. We groaned with disappointment when David's pick was bypassed. We ate popcorn and drank root beer while he told me about each of the players and the owner's strategies. It is all forgotten, except one thing—my fifteen-year-old, six-foot-one-inch son let me hold his hand while we watched television. I loved watching the NFL draft pick because I love my son. I love math because I love my son. I love Latin because I love my son. Love motivates me to learn these things.

Maybe you feel like your children reject your love. Many parents who want to homeschool through high school worry that they will "butt heads" with a certain child. This is normal at this stage—it's called the dialectic, discussed in *The Question* and referenced in the rest of this book. Young adults, much like toddlers, yearn to know the limits of their independence. If you recognize this struggle as healthy for the adults and the children, homeschooling shouldn't be any more difficult than normal life.

What if you are dealing with rebellion and your child doesn't respect you? If respect for authority is what you want to instill, stop reading this book. Get your child, find an ice cream shop, share a cone, and say, "You are and will always be my best beloved child. You have grown into a man so fast that my head is swimming. I've never been a parent to you at this age before, and as soon as I have practiced and am any good at it, you will be a different age, and I will need more practice. But there is one thing you should know: I will never abandon you to yourself. I will fight for you, alongside you, and with you. I will do whatever it takes for you to learn to serve others before yourself. Help me as I help you to make our relationship stronger." I have had to say something similar to my growing sons a few times.

If your child is rebellious, please step up to the difficult task before you. Get serious help, but don't relinquish your duty as a parent. Getting wayward adolescents out of the house by sending them to school will make you a peacekeeper rather than a peacemaker. Christians *make* peace. (Read Ken Sande's books to understand the difference.) Your children, your teenagers, and your young adults need to know that you will fight for them. Rebellion can be an understandable response from a youth who has been taught to be cynical. A wise adult looks for ways to empower adolescents while safeguarding them. This takes maturity and time that many do not allot and wisdom that is beyond the scope of this book.

It's difficult to walk through our own sanctification when someone we love is causing so much upheaval in the family. You will walk the road plowed by a child's rebellion no matter what, so don't cover it up. Instead, pray for the spiritual authority of the Holy Spirit to bathe your soul with peace and wisdom that passes understanding. If mental illness is revealed through these trials, please seek medical and spiritual counseling immediately.

You will walk the road plowed by a child's rebellion no matter what, so don't cover it up.

What if the rebellion is not constant but occasional? Keep these occasional tantrums in perspective. Even for those with high school students who love learning at home, the house of a homeschooler is infinitely chaotic and frustrating and, at the same time, the most beautiful thing in the world.

Parents will enjoy the rush of the whirlwind and should expect to be knocked about. Young adults have large bodies and lots of friends. Our home is always busy.

Young adults are delightful. They are still young and impressionable enough to be influenced by parents while old enough to be trusted and responsible for independent work. Don't give up your influence at the very time your ability to inculcate godly values is most effective. Young adults can work independently, engage in interesting conversations, fix things around the house, and amuse us with their fresh insights.

It may take some time for you to enjoy being with your children and to form new friendships for yourself, but it will come. Now, I can't imagine foregoing the blessing of homeschooling high schoolers—it's the time when students become confident learners and parents see the fruit of hard labor.

Can my children experience a diverse community through homeschooling?

Postmodernity has a different definition for diversity than my own. Diversity has been minimized to mean skin color or sexual preference or gender. To our family, diversity encompasses much more. Diversity means engaging with different ideas and experiences. University means to be united in diversity, which is not the same thing as political correctness.

In this way, homeschoolers are inherently diverse, even counter-cultural. We seem odd even to those who share the same skin color or religious background. We contribute significantly to diverse ideas by challenging mainstream assumptions about education. Like all minority movements, we welcome anyone who will consider our ideas. That is also one of the beauties of Christianity: all tongues and tribes are welcome.

As homeschooling has grown in numbers, it has also grown in diversity. As diverse parents lose confidence in school systems and gain confidence in the results of homeschooling, they are choosing to homeschool. A desire to provide religious and moral instruction remains the top reason to homeschool, but concerns over school environment and discontent with academic instruction in the public schools are also highly ranked. Many families with special-needs children find that they can meet their children's needs better at home.

Families who value cultural, ethnic, or racial diversity will find it among homeschoolers with a little extra effort.

Remember, politically correct diversity is not guaranteed at public and private schools, either. The benefit of homeschooling through high school is that young adults belong to multiple communities: church, family, neighborhood, sports teams, mission trips, work, and service. Parents may create opportunities for their children to interact with those who are different as well as those who are similar. Our family lived in a multiethnic community for ten years, so our older boys didn't need to leave the neighborhood to encounter diverse skin colors. Now, we live in a small southern town, which is full of northern retirees, so our younger boys spend more time among diverse age groups. We run small businesses where we work with people of diverse beliefs and cultural heritages. We also have the privilege to travel to other regions of the world, in part because we are not bound to a traditional school schedule.

If you value racial or socioeconomic diversity, seek out homeschool support groups, clubs, volunteer work, mission trips, and sports teams for your children. If you live in a rural area, look for homeschool groups in a nearby urban community, and vice versa. Attend a social justice meeting at a local church. Be sure to read literature that tells stories about people from all backgrounds, and use these books as an opportunity to discuss your own family's history and experiences.

As the globe becomes more ethnically diverse, the next generation will be less likely to notice cultural differences that are more obvious to my generation. Our children's respect for our authority will only be enhanced by embracing strangers and welcoming a diversity of ideas.

HABITS

Teachers talk about study habits because they are essential—even more so than the content of a subject. The word "student" means "one who studies." Hard work always trumps natural gifting. It is not the child who has the highest IQ but the child with the most self-control who becomes a respected adult. As confident parents teach their children to honor their authority, they also must help their students develop the habits that promote learning for a lifetime.

How do I structure a school day?

Replacing the idea of school days with lifetime learning is one of the hardest habits to break. You probably sat in a classroom for twelve years. But school and education are not the same thing. As you develop daily habits in your home that strengthen academic skills, remember that education does not require sitting in rows.

Ask any group of homeschoolers about structure and you will find a wide range of views. Some families believe in "unschooling": education that is driven by the child's interests at the time. They view this as the best way to nurture the natural curiosity of a child. Other families copy the very structured model of the schools they themselves attended, complete with school desks and hour-by-hour schedules. Those who use a highly structured model recognize that education is something you intentionally do with your student. But if education is always delivered in this manner, the soul of your child may be destroyed. On the other hand, those who advocate unschooling or student-driven education are eager to capitalize on a child's natural curiosity, sometimes at the expense of developing discipline and confidence needed to tackle a subject the student doesn't like.

I would advocate that a healthy balance is required. In our home, I set the schedule for young children because they need to master the basics. As they grow older and reach the rhetorical years, one of the jobs of a parent is to be creative and study topics beyond our natural interests. Early, rigorous training is rewarded when the older student has the character to pursue difficult material independently.

Does that mean young children should have a stricter, longer academic day than a high school student? No. The amount of structured time depends on the parent's goals and the student's abilities. My goal is to make intentional learning a daily habit for our children. When they are younger, they complete their chores and active studies first. Then they may embrace the needs of the day and the interests of the family members. In the evening when all are tired, it's time to be quiet and read for pleasure or prepare for the next day. We surround ourselves with ideas and activities because we are curious about life.

As young adults develop these habits, they have more freedom to do each day's task. As a younger child practices piano, an older student might be doing the dishes. While I'm cooking dinner, my teenagers may be writing an essay or working math problems. We may watch a movie together after reading and discussing a book and before they write a paper. Most mornings they still work around the house and study. Most afternoons we run errands, play sports, or work for wages. There is routine, but it is easily interrupted and then resumed because we have the authority to run our own schedules. Swimming, skiing, hiking, and camping are as much a part of the curriculum for a high school student as math, Latin, and SAT practice. For our family, construction projects, art, and travel are also included in the curriculum.

To help you rethink "education" entirely, read Anthony Esolen's book *Ten Ways to Destroy the Imagination of Your Child*. Cry and repent at the loss of childhood, and be equipped to overcome all the bad ideas confusing postmodern authorities about life and education and children. You will have to re-program and prepare yourself for lots of wrestling with the consequences of ideas as your family replaces industrial education with classical education.

So how do confident parents develop habits that structure an effective school day? They don't; it's too small a goal. Instead, they structure a lifetime of learning, which means some days and some months and some seasons look like school at home, some look like goofing off, and some look like suffering. Life is a big bag of living.

Life is a big bag of living.

How can I teach my child when I didn't do well in school?

First, be strong and decide your student will have a better education than you received. Then be ready for the great surprise—you will finally become well educated as you study with your children! As an adult, your ability to learn will be magnified. As a motivated parent, you will find that your life experience makes a K–12 education look a lot easier than you remember. I like homeschooling because it educates two generations at once.

The classical model emphasizes skills rather than content. You choose the content your family will study in order to learn the skills you want to teach. Work to master the basic skills of learning with your teenager—learning vocabulary, questioning ideas, and then presenting truth—and you will find that, together, you can tackle any subject. Both generations can recover a classical education at the same time. You can start at any age, any season, any time of day. Prepare yourself for deeper conversations by doing some of the assignments yourself. Your student will see you struggling with difficult material and succeeding, demonstrating to your child that you value education enough to pursue it as an adult. Start with strengthening the basics. Give yourself and your student the time needed with easier material so that the difficult becomes approachable.

Parents fear homeschooling high school students because they worry that they must develop a certain kind of transcript or study subjects the government mandates or read books with intimidating titles like *Physics*. Remember the first two responsibilities of a confident parent?

First, you are your child's authority. No one will fire you or take your children if you homeschool your own way. Homeschooling is in every state, even though some states have control over part of the curriculum. If you live in one of the areas of the country where homeschool parents must comply with academic regulations, be sure to join a local support group that will help you select coursework.

Second, know that working on good study habits is more important than checking off a list of credits. You may feel anxious when you hear other adults talking about their child's Advanced Placement classes, but you will rejoice when your child conquers a task that is difficult for him. Homeschooling has emotional hills and valleys just like anything else. If your child struggles with multiplication, throwing more difficult content his way will not solve the problem.

Homeschooling has emotional hills and valleys just like anything else.

You may feel inadequate helping your student in certain subjects. If your child can't study physics on his own, then study something simpler that prepares you both to study physics. Select material to study based on your abilities. If a student is struggling, start with easier materials in order to develop good study habits with your child.

If your high school student is prepared for physics, then he can study physics on his own, with a tutor, with a study group, in a Classical Conversations' seminar, or in an online course. There are many resources for capable high school students. Your role may be to encourage them to find additional resources rather than to actually tutor the subject, but the classical model can help your whole family strengthen academic skills.

The classical model recognizes that all people are capable of learning. If you are weak at academics, identify one of your strengths. Evaluate what habits and skills make you strong in that arena and then duplicate the same habits in weaker arenas. For lots of specific examples, read *The Core,* which describes how anyone can learn to tackle a new subject at any age.

Seasoned homeschooling parents recognize how quickly they became strong in academics by repeating remedial subjects with their younger children. This gives parents the confidence to lead students through the challenge of difficult high school subjects. If you start homeschooling an older child, you do miss out on the early years of preparation as a parent, but don't discount all those years of homework help. Many parents pull older children out of school because they find they are working long nights on homework together anyway. You may be more prepared than you realize.

Prepare yourself to teach by reading good quality children's books. If your child is studying tenth-grade biology, get a fifth-grade science book for yourself so you can quickly and easily add to the topic's conversations. You may find reading a dozen children's books on human anatomy can replace a thick high school text. Be inventive and resourceful. These are more skills homeschoolers add to their repertoire!

I spent our children's first twelve years reading aloud every night. We didn't own a TV when our first sons were little, so books occupied our many hours of family time. Picture books and nursery rhymes led to Caldecott- and Newbery-winning children's literature, followed by short stories and then novels by popular authors like Dickens and Brontë and Austen, a long time before Caesar and Cicero and Augustine and Jefferson. We read them over and over again so the words became familiar and the styles internalized and the struggle to understand more difficult material reduced.

Building precept upon precept is the only way to become highly skilled at anything. Patiently wrestling through academia takes time, daily, yearly, and for a lifetime. If you feel like the end-of-grade exams or the SAT or a diploma is the measure of your student's education, the pressure can make you choose pragmatism over excellence. Don't just get through material—learn the material well.

If your high school student is struggling to write well, he may need to go back to the basics. Notice the tension here. We want our high school students to take college prep courses because they look good on the transcript or resumé. In contrast, a remedial English class looks remedial! So, often we sacrifice what our students really need in favor of what others value. If our goal in teaching English is for our children to understand English, perhaps we need to study remedial English with them. Otherwise, we are acknowledging that knowing English is not the goal; we'd rather earn the mandated credit and move on. Instead, I want to communicate to our children that it is important for them to have a thorough understanding of their own language.

You may be wondering, "How can I help my child study English grammar when I never learned it?" Well, I didn't learn English grammar in school either: I learned it with our children. I recommend tackling it just as I described above with literature: start with the basics and move to the more complex. Try working through *The Writing Road to Reading* by Romalda Spalding (Harper Collins, 2012), *Our Mother Tongue* by Nancy Wilson (Canon Press, 2004), and some consumable grammar books from the grocery store with your high school student. You will find that this low-level information is transformational to your student's abilities.

Balance easy subjects with challenging subjects so the difficult academics are manageable. When I was in public high school, I didn't have time to build decks, travel, work, and contemplate ideologies with my classmates. I completed my assignments and went to a selective college and promptly discovered I had never learned how to learn. I had never been expected to do more than regurgitate information found in textbooks. I had been trained to find answers rather than understand problems. I want our sons to be able to do both. We balance between difficult subjects with a lot of new *content* to master and easy subjects on which to practice new *skills*.

The physical science text the boys use for high school is easy to read without a lot of difficult math. This affords us the time to learn how to write lab reports and research papers. The next year, our biology text is more difficult to read with a lot of new vocabulary (what classicalists call *grammar*). The emphasis is on memorizing copious data and writing simpler lab reports. You can't master everything at once, so we pick a skill to focus on and are happy doing our best with the rest. Likewise, we may quickly read a lot of books related to Americana in order to survey American history and literature while we study American government or economics more in depth.

Daily math problems should always be at the student's level or below due to the heavily ordered nature of math. More challenging math problems may actually come from a science project, a formal logic course, SAT math prep, or a book in non-Euclidean geometry. Or the student may pull just a few problems from an advanced math book on days when he flies through his daily text with no errors and everything is neatly written down. I personally use the daily math lessons to teach our boys the habit of learning a little more every day. I use our math books to teach our children time management, neatness, and study strategies, rather than math. Intentionality is important in developing good habits.

Even for experienced homeschool parents, learning alongside your student is not always easy. I know better, yet I often say to our children, "Just do it and get it over with." What does this phrase teach?

1) Our children know that I am making them do something that is not important.
2) Time is being spent rather than redeemed.
3) I am letting someone or something or some system I probably do not respect dictate how our time is used.
4) I may be having a bad day with no time to help.

When we have difficult days, I don't give up and let someone else have the joy and privilege of leading our children. Instead, I recognize that difficulties are promised to each of us and avoidance doesn't lead to sanctification. Difficult situations force me to mature. Romans 5:3–4 says, "We glory in tribulations also: knowing that tribulation worketh patience; and patience, experience; and experience, hope." I also know our children are watching my response, and avoiding sanctification is not a lesson I'm interested in teaching.

Can my children get into college?

There are two related questions: 1) Do colleges want homeschooled students? and 2) Should college be the goal?

As to the first question, colleges and universities have recruited homeschooled students for some time now. These graduates have proven to be bright, self-disciplined students who are well-prepared for the college experience. When Classical Conversations conducted a 2013 survey of the program's alumni, not one of the two-hundred-plus students who completed the anonymous survey reported being unable to attend college because they had not been accepted at the school of their choice. Again, see Brian Ray's book *Home Educated and Now Adults* for more information.

Colleges today are familiar with the process of evaluating and admitting homeschooled students. I know a homeschooled girl whose four oldest brothers all went to West Point after being homeschooled. The military academies welcome homeschooled students and have web pages and information specifically for homeschooling families. (They do have stricter requirements than most schools, and if you are interested in having a child attend, you need to start preparing as early as reasonable. Ask questions of other homeschoolers in your area, and you will find a community of partners willing to help.) If you choose to pursue a college degree as the next step in your student's education, a wealth of resources exists, both online and within the community of experienced homeschooling parents.

Let's look briefly at what it means to be prepared for a college degree. It means being able to read a lot of material quickly, study material you don't particularly enjoy, ask questions of professors, and turn assignments in on time. These tasks require a respect for routine. The high school student needs to practice these skills for at least thirty hours a week if they are going to spend more than forty hours a week on college assignments. A good student prioritizes time and sacrifices interests while learning to memorize copious amounts of information, discussing difficult vocabulary, and expressing ideas clearly and concisely. I just described a classical education! The habits of getting work done well and with understanding allow a student to embrace adult education.

Now, let me address the second question. As our last two children approach college age, I have wondered if college should be the goal for our boys. I have often shared that when I began homeschooling, getting my boys into college on scholarships was my goal. I needed the world to verify that homeschooling made for a successful education. At the time, I would have counted homeschooling a failure if our sons had not gotten into college. I worked very hard with our first two children to meet this goal, and we succeeded. Now that they are grown and we are about to launch two more sons, I feel college preparation is too small a goal.

Throughout our elder two boys' childhood, I would have said I wanted them to be Christians, but my actions indicated that I wanted them to be collegians. With my younger sons, my only goal is to raise virtuous men, which makes teaching Latin seem like a breeze. Virtuous men have no problem going to college because they are studious. They have no problem finding employment because they return honest hours of work for honest wages. They have no problem starting businesses because they can sacrifice to make others' lives better. They have no problem serving in missions because they can delay personal desires. In the past, Christendom knew that the point of education was to inculcate virtue, but today it would be hard to convince educational associations that, as wonderful as STEM (science, technology, engineering, and math) or the Common Core may sound to them, virtue should be the goal of education.

With my younger sons, my only goal is to raise virtuous men, which makes teaching Latin seem like a breeze.

Most readers will agree with me that they want their children to be honest, intelligent, compassionate citizens. Somehow, we say it but our actions don't convey that we mean it. Raising our children well doesn't mean that I set a lower value on academics. Instead, it means I don't forget that sound academics should glorify God. Jesus loved the world so much He gave His life for it. I take that to mean that I too should take an interest in the things He created. My love of Christ drives me to want to study everything He made. All things were made through Him; hence, I am curious about all things. Earning a better living or getting good grades or receiving a college scholarship may be the result of obeying Him in all things, but these are no longer my goals for our sons.

CONTENT

If your student has learned to honor your authority, and you have taught him self-control through good habits, the academic content is the easiest portion of this triad. Students will trust that their parents have a good reason for the assignments even if they seem irrelevant. I remember David asking me "Why do we have to read Caesar's *Battle in Gaul*?" I thought he was questioning eight years of Latin studies, so I launched into my usual explanation of the benefits of studying history, literature, and language all at once when he interrupted me: "No. I want to study Latin. I just can't figure out who will talk to me about ancient battle strategies." I laughed and told him to get back to work. That year we had two new students join his Classical Conversations seminars who actually pored over history books about war and political strategy. Fortunately, all the students in the seminar enjoyed Latin studies, so every Tuesday he spent a big chunk of time in meaningful conversation about the very topic he thought no one cared about. I was delighted to be included in the education of these fourteen-year-olds.

Confident parents know that if their family can work as a team and their young adults have witnessed the effort needed to complete difficult tasks, their academic framework will be strong and able to support even heavy coursework.

How can I teach high school subjects when I'm no expert?

Education used to mean the passing of wisdom and virtue from one generation to the next. Adults passed on important ideas through a lifetime of activities and conversations with children. Now, education has come to mean experts lead students through one or two subjects for a few months and then move on to the next group of children. We are working to reclaim the traditional kind of classical education in our homeschooling community.

Our sons do know things that I don't know, and they want to study things without me. Sometimes, they like to find their own tutors and mentors. They have had tutors who are better at teaching music, art, Latin, and writing than my husband or I. Sometimes we hire experts that we find, sometimes the students find experts they want to study with, and sometimes parents in our community of homeschoolers share their expertise. Our sons have taken online classes and classes at universities. Rob and I have not been their only teachers. We welcome other teachers in various subjects, but not if it causes us to neglect the boys' souls, our family's structure, or time for our young adults to pursue their passions. We know the importance of depth, not simply breadth, when it comes to mentors.

Our sons choose from a multitude of homeschooling companions who like to get together at night to study astronomy or read Latin before eating dinner and watching the latest movie. This is possible because we have found families who enjoy the same things we do. High school students should look at everyone they meet as a potential teacher.

Many parents are concerned that if they homeschool through high school they must learn everything they want to teach their students. Instead, think of yourselves as the managing director who helps to provide resources as needed, lend an ear for discussion, and challenge your student when he is making errors. As a parent, you simply need to protect the time your student needs for his pursuits and help your student stick to the task at hand.

In modern education, a master teacher is a specialist or an expert in a given, usually narrow, field. To a classical educator, a master teacher is a master learner who models good study habits. The master teacher is excited to learn new things and to share them with the community. A master teacher assesses whether a student needs to define new vocabulary, attempts to discern gaps in the student's understanding, and gives the student a chance to express his knowledge. Classical educators attempt to understand the arts of **grammar** (vocabulary), **dialectic** (clear reasoning), and **rhetoric** (wise choices) and their application to quality content, whether an ancient piece of literature or a new brownie recipe.

To a classical educator, a master teacher is a master learner who models good study habits.

I'm thankful for those who do difficult research and academic analysis, but I want our sons to learn more than knowledge. They need to learn wisdom, and that is where the rhetoric stage, which requires consistent mentoring throughout high school, is so important. Wisdom comes from being able to integrate knowledge about science, math, literature, and history so that we have a complete and whole understanding of the world in which we live. This is the knowledge toward which the classical "master teacher"—a parent just like you—is best equipped to guide a young adult.

What if my child is gifted or has special needs?

Let's look at the extremes in academic abilities, from students who have the least abilities to those who possess great intellectual advantages. For both extremes, I still say you can homeschool because both cases require a parent to be in charge, whether pulling together a team of specialists or creating an advanced learning opportunity for your child. Academic curriculum abounds for either type of student. Online delivery and FedEx can both bring content to anyone. Just Google "homeschooling special needs" or "homeschooling gifted children" and you will find a bewildering array of options. Your job is to orchestrate a life of learning, with an emphasis on strengthening weaknesses required for healthy living while lighting passions that provide purpose.

First, let's address the gifted child. Students who are exceptionally passionate or gifted can rarely be stopped; they are going to pursue their talents. That's why you already know they have talent—it stands out and they talk about it all the time. They need a parent to balance and direct them to accomplishments that do not come so naturally. Our role is to encourage our children to strengthen weaknesses in order to become competent adults. As high school students, they require exposure to a broad knowledge in a range of subjects and skills.

Parents help students both pursue their strengths and make progress in weak areas. For example, the math prodigy must keep writing so that he can clearly express his ideas to others. Parents teach children skills they naturally repel, like brushing their teeth and making their beds as young children, completing writing and math assignments as adolescents, and honoring work or sports commitments when they'd rather go to a party as young adults. Even the most gifted students have times when they need more than their own will to motivate them. We've all met the absent-minded professor or the prima donna. He will not be hired to teach if he cannot show up on time, and she will be overlooked for the next production if she cannot take directions.

On the opposite side of the spectrum, the student who has special needs deserves a longer incubation period with more protection from unrealistic expectations so she can focus on things that are crucial to learn. That doesn't mean she will never leave the house, it just means more extensive preparation is required. If you listen to parents on YouTube who have homeschooled children with special needs, you will hear a common theme of families spending more time on fewer subjects with less pressure to perform. The classical model works with these high school students too, as you focus on teaching skills that have broad applications by practicing on just a few subjects. Classicalists use content that provides a liberal arts curriculum, but we really just teach students to memorize (grammar), think (dialectic), and tell stories (rhetoric). These skills are a perfect fit for any range of academic abilities. For more help tailoring a classical education to a special-needs child, check out Cheryl Swope's book *Simply Classical: A Beautiful Education for Any Child* (Memoria Press, 2013).

What about credits, transcripts, and diplomas?

Often, parents are intimidated about homeschooling through high school because they worry about the administrative elements such as diplomas, transcripts, standardized testing, college placement exams, and career assessments. The good news is that homeschooling parents have more assistance than ever when assembling these important documents.

Confident parents know they have the authority to list the credits they want on a transcript as long as the document is honest and clear. As you work on establishing credits, remember that they vary from district to district and from state to state. In general, one credit is assigned for 150 hours of study and a half credit is 75 hours. But what if your student is a genius and gets through the whole algebra text perfectly in seventy-five hours instead of the average 150? How many credits should he receive? Or, what if your child with a medical condition needs 180 hours to complete half of the text because he is too weak to stay awake? Should he fail, or should he get an extra credit for perseverance? Thankfully, homeschool families have discretion in making these important decisions.

I like credits; I use credits; I think credits are a quick review of completed coursework. I just don't think they mean as much as others seem to think. There are many ways to assess a student's progress. Tests and grades and credits are very helpful. But so are kind words, working beyond the scope of the assignment, and challenging assumptions even if that leads to different assignments than previously planned.

Use the general rule about number of hours or use the completion of a particular textbook to help guide you with credits. Then, remember to challenge your children to do their best and to affirm them in more ways than the awarding of a credit. For more details, look into a website like ACADEMICRECORDS.NET or a book such as *Transcripts Made Easy* by Janice Campbell.

Organizations like Classical Conversations and the Home School Legal Defense Association have aggregated information about state testing requirements and the college application process for homeschoolers. The homeschool market has grown sufficiently to support supply companies that specialize in creating graduation products just for homeschoolers, from mortarboards to diplomas. Many state homeschool organizations host a special graduation event in the spring that is available to all homeschool families in the vicinity. College websites often have a separate section explaining their requirements for homeschooled applicants, and many admissions officers actively recruit homeschool graduates. As a homeschooling parent, you do have to think like an administrator at times, but you have the advantage of several generations' worth of experienced homeschoolers who can make your burden light.

* * *

As I finish this chapter, I find myself in my usual place: sitting across the table from David, answering his occasional math questions while I do my own work. But our setting is not usual. We are in a hotel in Ohio in November, waiting for David to go to rugby practice. He is working out with a men's development team even though he is too young for their housing program. They were happy to let him attend if a parent would stay with him because they only provide housing for men over eighteen years old. Instead of spending all day with the same people at school, he is practicing with men from all over the world, studying math, Latin, and chemistry, marveling at suburban shopping centers, and competing with his brothers in their online fantasy football team. He spent the first week here with his dad, and now I am here with him for two more weeks. Meanwhile, Rob is back at our home enjoying time with William. We spent lots of time at home together when they were children. Now we are enjoying a different mix of family life. High school is the season for unusual learning opportunities, and we want to make the best of them.

Whether you think of yourself as a coach, managing director, or tutor for your high school student, developing a confidence in your authority, instilling good habits in your household, and choosing appropriate content are your prime responsibilities. Your student's responsibilities are to honor your authority, develop study skills, and learn a mix of interesting and necessary topics. If you are really fortunate, you may even get to hold hands with your son while watching the NFL draft picks.

CHAPTER TWO

RHETORIC DEFINED

"...it is absurd to hold that a man ought to be ashamed of being unable to defend himself with his limbs, but not of being unable to defend himself with speech and reason, when the use of rational speech is more distinctive of a human being than the use of his limbs. ...A man can confer the greatest of benefits by a right use of these, and inflict the greatest of injuries by using them wrongly."

—Aristotle, *Rhetoric* (1.1)

The last chapter described how confident parents can overcome obstacles. In this chapter, the focus moves from obstacles to the opportunities that await when you confront your fears. Educating classically through the high school years is rich with possibilities. I talked in *The Core* about the need to focus on specific grammatical content. In *The Question*, I addressed the awe and wonder that students experience when their middle school years center on questions. These foundations make guiding your child's classical education through high school not only possible but also rewarding beyond your wildest imagination, especially if the coursework is surrounded by conversations. As you learn the art of **rhetoric** alongside your high school-aged students, you'll be developing the skills to have a rewarding and fruitful conversation about any subject you encounter.

Let's start by reviewing what "classical education" means. The words can sound intimidating, but they refer to a style of learning that is innate for each of us. Classical education recognizes that as humans, when we learn something new, we progress through three stages. The classical model names these three stages **grammar**, **dialectic**, and **rhetoric**.

Grammar is all about words and naming. Memorization is the most important tool in this stage, because when we begin to learn something new, we start by collecting concrete facts about it. In gardening, you learn terms for soil acidity, sunlight, and spacing of seeds. In plumbing, you learn the parts of a toilet and how to recognize different types of pipes. In auto repair, you learn the parts of an engine. In English, you learn vocabulary and memorize the parts of speech. In chemistry, you memorize the periodic table of elements. Because young children love to sing songs and parrot words back, the grammar stage comes naturally to children in the elementary years; however, everyone practices the art of grammar when they encounter something new. My book *The Core: Teaching Your Child the Foundations of Classical Education* explains the grammar stage in depth.

Dialectic is all about questions and relationships between ideas. When we learn something new, after we gather facts, we examine and analyze the facts we have collected, and we figure out how they fit together by asking questions. In gardening, you learn what plants grow well in what types of soil. You ask what will cause a plant to die in one environment and thrive in another. In plumbing, you learn how the parts of a toilet fit together. In auto repair, you learn how one part of the car affects another part. In English, you learn how the parts of speech fit together to form sentences, and you analyze others' writing and ask what makes a sentence "good." In chemistry, you ask how elements interact or why salt is used to extinguish electrical fires. The dialectic stage comes naturally to pre-teens who love to ask questions and debate ideas, but everyone of any age must practice this art when they learn something new. My book *The Question: Teaching Your Child the Essentials of Classical Education* breaks down the dialectic stage into manageable steps for a classical education at home.

That brings us to rhetoric, which is the main focus of this book. Rhetorical skills come naturally to young adults who are ready to progress from asking questions to making arguments, and from analyzing others' ideas to presenting their own. **Rhetoric** is all about conversations and expressing truth. Rhetoricians write essays, present hypotheses, lead discussions with others, and act on the knowledge they have gained about a new subject. In gardening, you might plant a tomato, harvest it successfully, and prepare a salad for your family. In plumbing, you repair a broken sink and teach someone else how to do the same. In auto repair, you explain to a worried customer what is wrong with his car and how to fix it. In English, you use your knowledge of sentence and paragraph structure to write a compelling essay about justice and freedom. In chemistry, you teach someone else how to balance an equation, or you use your knowledge of chemical reactions to bake bread, purify water on a camping trip, or develop a more fuel-efficient car. Notice how this stage of learning comes at the same time that high school students are ready to seek mentors, find practical applications for their learning through a part-time job or internship, and use their skills to benefit others by volunteering or taking part in a mission trip or service opportunity.

> *We must teach our students to be both wise and humble as they attempt to separate truth from lies and persuasion from manipulation.*

As a mom of four boys, sports analogies come easily in my house. If they do for you, then you can think of your family's pursuit of truth through classical education as a football game. As you study vocabulary and memorize facts in the grammar stage, you are mastering the basics of the game. You trust your coach to provide you with the foundational skills you will need later. As you learn logic and practice asking good questions in the dialectic stage, you are refining your defense. You want to be able to recognize and tackle faulty arguments wherever they appear. As you learn public speaking and persuasion in the rhetoric stage, you are developing your offense. You want to be able to defend and carry the truth to others. For this reason, we must teach our students to be both wise and humble as they attempt to separate truth from lies and persuasion from manipulation.

Is rhetoric truth-serving or self-serving?

Most of us today think of rhetoric as a collection of sound bites in political debates: political pundits propounding propositions. One of the most common punch lines in popular jokes has something to do with either lawyers or politicians being liars. One reason is that these two professions stand out among careers that use public speaking. They can use the tools of rhetoric without being wise about its ends. Alternately, where "rhetoric" is not being used as a series of sound bites, we find it being used to emotionally manipulate us: images of sick animals parade before us while melancholy violins play in the background, demanding through our stomachs—not our brains— that we give the necessary twenty-nine dollars a month to save that sad-faced puppy or kitten on the screen. The organization behind this ad may base its actions on logical reasoning and be supported by ethical individuals, but logic and character do not play a major role in this kind of advertising. Instead, ad campaigns rely on proven emotional triggers to prompt action.

If we are going to teach students how to share their knowledge with the world and to be wise leaders, it matters that we reclaim the art of rhetoric as a means to seek truth for ourselves and to point others toward truth. Students are sensitive to that distinction as well. Matt Bianco, a homeschool dad who lives near our family, tutored my son William in twelfth grade. One weekend, Matt took the students to meet with other groups of students at a camp near Staunton, Virginia. The group of about fifty students and a handful of parents spent the afternoon and evening together, which culminated in a lively discussion as they sat around the fire. The next day, they were going to the nearby Blackfriars Playhouse to attend a performance of *Julius Caesar* at the American Shakespeare Center. In preparation, Matt wanted to lead the group in a discussion of whether Brutus should have assassinated Julius Caesar. As the conversation persisted, however, he discovered that the students had different plans.

"What is the theme of Shakespeare's *Julius Caesar*?" he asked.

"Loyalty!" one student responded.

"Patriotism," said another.

"Rhetoric," said another. This response was immediately followed by agreement from several other students.

With this prompt, the conversation turned to a discussion of the nature of rhetoric. The members of the group were divided over whether an act of persuasion should only be called rhetoric when a virtuous person is persuading someone toward truth, goodness, or beauty, or whether persuasion should still be called rhetoric when it is being used as a tool for deception, manipulation, or trickery. They understood intuitively that the *tools* of persuasion can be used for good or for evil.

When a speaker errs in the way he uses these tools, rhetoric turns into sophistry (persuasion for the speaker's gain rather than for truth). The Bible

The tools of persuasion can be used for good or for evil.

records an early incident that helps us to see the difference between rhetoric and sophistry. In Genesis chapter 3, the serpent asks Eve if God had actually told her not to eat from the trees in the garden. Eve responds that God had said they could eat from every tree but one: the Tree of the Knowledge of Good and Evil, which they must not eat, lest they die. The serpent tells her that she will not surely die. The last and most convincing thing he says to Eve is, "Ye shall not surely die: For God doth know that in the day ye eat thereof, then your eyes shall be opened, and ye shall be as gods, knowing good and evil." If rhetoric were defined simply as the art of persuasion, the serpent would have to be judged as a mighty rhetorician, for Eve does, in fact, eat from the forbidden tree, and her husband, Adam, quickly follows suit. However, the serpent has distorted the truth of God's character, so he is demonstrating sophistry rather than rhetoric.

In fact, perversions of rhetoric like propaganda, brainwashing, demagoguery, and double speak are all the more reason for students to study rhetoric. As Edward Corbett writes in *Classical Rhetoric for the Modern Student*, "citizens might thereby be put on their guard against the onslaughts of these vicious forms of persuasion"(25). Just as we should teach formal logic in order to prevent children from being taken captive by lies, we should teach rhetoric so that students may captivate others with the truth in high school and beyond.

The author of one of the first English treatises on rhetoric, Thomas Wilson (c. 1525–1581), lived during the Renaissance. Wilson studied rhetoric as a student at Cambridge, and at the age of twenty-eight he published *The Art of Rhetoric*. A few years after writing the book, Wilson had the opportunity to put its principles to the test when he found himself charged with heresy and imprisoned in Rome during the Spanish Inquisition. Wilson needed to craft a convincing defense, but he would not deny his faith. His rhetorical skill enabled him to do both. He survived the Inquisition, and he practiced the art of rhetoric throughout the rest of his life. At various points, he served as a diplomat and then Secretary of State under Queen Elizabeth. He wrote about economics. He also translated the orations of the great speaker Demosthenes from Greek into English, using them to make a political argument about England's relationship with Spain. He was known to be industrious and diligent, and his memory was highly regarded by his contemporaries.

In the introduction to *The Art of Rhetoric*, Wilson wrote,

> Neither can I see that men could have been brought by any other means to live together in fellowship of life, to maintain Cities, to deal truly, and willingly obey one another, if men at the first had not by art and eloquence persuaded [them of] that which they full oft found out by reason. (Wilson, *The Art of Rhetoric*, p. 42, spelling modernized)

He understood that his many vocations all relied on his ability to persuade others of the truth. We want our students to engage with the world, but Wilson reminds us that one cannot lead without the ability to persuade others to follow.

I think of what Paul said in Romans 8:38–39, explaining the early Christians' willingness to die on behalf of their Lord: "*For I am persuaded*, that neither death, nor life, nor angels, nor principalities, nor powers, nor things present, nor things to come, nor height, nor depth, nor any other creature, shall be able to separate us from the love of God, which is in Christ Jesus our Lord" (emphasis mine). Paul and his fellow believers were inspired to do great things because they had been persuaded of the truth. As a parent and a teacher, I hope all of my students will have a passion for persuading others.

Rhetoric is the use of knowledge and understanding to perceive wisdom, pursue virtue, and proclaim truth.

My personal goal for this book is, therefore, to persuade you to accept this nobler definition of rhetoric that draws from Aristotle's insights but weighs them in light of biblical teachings: *Rhetoric is the use of knowledge and understanding to perceive wisdom, pursue virtue, and proclaim truth*. I know it sounds complicated, but in the next few sections, I will explain each of these elements in greater detail.

THE USE OF KNOWLEDGE AND UNDERSTANDING...

Rhetoric has to be built on something. You cannot effectively persuade someone of the truth until you know what the truth is. Think about a blender: if you turn it on without first filling it with suitable ingredients, it makes a horrible sound and produces nothing edible. Where do the ingredients come from? The first two stages of learning. If you remember, the grammar stage of classical education teaches your child to acquire lots of knowledge and facts about the world. The dialectic stage teaches your child to assess and order that information so that he begins to understand it. Rhetoric is the culmination of what your student has practiced in the early years of his education.

Modern education encourages students to think that what they learn has no practical application; that each subject exists in isolation, and there is no crossover. A classical education teaches the exact opposite. Everything studied in the grammar stage sees its fruit in the rhetoric stage. Your student will use his knowledge and understanding to develop wisdom. Memorizing the names of the U.S. presidents (grammar) will give him the vocabulary he needs to study the U.S. Constitution and compare it to the Magna Carta (dialectic). Having defined and compared governing documents from different parts of the world, he will be able to make a wise judgment about the meaning of good governance and apply that knowledge to his work or family (rhetoric). The same process applies in any subject. Furthermore, knowledge learned in one subject may find application in a completely different subject! The facts your child learns about math might help him understand a principle in economics or physics. His knowledge of history facts might help him discover truth about a style of fine arts or a foreign language. Translating Caesar's *Gallic Wars* helps students to understand Napoleon better and his goal to create a new Roman Empire. Drawing a line through a scatter plot and determining the slope helps them determine if there are cause and effect relationships between things like the money supply and inflation, GDP growth and unemployment, and corporate profitability and stock market returns. Knowledge of the exuberant spirit of the Renaissance helps him understand Michelangelo's *David*.

...TO PERCEIVE WISDOM...

When we talk about wisdom, we can look to King Solomon as an example, a man internationally renowned for the wisdom given to him by God. His wisdom extended across today's modern subjects, from music and poetry to science and history:

> And God gave Solomon wisdom and understanding exceeding much, and largeness of heart, even as the sand that is on the sea shore. And Solomon's wisdom excelled the wisdom of all the children of the east country, and all the wisdom of Egypt. For he was wiser than all men; than Ethan the Ezrahite, and Heman, and Chalcol, and Darda, the sons of Mahol: and his fame was in all nations round about. And he spake three thousand proverbs: and his songs were a thousand and five. And he spake of trees, from the cedar tree that is in Lebanon even unto the hyssop that springeth out of the wall: he spake also of beasts, and of fowl, and of creeping things, and of fishes. And there came of all people to hear the wisdom of Solomon, from all kings of the earth, which had heard of his wisdom. (1 Kings 4:29–31)

We want our high school students to use their knowledge and understanding... to know God and to make Him known.

Solomon was a Renaissance man before the term was coined! More importantly, he understood that wisdom comes from God. Wisdom enables us to see connections between ideas and relate all knowledge back to our Creator. As Saint Augustine wrote in *On Christian Doctrine*, "let every good and true Christian understand that wherever truth may be found, it belongs to his Master" (book II, chapter 18). We want our high school students to use their knowledge and understanding not for personal gain or fame, but as a way to know God and to make Him known. All our study and practice of rhetoric should have this purpose in mind.

...PURSUE VIRTUE...

As our sons have become men, they have learned to live with the consequences of their actions. That is how the world judges them. Their choices also reveal what they truly value. Remember, "He that saith, I know him, and keepeth not his commandments, is a liar, and the truth is not in him" (1 John 2:4). Rhetoric is about words, of course, but it is also about actions. We want our children to act rightly and to persuade others to do the same. One of the great Roman writers on rhetoric, Quintilian, put this idea succinctly when he said, "At any rate let us banish from our hearts the delusion that eloquence, the fairest of all things, can be combined with vice" (*Institutio Oratoria*, volume 4, book 12). An elegant and persuasive speech delivered by a just man moves people to act.

...AND PROCLAIM TRUTH...

"But sanctify the Lord God in your hearts: and be ready always to give an answer to every man that asketh you a reason of the hope that is in you" (1 Peter 3:15).

As students enter the rhetoric stage of education, they are on their way to becoming leaders of men. To lead rightly, they must proclaim truth to those around them, whether they are politicians, statesmen, missionaries, business owners, parents, or simply members of a community. Nancy Pearcey makes a similar argument in her book *Saving Leonardo*:

> The central challenge of our age, says Catholic philosopher Louis Dupré, is the lack of integrating truth. "We experience our culture as fragmented; we live on bits of meaning and lack the overall vision that holds them together in a whole." As a result, people feel an intense need for self-integration. Christianity has the power to integrate our lives and create a coherent personality structure—but only if we embrace it as the ultimate, capital-T Truth that pulls together all lesser truths. "Faith cannot simply remain one discrete part of life," Dupré says. It must "integrate all other aspects of existence." Anything less is neither beautiful nor compelling enough to ignite our passion or transform our character. (44; quoting from an interview in *The Christian Century*)

As educators, it is our job to give students the confidence, through repeated practice in a variety of subjects over an extended period of time, to proclaim truth no matter what situation they encounter.

How do I incorporate rhetoric in my child's education?

I wanted to start out with the big picture so that you will catch the vision of why we would want our sons and daughters to become great rhetoricians. But, I know that parents also want to know how to make this part of their daily schooling. What does it look like to use knowledge and understanding to perceive wisdom in science? What does it mean to use knowledge and understanding to pursue virtue in mathematics? What does it mean to use knowledge and understanding to proclaim truth about history? The rest of this book will go through subject by subject and show you practical ways to implement the study of rhetoric with your student. The rest of this chapter provides you an overview of rhetoric as an art of learning.

We often start our discussion of rhetoric with the Greeks because they were some of the first to systematize the study of it and arrange it in an orderly form. I compare what they did to what some homeschool moms love to do, which is to break big ideas into small, manageable steps—a sort of "Five Ways to Organize Your Homeschool Day"—but with togas instead of denim jumpers, as the stereotype goes. Aristotle, in particular, divided the art of rhetoric into five canons. The word comes from the Greek *kanon*, which refers to a measuring line or standard of excellence. The five canons are invention, arrangement, elocution (style), memory, and delivery. To be excellent rhetoricians, our students should aim for excellence in each of these areas. Here are a few helpful ways to think about each canon:

Canon	Guiding Question	Action
Invention *Inventio*	What should I say?	Discover ideas, research, and plan.
Arrangement *Dispositio*	In what order should I say it?	Arrange ideas in a logical and organized manner.

Elocution (Style) *Elocutio*	How should I say it?	Express ideas in the style that is most persuasive in appealing to the audience.
Memory *Memoria*	How should memory inform my presentation?	Add memorable features to your essay or speech. Commit ideas to memory.
Delivery *Pronuntiatio*	How should I present this truth in speech and action?	Deliver ideas in oral or written form.

The five canons give us a form to use when we talk about the art of rhetoric, and you can use them to practice rhetoric with your student. Each subject-specific chapter that follows will be organized around the five canons, so this section simply gives you a preview; each time you cycle back through the canons, you will discover something new about them.

INVENTION

Before your student begins to speak, write, or create something, he must first identify the truth he wants to present and the audience to whom he will be communicating it. In my last book, *The Question*, I outlined five types of questions your student can ask to help him figure out what to say. He should (1) define terms, (2) compare ideas, (3) ask about the relationship between ideas, (4) consider circumstances, and (5) review any available testimony about the subject. He might practice this canon by conducting research in a library or on the computer; he might gather ideas by talking to a group of people, or he might analyze the logic of an argument. Although he may begin alone, he should always invite others into his process of invention. I named this book about rhetoric *The Conversation* because a conversation is one of the best places for a student to clarify his ideas and learn how to relate them to someone else in a way that is thoughtful and accessible. In *The Office of Assertion*, an approachable book on rhetoric and writing, Scott Crider writes "We tend to assume that our argument is self-evident, either because we ourselves already understand it and simply expect others to, or because we have not thought enough about it to see that its terms might need to be defined and its ideas elaborated" (19). If you invite the greatest scientist in the world to speak to a five-year-old, you will have wasted your time unless the scientist can tailor his message to the child's level of understanding. Audience matters. Even essays that only you or one other person will read should be planned from the beginning with an audience in mind.

ARRANGEMENT

After determining what he wants to say, your student will need to decide in what order he should say it. It may be easiest to understand how arrangement works when your student is writing an essay. After all, modern educators, too, instruct students to create outlines before they begin to write. But, your student also needs to practice arrangement if he is creating a poster for a science fair. After all, he will need to think about the best way to lay out the graphs and information in the space he has been allotted. Likewise, a scientist learns to arrange experiments rightly so that he tests the appropriate variables in the appropriate order. A mathematician arranges a mathematical proof so that it follows a logical sequence, and your math student should do the same. A choreographer arranges a series of dance movements. A graphic designer arranges headlines and images to achieve a desired effect on the viewer.

Audience and purpose should always inform his decisions. As an example, a journalist writing a newspaper article will put the most important ideas at the very top (called an "inverted pyramid" structure) so that fast-moving readers will not miss them. By contrast, a novelist may save a surprising twist for the very end, wanting to keep his readers guessing. Rhetoric is always relational. You can't persuade a brick wall or a sponge. So, remind your student that no audience wants to be treated like a sponge. A human will rarely absorb everything you say if you ignore his or her needs and experiences.

Studying arrangement in this way allows you to talk about choices and consequences with your student. This train of thought should also lead your student to consider how he arranges his own life. Perhaps he is seeking more independence and wants to take charge of his own schedule for completing his studies. I once gave an 18-year-old seasonal employee keys to a car and a credit card to use for business purposes. As he was moving on to more permanent employment, he handed the keys back to me and thanked me for trusting him more than anyone he had ever met. He was stunned that a stranger would give him so much responsibility. I was pleased because I noticed he rearranged his whole life to serve our family that year. Actions are as much a part of a conversation as words.

ELOCUTION / STYLE

The next consideration is the canon of elocution, in which your student asks, "How should I say it?" Should the presentation be spoken or written? Should it be formal or informal? How specialized should the vocabulary be? Students will learn to dress up their writing and speaking with rhetorical devices, such as metaphors, similes, and parallelism, but they must also learn when *not* to use these devices and how to avoid overusing them. Aristotle writes this:

> It is appropriate enough for a poet to talk of "white milk," in prose such epithets are sometimes lacking in appropriateness or, when spread too thickly, plainly reveal the author turning his prose into poetry. Of course we must use some epithets, since they lift our style above the usual level and give it an air of distinction. But we must aim at the due mean, or the result will be worse than if we took no trouble at all; we shall get something actually bad instead of something merely not good. (*Rhetoric* 3.3)

The style of a sermon will differ from the style of a political debate or of a commencement speech. The audience and the subject matter determine the stylistic devices the writer or speaker should employ to move the audience to new thoughts or actions.

Elocution may be as simple as showing compassion for the reader by proofreading an essay or as complex as creating an extended metaphor in a poem or putting a fine glaze on a piece of pottery. The danger for student rhetoricians is that they may mistake ornamentation for appropriateness and neglect clarity. Remind your student to put his audience's needs ahead of his own desire to show off. At the same time, do not expect perfect elocution right away. Like anything else worth doing, elocution requires practice and the willingness to do it badly at first. Expect extremes, and then take the time to correct them.

MEMORY

The fourth canon of rhetoric is memory, which, in ancient times, referred literally to the act of memorizing a speech. Great orators memorized their words so that they could throw their entire bodies into presenting the speech and speak naturally. Contemporary students of rhetoric can think about memory in several different ways. First, when students communicate about a subject, they should draw from memory, making use of what they and the audience already know about the subject. Find common ground with the audience. Whenever possible, lay out the context surrounding your argument or idea.

Second, students should seek to make their communication memorable for their audience. This might mean giving a clear "road map" at the beginning of a speech, telling the audience what key words to look for so that they can remember main points. It might mean limiting a presentation to three main ideas rather than providing seven or ten. It might mean using repetition to drive home an argument. You may notice that in this section I am identifying each aspect of memory by using numbers. This technique makes it clear when I move on to a new point.

Third and finally, students may actually memorize a speech or a presentation if doing so will allow them to focus more on their audience. Non-verbal communication, including eye contact, is extremely important if you are trying to persuade someone that you are trustworthy. Even if your student is not memorizing a speech to present to a large audience, he should "be ready always to give an answer to every man" about the gospel, and that means thinking about his answer, working out the best way to say it, and being prepared to speak it aloud to another person. What is that if not a feat of memory?

DELIVERY

The final canon of rhetoric is delivery: "How should I present this truth in speech and action?" As your student prepares to engage the world in more ways than ever, with less supervision than ever, you as the parent will have the opportunity to talk to him about the way he presents not only his words but also himself. Is his attire appropriate to his situation, and does it convey respect for the people he will encounter? Does his body language demonstrate confidence, interest, and integrity? I once agreed to allow my Challenge students to celebrate National Pajama Day by wearing pajamas to class. (They used very persuasive arguments to convince me this was a good idea.) Unfortunately, it was also the day they were presenting memorized historical speeches. One of my students delivered a flawlessly memorized rendition of Martin Luther King, Jr.'s "I Have a Dream" speech, complete with booming voice and Southern accent. Unfortunately, he delivered this speech in Cookie Monster pajama pants. His attire made it difficult for the audience to focus on the content and delivery and to be moved.

Encourage high school students to practice public speaking through debate, mock trial, or science fairs, not because all of them will have careers that require public speaking, but because the skills they acquire will serve them well in any situation. And remind them to wear the correct attire!

PERSUADING THE HEART, MIND, AND SOUL

The five canons of rhetoric provide a form for implementing rhetoric in your student's education, but we still need to talk about what makes something persuasive. Aristotle used three categories he called **logos**, **pathos**, and **ethos**. Each one appeals to a particular sensibility that we can simplify to mind, heart, and soul.

The Greek word *logos*—think of the word "logical"—is the same one that appears in John chapter one, "In the beginning was the Word, and the Word was with God, and the Word was God." *Logos* ("word") also means a plea, an opinion, or a reasoned argument. In classical rhetoric, *logos* refers to propositional truth, an argument that appeals to the mind of the listener. Aristotle calls it "persuasion [...] when we have proved a truth or an apparent truth by means of the persuasive arguments suitable to the case in question" (*Rhetoric* 1.2).

Pathos—think of the word "pathetic"—refers to an emotional appeal, an appeal to the heart. When we speak of *pathos*, as when we speak of rhetoric, we are referring to an emotional appeal that leads toward truth. There is a marked difference between a story that moves us to rightful compassion or celebration and a story that manipulates the emotions for personal gain. We must be careful not to lump the two together too tightly. Charles Dickens inspired his readers to compassion by appealing to our love for Tiny Tim in *A Christmas Carol*. Harriet Beecher Stowe inspired her readers to speak out against slavery by appealing to an emotional bond with the slaves in *Uncle Tom's Cabin*. In the Bible, Nathan inspires David to repentance by appealing to his concern for justice.

When an emotional appeal is connected to truth and produces a right response, it can be called *pathos* and is an act of rhetoric. When an emotional appeal is divorced from truth or out of balance with the logic of the appeal, it can constitute emotional manipulation. Dorothy Sayers describes this well in her essay "The Lost Tools of Learning":

> Has it ever struck you as odd, or unfortunate, that today, when the proportion of literacy throughout Western Europe is higher than it has ever been, people should have become susceptible to the influence of advertisement and mass propaganda to an extent hitherto unheard of and unimagined? Do you put this down to the mere mechanical fact that the press and the radio and so on have made propaganda much easier to distribute over a wide area? Or do you sometimes have an uneasy suspicion that the product of modern educational methods is less good than he or she might be at disentangling fact from opinion and the proven from the plausible?

I think of all the products being made today with planned obsolescence or the common practice of sending a sales team to promote a product with guarantees that the service department could never keep. Practicing rhetoric, truth with words, will prepare our students to recognize integrity in daily living.

Finally, *ethos*—think of the word "ethical"—refers to the character or reputation of the rhetorician. Ethos appeals to the soul of the man. Aristotle writes in *Rhetoric*, "It is not true, as some writers assume in their treatises on rhetoric, that the personal goodness revealed by the speaker contributes nothing to his power of persuasion; on the contrary, his character may almost be called the most effective means of persuasion he possesses" (1.2). Today, although we attempt to determine the character of a speaker by the quality of his speaking, we are often disappointed to find that the smoothest speakers lack a basic ethical compass in their lives, no matter how persuasive their speeches might be. What if a pastor preached a sermon about training up children but his own children were out of control? What if you went to a financial planner who exhorted you to live on a budget while he was personally in debt? Remember our definition of rhetoric: *Rhetoric is the use of knowledge and understanding to perceive wisdom, pursue virtue, and proclaim truth.* As our students pursue virtue to become men and women of character, they will become more persuasive writers, speakers, and leaders, no matter what vocation they pursue.

PART TWO

THE RHETORICAL ARTS

CHAPTER THREE

READING

"In great literature—poetry and fiction—we see ourselves, our friends, our enemies, the world around us. We see our interests portrayed in bold relief—our questions asked better than we can ask them, our problems pictured better than we can picture them by ourselves, our fantasies realized beyond our fondest dreams, our fears confirmed in horrors more horrible than our nightmares, our hopes fulfilled past our ability to yearn or desire."

—James Sire, *How to Read Slowly*

As classical educators and parents, we sometimes forget that we really only need four things in order to educate someone. We need pencil, paper, good books, and time for great conversations. We do not need a Smart Board or a flashy PowerPoint presentation or even a doctorate degree in literature. Instead, we should learn to cultivate the art of good conversation, to ask good questions, to listen, to reflect, and to ask more questions. We know how to share stories with our very young children. If you ask most people to tell you a fairy tale that they remember from childhood, they can narrate the story of *Little Red Riding Hood* or *The Three Little Pigs* or *The Little Red Hen* or *Sleeping Beauty*. These stories bind us together as a community because they create a shared language. When children become fluent readers, we cheer for their accomplishment, their newfound independence, and, unfortunately, we stop sharing books together. Instead, we need to learn how to share adult literature with our children so that we continue to have community through a shared language. In the Western world, generations of families grew up on two texts—Shakespeare and the Bible. I am not arguing that we should return to these two texts alone, but I am suggesting that we should reclaim the notion that reading the same works, even if only a perennial few, creates community.

People are uniquely wired to respond to stories. We instinctively know this when children are small. It is a rare child who does not look forward to a bedtime story. Indeed, many seem incapable of going to bed without one. For parents, it is easy to share reading with very young children, but we struggle when it is time to read and discuss literature with older students. In order to make the transition, we should ask ourselves what makes it so easy to share books with young children. One answer is that we know exactly what to read. The selection of nursery rhymes and fairy tales has been remarkably steady for over a hundred years. Once we get past fairy tales, however, our society no longer knows what books to share with children. Should we force children to read dusty old books? How do these relate to life in the modern world? Should we allow them to read only books by contemporary authors? How will we know if these books are any good? How will we know if they have anything important to say or if they will stand the test of time? As classical educators, we can remove some of the confusion. We can make rather easily a list of the accepted classics of world literature that were read in classrooms until the 1950s. We can stake our claim that these are the accepted classics and that we will have the classics and only the classics, thank you. However, this position ignores the underlying problem in modern education—the fact that we have forgotten why it is important to read fiction.

Many contemporary educators focus only on literacy, insisting that everyone must learn to read. Classical educators and parents have done a remarkable job of reclaiming reading instruction for young ones by reviving the lost art of teaching phonics. The confusion arises when we are faced with the next step. What do we do with them once they know how to read the words on the page? Most educators then begin to talk loudly about reading comprehension. Why all the focus on reading comprehension? The obsession of parents and educators with this particular phrase reveals their underlying assumptions about the goal of reading. They want their students to read to acquire information. Even though this seems like a practical goal, it is strangely impractical because the readers don't know what to do with the knowledge they have acquired. They seem to believe in a mystical connection between literacy and destiny. We have conflated reading with the pursuit of success and the acquisition of power. Children who learn to read will stay in school and get good jobs certainly, but, more importantly, our society believes that they will have power because knowledge is power. Perhaps this is thinking too much of too little. Albert Jay Nock insists, "Surely everything depends on what he reads and upon the purpose that guides him in reading" (*Climbing Parnassus*, 154).

Those who battle against illiteracy forget that literacy is only the beginning of reading. They forget that proper progress requires readers to mature beyond comprehending the words to being formed by them. The purpose of reading is for the reader to experience the emotions and actions of the characters vicariously so that they can practice judgment and virtue. In a postmodern world, these are forbidden words. Many of us were not allowed to discuss wisdom and virtue in our school classrooms, so we are ill-equipped to have these conversations with our own children and students. However, as classical educators and parents, we must reclaim the notion that literature allows young adults (and older adults, too) to practice wisdom and virtue through fictional examples so that we will be strengthened to resist temptation in reality. We must learn to govern ourselves wisely.

"Going Deeper into *Out of the Silent Planet*" by Courtney Sanford

To lead students into a deeper discussion of a novel, I use a tool for subject integration called a **topic wheel**. It is not actually a wheel, but rather a simple diagram I draw on the board. I draw a circle in the center of the board and then I draw seven more circles around the center circle. I fill in the center circle with the title of the book, and then I label each of the surrounding circles with another subject.

While leading a Challenge II (tenth grade) discussion of *Out of the Silent Planet*, I drew my circles and wrote the title in the center. I labeled the circles with subjects we were studying or had studied: biology, art, math, language, literature, theology, and philosophy. My work was finished. It was time for the students to do the thinking while I took notes.

I pointed to "biology" first and asked if there was any biology in the book. The students explained the differences in plant life on Malacandra and on Earth, and the different physical properties of water in each place. They also compared the three humanoid species to humans. On Malacandra there are hrossa, séroni, and pfifltriggi. The séroni were most like scientists.

After giving everyone a chance to contribute their ideas, I moved to the second empty circle and asked what references to art there were. One student remembered that the hrossa were poets. One remembered that there were mosaics that recorded the history of the whole planet.

In the next circle, I asked students to try to remember any math in the novel. All the students said that there must have been very advanced math used to design a spaceship that could travel to Mars. Dr. Weston would have known the math; he was a physicist who developed the spaceship.

Our next task was to fill the circle labeled "language." The students remembered that the hero of the story, Ransom, is a philologist, one who studies the structure and history of languages. Not the normal hero of an adventure story, but when traveling to new lands, it really does pay to know how to learn a language. Ransom was able to learn the language and communicate with the native species rather well. Those who did not know how to learn a language, Weston and Devine, made fools of themselves by speaking loudly and in baby-talk to the natives. As a class we felt certain that we would not be so foolish, we would have the skills to learn the language because we are studying Latin.

When it came to the literature circle, the students compared this novel with another C. S. Lewis novel, *The Lion, the Witch and the Wardrobe*. The students compared Malacandra to Narnia: both are fantastic lands with strange creatures and both are ruled by very wise and mysterious beings, one a lion and one an Oryarsa.

> This, of course, led us right into the final empty circle: theology. In Malacandra, there had been a type of angel (an Oryarsa) who had become "bent," or turned bad. He is like Lucifer. He could no longer communicate with other Oryarsas of other planets. So the "silent planet" is ours: Earth. What does it mean that we are the silent planet? All this time we thought we were the only intelligent life forms there were, but Lewis is asking us to consider a new idea: we aren't the only ones, but the others won't speak to us. My students were also intrigued with Ransom. His name makes you think he would be a human sacrifice. Was he a Jesus character? Was his life going to save others?
>
> Finally, I asked them to consider philosophy. What is philosophy anyway? They defined it as trying to figure out whether you really exist and what is real. One student even said that philosophy is a love of wisdom. "What is the philosophy in this story then?" I asked them. There may be other planets and other species, and some might know how to get along better than we do. Humans aren't the best species, one student said. We don't respect differences among ourselves like the inhabitants on Malacandra do. They seem wiser. There may be species that we can't see, like Oryarsa, or angels, or God. The students thought that maybe non-Christians might be open to knowing about God after reading this book. It might help them consider the possibility.
>
> What a great discussion! We began with a book and seven empty circles. Like a parable, it is a simple way to think deep thoughts.

Now that we have considered why we want our older children to read, we must decide what they should read. We could become strict, reactionary classicists and simply tell the world: "We will continue to read the classics because they have always been the classics. As classical educators, we are the inheritors and preservers of this literary tradition." This answer will not satisfy our souls. We must answer the deeper question, "*Why* are we reading?" The *what* will follow. With practice, we will learn to recognize whether or not a literary work helps us to train students to recognize and love truth and whether it helps them to gain wisdom about how to live well.

So, how do we go about reading well with our children? The first step is to begin reading.

So, how do we go about reading well with our children? The first step is to begin reading. To make a proper start, we should do exactly what we do for our students. We start at the beginning. We would never hand our newly reading student a copy of *Paradise Lost*, so we should not expect that of ourselves. We should plan to progress from good children's literature (consult the older Newbery-award winners) to short stories (adult literature that can be read in smaller chunks) to classics of adult literature. Reclaiming an education takes time and patience and a careful progression from simple to complex.

After reading, start with simple questions. Who are the characters? What did they do? Why did they do it? Were they right? If so, what were the results? If not, what were the consequences? Then, to move your student toward reading rhetorically, you can use the five canons of rhetoric as tools to help you interpret literature. It is easier to see how this works with a concrete example.

EXAMPLE 1: *THE SCARLET LETTER*

PARENT: How did you like *The Scarlet Letter*?
STUDENT: I hated it.
PARENT: Why?
STUDENT: I wanted it to have a happy ending.
PARENT: Isn't it a novel about adultery?
STUDENT: Yes.
PARENT: So, you wanted there to be no consequences for their sin?
STUDENT: No.
PARENT: But you wanted them to live happily ever after? In other words, you wanted Dimmesdale, Hester, and Pearl to leave the community and start over together?
STUDENT: Yes.
PARENT: Why?
STUDENT: Because they loved each other.

PARENT: Wasn't she already married?
STUDENT: Yes, but her husband was absent and then unkind.
PARENT: So, are you saying that she wasn't really married?
STUDENT: Of course she was married, but she should be allowed to find some happiness.
PARENT: Did she find happiness with Dimmesdale?
STUDENT: No.
PARENT: Why not?
STUDENT: Because the Puritans were so judgmental.
PARENT: So you're saying that she was unhappy only because the community treated her badly?
STUDENT: Yes.
PARENT: What would be a happy ending for these two and their child? Can they stay in the community?
STUDENT: No. They would have to leave and start over together.
PARENT: Do you think they will be happy living outside the community?
STUDENT: I don't know. I guess that's not really a choice.

Notice that this parent did not begin the conversation by telling the student that he was wrong or by lecturing him on the evils of adultery. Instead, she had a conversation and asked questions. This conversation illustrates a remarkable clarity about the purpose of literature that stands in stark contrast to the confusion of contemporary educators. Go back and reread the dialogue, pausing to consider what makes this conversation possible. The teacher did not believe that the end goal was to produce a student capable of reading comprehension, one who quickly and flawlessly regurgitates the bare facts of Hester and Dimmesdale's story. Instead, the wise teacher of literature knows that the purpose is character formation. This teacher understood the connection between reading well and living well. The student in this story missed the point of Hawthorne's novel—the only way of redemption for these characters is through repentance. If they flee to the woods, their sin and misery will only be multiplied. They must turn aside from their mistake and be restored to the fellowship of the community.

Even more powerful than Hester's repentance is that her example of repentance leads the student to repent. As a result of reading *The Scarlet Letter* and having a conversation with a loving mentor, he has become a different person. He can recognize the pattern of temptation because of the example of Hester and Dimmesdale. The first principle he learned is this: it is easy to slip into the justification of sin when we have been wronged. Don't we do this every time we apologize like this: "I'm sorry I called you names, but you made me angry." Now he will be able to recognize temptation. The second principle he learned is that we justify our actions out of selfishness. After all, doesn't Hester have a right to claim some happiness in this life? Careful readers of *The Scarlet Letter* must consider that this is the wrong question. What we might ask instead is "Are Hester and Dimmesdale more important than the community?" The third principle the student above learned is that the consequences of our actions are never limited to ourselves. Of course the affair between Hester and Dimmesdale has consequences for both of them, but it also has consequences for their child, for every member of Dimmesdale's congregation, and for their entire community. As students mature, reading more and more widely, they will see this same theme again and again. As we look at the canons of rhetoric in detail, you will see more clearly how this works.

Invention

What is the primary argument of *The Scarlet Letter*? Novels never illustrate the thread of their argument in the form of a logical syllogism or even the truncated form of an enthymeme, which is frequently used in political speech. However, the careful reader must learn to recognize and articulate the argument(s). What if we attempted to summarize the book as a logical syllogism? It might read something like this.

> All people who have committed a sin must face the consequences of their sin.
> Hester Prynne and Arthur Dimmesdale committed the sin of adultery.
> Hester and Dimmesdale must face the consequences of their sin.

If this is the unassailable logic of the book, then why do so many students sympathize with these lovers? Perhaps the lesson is that we want to remove the shame of our actions without doing anything to repair the damage. We want redemption without repentance. Our recognition of the argument allows us to reorder our sympathies away from sin and toward virtue.

Arrangement

Take a look at how the author begins and ends the book. For our example, how does *The Scarlet Letter* end? How does Hawthorne's choice of an ending contribute to our interpretation of his argument? This novel ends with the Hester's return to the community. She becomes the counselor to many women, particularly those who experience "the continually recurring trials of the wounded, wasted, wronged, misplaced, or erring and sinful passion—or with the dreary burden of a heart unyielded, because unvalued and unsought" (340). In the eyes of the townspeople, the letter "A" no longer means "Adulteress" but "Able." Because her mother chooses to repent and return to their community, Pearl does not become the child of the wilderness, living outside of society. She is able to make a life within civilization. Paying attention to the arrangement of the book contributes to our understanding of the meaning of the story. Modern readers struggle with this book. Because they do not understand Christian theology or sometimes even basic morality, they we are easily distracted by the argument that this book is simply a criticism of those nasty old Puritans who were so fond of shaming people. What if the book is actually about sin, the consequences of sin, repentance, and restoration to right fellowship with the community? What can we learn from their experience so that we can live well in our own communities?

Elocution

So far, we have focused on live conversations, but a rhetorical reading also requires older students to learn to have a conversation with the book itself—with the language and style the writer employs. In order to do this well, they should be encouraged to write in their books. If we want them to become lifelong learners, we should encourage them to begin having a conversation with the author. Very active readers often have elaborate systems for marking up a text. Some use pencil to write marginal notes while others rely on elaborate highlighting systems. Whichever system

If we want them to become lifelong learners, we should encourage them to begin having a conversation with the author.

students use, they should be trained to think of their reading as a conversation with the author instead of regarding themselves as passive receivers of a message. How can they avoid error in the words of others if they do not learn to read with discernment? They should circle words with unfamiliar meanings, write question marks in the margin if they don't understand or don't agree with the author's point, underline or highlight compelling passages, record their responses in the margins, and more. In other words, reading conversations are not limited to the book club meeting or to the classroom—they also take place, in a limited way, between reader and author. Many proficient readers report that they regard books as personal friends.

Memory

As students continue to read widely, they will begin to build a rich storehouse of memory. Then, they can read *The Scarlet Letter* in light of other stories about sin and its consequences, wisdom, virtue, and living in community. What can we learn from other tales of adulterers? From David and Bathsheba? Arthur and Guinevere in the legends of Camelot? John Proctor and Abigail in *The Crucible*? Helen and Paris in *The Iliad*? Do we have other examples of people who have been tempted but did not succumb? What about Joseph in Egypt? Jane Eyre? Tom Robinson in *To Kill a Mockingbird*? What can we learn by comparing these stories? This is one way in which the student becomes a rhetorical reader.

Delivery

Now that they have read and understood the story, what are students to do about it? They must share their ideas with others. They can learn to ask good questions so that they can lead the class discussion, they can write a persuasive essay that presents an argument attacking or defending the actions of one of the characters, they can deliver a speech that presents their arguments, or they can write their own story.

The above description of a rhetorical reading of *The Scarlet Letter* is necessarily simplistic. This interpretation of the novel is certainly not the only way in which to read it. I have presented one side of the story—the novel as a tale of repentance and redemption. In an actual classroom, some of the students would argue that this is not the meaning of the novel at all. They would present an alternative for the class to discuss. The disagreement would lead to a healthy conversation in which everyone's understanding of *The Scarlet Letter* would be altered, enriched, and amplified. The teacher may be swayed by persuasive arguments that the book portrays the exact opposite. In a few years, when I read the novel again, I may see something completely different. This is one major shortcoming of many modern literature guides. Instead of training students in the skills of conversation, they offer their own interpretation of the work. Because the author of the guide is an expert, the student assumes that she has articulated the correct interpretation of the novel. The student then shuts down instead of wrestling with the ideas in the book to weigh whether or not the commentator is correct in her assessment. We must concentrate on training students in the art of asking good questions so that they can participate in lively conversations about big ideas.

> *We must concentrate on training students in the art of asking good questions so that they can participate in lively conversations about big ideas.*

EXAMPLE 2: *A CHRISTMAS CAROL*

Now let's consider another example of rhetorical reading—*A Christmas Carol* by Charles Dickens. The conversation should begin with a retelling of the basic story, even if it is a familiar one. Most students could quickly tell the story of Ebenezer Scrooge, an old miser visited by three ghosts on Christmas Eve—the Ghost of Christmas Past, the Ghost of Christmas Present, and the Ghost of Christmas Future. In the morning, he repents of his selfish ways, gives generously to his employee Bob Cratchit, and joins his nephew for a proper celebration of the birth of Christ. After a brief narration, students can start a conversation about the book, guided by the canons of rhetoric.

Invention

What is the main argument of this book? Here it is as a syllogism:
All people who have the means should help those who are in need.
Ebenezer Scrooge is a person who has means.
Therefore, Ebenezer Scrooge should help those who are in need.
In *A Christmas Carol*, it is Dickens' task to persuade the audience to pursue charitable actions.

Arrangement

What is the best arrangement of the plot to move the audience to the desired ends?

It turns out that Dickens employs a relatively simple arrangement for this short novel by dividing it into three sections, one for the visit of each ghost—the Ghost of Christmas Past, the Ghost of Christmas Present, and the Ghost of Christmas Future. Each ghost makes an emotional appeal to Scrooge. The Ghost of Christmas Past uses scenes from Scrooge's early years to induce regret concerning his lost opportunities. The Ghost of Christmas Present evokes envy, pity, and shame in Scrooge by showing him the jovial Christmas of Scrooge's nephew, the failing health of Tiny Tim, and the broader vision of suffering in the world conveyed by the repulsive children concealed under his robe who represent Want and Ignorance.

Elocution

In his call to action, Dickens employs the sentimental style that appealed to his Victorian readers. At the end of *A Christmas Carol*, many readers are moved to tears by the plight of young Tiny Tim. Dickens' masterful emotional stroke is delivered by the picture of an empty chair with a crutch leaned against it. This contrasts powerfully with the immense joy and cheer readers experience when Scrooge realizes he has been saved from himself.

Memory

The emotional effect has a double impact on the memory. It reminds us of all the times we were blessed by someone's love, in life and in stories. The couple in *The Gift of The Magi*, Pa and Ma in the Laura Ingalls Wilder series, and the family in the stable all remind us, with Scrooge, that we are not our own but we are our brother's keeper. Scrooge, along with the host of characters in our memory, equally inspires us in the future as we stumble into opportunities to serve and thank others. I personally think the greatest moment in film history is when Alastair Sim, who plays Scrooge in an early black and white version, stands on his head because the normal world is full of too much joy for any human to bear, and so we must do something foolish or perish from the weight of glory. Cartwheels and handstands and heel kicks and high fives form a happy heart.

Delivery

The examples of *The Scarlet Letter* and *A Christmas Carol* afford us the opportunity to examine closely the first three canons of rhetoric, to study how the author's logical invention of an argument, skillful arrangement of an argument, and purposeful style can move the audience to change their thinking and behavior. If classic novels were simply self-contained and we read them only to get information about the characters, then we could agree with some contemporary educators that students do not need fiction. Cultivating rhetorical readers is the opposite of reading for information. We assume that authors are making an argument that will persuade us and change us. It is not only the characters who are changed, but the readers also. Dickens has raised Scrooge's awareness of the suffering around him, but he has also raised the same awareness in his readers. Not only does he change Scrooge's thinking, but also his behavior; he is moved to take charitable actions. Many readers in Dickens' own London were moved to assist widows, orphans, and others because they read one of his novels. Many readers today will also be moved to help the needy in their communities.

> *We assume that authors are making an argument that will persuade us and change us. It is not only the characters who are changed, but the readers also.*

These two examples of the canons of rhetoric applied to specific stories make it easier to create a list of universal questions that will help you and your student become rhetorical readers.

UNIVERSAL QUESTIONS

Invention—What is the author's main argument?

Above, I represented the arguments of Hawthorne and Dickens as formal logical syllogisms. There is no need to do this with every work of fiction that you read with your student, but it does help illustrate that every author is making an explicit argument about how we should view the world.

Modern guides to literature would refer to this exercise as the discovery of the theme. However, the use of the word "argument" broadens the scope of this discovery. The argument presents an interpretation of the world and calls the reader to respond with a change in thinking or behavior. The theme of *The Scarlet Letter* is adultery. The argument is a call to repent and to be restored to the community. The theme of *A Christmas Carol* is good will. The argument is a call to distribute charity. Similarly, many modern texts about literary analysis focus on the character as a simple matter of description. The goal is to know the character or understand what motivates him. Understanding the argument involves knowing the character and his motives but also evaluating his actions. We must decide whether or not the character has acted well or whether or not the author has presented the correct view of the universe.

Arrangement—How does he structure the argument?

Does the book begin at the beginning and proceed chronologically or does it begin in the middle (*in media res*) and fill in the details through flashback?

Modern literary analysis texts encourage students to focus on the plot. The word "plot" is similar to arrangement, but is more limited in scope. Plot is limited to the progression of the action of the play. The classical, rhetorical word "arrangement" implies a conscious study of the author's choices and how those choices serve to make his argument more persuasive.

Elocution—How does the author present his argument?

Does the author use high style (long words) or low style (simple words)? Does he use figurative language, like metaphors and symbols, or plain language?

Modern works of literary analysis tend to separate the elements of style into separate categories like tone, diction, and symbolism. This separation of the elements fragments the understanding of a work. A rhetorical analysis looks at the author's tone, diction, and symbolism to understand how he builds the persuasive argument.

Memory—What memories should this book retrieve?

What do the canons of *memoria* (memory) and *pronuntiatio / actio* (delivery) have to do with reading fiction? In one sense, memory can be defined as the effective memorization of a speech so that it may be delivered smoothly and effectively. However, texts explaining the art of rhetoric also use memory in a broader way. In earlier generations, people carried commonplace books to record important or well-expressed sentiments. Recording these thoughts was a way of showing that the thoughts now belonged not just to the author but also to the reader. This transference of ownership does not happen with a Google search. The effective rhetorician has read widely and memorized many examples and sayings so that she can properly bring them into persuasive speech, speech that serves to comfort or to counsel or to confront. This is wisdom.

Delivery—What can reading aloud teach me about this book?

Training in memory and delivery becomes more obvious when we study plays or poetry.

The effective rhetorician has read widely and memorized many examples and sayings so that she can properly bring them into persuasive speech.

Reading a Shakespeare play alone in one's room falls far short of reciting a soliloquy or reading an entire play aloud with companions. In fact, classical education that aims to provide rhetorical instruction in reading necessarily must devote much time to reading aloud. Many students who struggle with Shakespeare do so because they are introduced to Shakespeare by reading. His plays must be performed. Instead of assigning students to read Shakespeare's plays silently, we should have them read the plays aloud to their families, read the plays aloud with their classmates, listen to recordings, watch movie versions, and attend performances together. With this approach, we will "kill two birds with one stone." First, students will comprehend the plays more readily. The vocal inflections and the physical gestures of the actors will give the students clues to the meanings of difficult words. I have had more than a few students attribute their success comprehending Shakespeare to the fact that their parents read aloud Psalms from the King James Version of the Bible. Not only does the performance of the plays improve their comprehension but it also allows us to train students in the rhetorical skill of delivery. Students who regularly listen to good speeches will be better speakers. In other words, good delivery is better *caught* than *taught*.

EXAMPLE 3: "BATTER MY HEART, THREE-PERSON'D GOD"

We have now considered the ways in which to read prose and plays rhetorically. What about poetry? Because poetry is more difficult for most students and adults, it is even more important to read it rhetorically, using the five canons. To illustrate, let's look at a sonnet by John Donne.

Holy Sonnets: "Batter my Heart, Three-Person'd God"
By John Donne

Batter my heart, three-person'd God, for you   1
As yet but knock, breathe, shine, and seek to mend;
That I may rise and stand, o'erthrow me, and bend
Your force to break, blow, burn, and make me new.
I, like an usurp'd town to another due,   5
Labor to admit you, but oh, to no end;
Reason, your viceroy in me, me should defend,
But is captiv'd, and proves weak or untrue.
Yet dearly I love you, and would be lov'd fain,   9
But am betroth'd unto your enemy;
Divorce me, untie or break that knot again,
Take me to you, imprison me, for I,
Except you enthrall me, never shall be free,   13
Nor ever chaste, except you ravish me.

The first reaction on the part of many students will be, "I really don't like poetry. It's too hard. I don't have any idea what he is saying here." This difficulty reinforces our need to use the canons of rhetoric to interpret literature. You might be able to guide students through a rhetorical reading of a familiar book like *A Christmas Carol* without naming the canons of rhetoric and consciously applying each one. It is much more unlikely that you could stimulate and guide a great conversation about a harder piece like Donne's sonnet. Having practiced the tools on more accessible literature, you will have them at your disposal to help students understand and appreciate a challenge.

Invention

What in the world is Donne saying here? At first, what we see are images of violence and force. In plain language, Donne is saying that he cannot be changed by God's gentleness with him. His sin and estrangement from God are so great that God must use violence in order to change his sinful nature and restore the fellowship between them.

Arrangement

In what kind of form has Donne arranged his poem? He had many choices when he began. He could have written the poem in free verse. He could have chosen not to have a regular meter or rhyme scheme. In fact, he could have chosen not to write a poem at all. But, the fact is, he has chosen to write a poem that follows a strict form—that of a sonnet. If students are unfamiliar with this form, you must first begin by helping them to define it. How many lines are in the poem? Fourteen. What is the rhyme scheme? The rhyme scheme of a poem is identified by classifying the last word of each line with a letter: *abba abba cdcdcee*. The *a*'s represent one set of rhyming words, the *b*'s another, and so on.

At this point, you are simply teaching the students to be keen observers as they read, the first step toward reading rhetorically. To move them forward, you must help them see how the arrangement of a literary work serves the argument. Refresh your memory about how we did this with the two examples above—*The Scarlet Letter* and *A Christmas Carol*. How does it help us to know the sonnet form and to define it? We must now consider how other writers have traditionally employed the sonnet form. What students will discover is that the sonnet has almost always been used for composing poems to one's love. Why would Donne choose the form of address between a man and a woman to reflect his relationship with God? What does this tell us about how he views that relationship? Donne is certainly not the first to conceive of the relationship in this way. In Scripture, Jesus tells the parable of the ten virgins waiting for the bridegroom. Later, Paul repeatedly refers to the picture of the bride and bridegroom as the picture of Christ and His church (see Ephesians 5, 2 Corinthians 11). How does Donne's poem contribute to our own understanding of that relationship? What makes that relationship similar to one between a husband and wife? What makes it different?

Elocution

What kind of words does Donne use to convey his argument? The first few lines of the poem create a powerful contrast between gentleness and violence. On the one hand, he portrays God as one who knocks, breathes, shines, and seeks to mend. On the other side, he talks of God as one who can batter, break, blow, and burn him. Donne skillfully employs multiple stylistic devices at once. Compressing one-syllable action verbs together with no conjunctions—a stylistic device known as *asyndeton*—contributes to our sense of the relentless and forceful action needed to effect this transformation. Donne also employs *alliteration*, a device in which the words all begin with the same sound. The repeated harsh sound of the initial consonant reinforces the violence—batter, break, blow, burn. The contrast between gentleness and force is created by the close juxtaposition of the gentle verbs with the harsh verbs, a stylistic device known as *antithesis*.

Memory

The art of memory is best practiced with poetry. In previous generations, children memorized poetry every year to present at the final school exhibition. Memorizing and reciting poetry was as important in a rhetorical education as learning to craft and deliver one's own original arguments. When our children are small, they frequently memorize and recite the most basic forms of poetry—nursery rhymes. Even without understanding the words, they delight in the repeated sounds. We often have them recite poems as a way of practicing their speaking skills. As they grow, we forget the importance of these exercises. A comprehensive training in the art of rhetoric would bring all of these skills together.

What if a unit in poetry studies looked like this? "First, copy the poem into a beautiful journal. Do this in your best handwriting and complement it with a beautiful drawing. Next, memorize the poem and deliver it to your family members, your class, and a few close friends. Lead a class discussion on the meaning of the poem and how each of the stylistic devices in the poem contributes to the meaning. Finally, write a sonnet like 'Batter My Heart.' Be sure to describe a loving relationship that is not that of a man and a woman. Copy Donne's form and style, but make it your own." These exercises would make for a robust rhetoric curriculum. I hesitated to include these assignments because it would be all too easy to convert these into a poetry checklist. I can picture parents and teachers listing each of these steps in the daily planner so that they can check them off and close out the school day. This should not serve as a checklist. Instead, we want to help students discover the delights of poetry. If we help them uncover a poem's meaning, we can awaken a love of poetry. If we help them appreciate the sounds by listening to the recitations of others, we can help them hear the beauty of poetry. If we train them to recite poetry, then we give them a lifelong delight of poetry.

Delivery

What about the final canon of rhetoric—delivery? Outside of reciting poetry and performing in plays, how do we practice delivery with reading? The first step is to practice reading aloud. Earlier this year, a friend enrolled her son in policy debate. After the first tournament, she looked to his coach for some ways to help him improve his public speaking. The advice was surprising. The coach advised her to have him read aloud to his family every day. In earlier generations, students practiced public speaking through recitations of famous speeches and poems long before they were asked to deliver their own, original oratory. We need to reclaim this lost art of reading aloud. Students can practice by reading Scripture aloud in church. They can practice at home by reading stories to younger siblings. They can practice in class by reading plays aloud or by reciting poetry.

It would be easy to dismiss all these things as utilitarian. In other words, you might misconstrue my argument by reducing it to a simple formula "practice reading aloud = good speaker/debater = good job." This is not the point of rhetorical instruction for the classical educator. First, we want students to recognize good literature and to delight in it. Then, we want them to learn truth from it. Finally, we want them to love others so much that they are compelled to share truth with them. Perhaps they will love reading so much that they will start a tutoring program for children who struggle with reading. Perhaps they will start a book club with members of their church or larger community. Perhaps they will read aloud to residents of a nursing home. They will learn to live well and to share their joy and wisdom with others. Along the way, we rebuild families

We want them to love others so much that they are compelled to share truth with them.

and communities that modern society has all but destroyed. We rebuild them by sharing stories together so that we have a common language with which to interpret the world.

Interpreting literature, *using the five canons of rhetoric:*	
Invention	What is the author's argument?
Arrangement	How does he structure the book to convey his argument to you?
	How does he begin the book?
	How does he advance his argument?
	How does he end the book?
Elocution	How does he present his argument?
	What kind of language does he use?
	Who tells the story?
	Is the narrator one of the characters in the novel?
	Is he the main character or not? Is he reliable or unreliable?
	Is he omniscient (having all knowledge) or limited?
Memory	How does the author add to the conversation about the book's topic?
	Who else has written about it?
	How does this work compare to other treatments of this subject?
Delivery	Now that you have read and understood the story, what should you do with your newfound knowledge?

CHAPTER FOUR

SPEECH AND DEBATE

"Both Cicero and Quintilian maintained that the most valuable background for an orator was a liberal education, because they recognized that such a broad education was best calculated to aid a person faced with the necessity of inventing arguments on a wide variety of subjects."
—Edward P. J. Corbett, *The Art of Rhetoric for the Modern Student*

A book about rhetoric would not be complete without a chapter on speech and debate. After all, the art of rhetoric is the art of speaking eloquently and persuasively. Most high school students form strong opinions and have a strong desire to share them. Unfortunately, they often want to air an opinion off the cuff without learning how to craft an argument. (In that respect, they may resemble TV and radio personalities and even contemporary politicians.) I was educated in public school where I only had to take one or two speech classes. A number of you may have tried mock trial or debate, but very few of you probably encountered these classes in the context of a full-fledged rhetorical education.

Many articles lament the deplorable communication skills of today's young adults. Some parents express concerns that technology is robbing our children of their voices. Others worry that the emphasis on STEM (science, technology, engineering, and math) comes at the expense of writing and speaking. We must help our children learn to think through issues and then express their thoughts to others. Just as the study of formal logic encompasses much more than "critical thinking," the art of rhetoric encompasses much more than the modern study of communication skills. A rhetorical education employs all of the liberal arts as students persuade others of truth. Students who wish to pursue speech and debate don't do so in a vacuum, simply studying how to craft a great speech or best their opponents in a debate. They must be aware of a wide range of subjects such as literature, government, science, economics and history. Otherwise, they will become proficient in communication skills but will have nothing to say. In addition to gaining familiarity with a wide range of knowledge, students must be able to craft a logical argument (skills developed during the dialectic stage through asking questions, defining terms, and comparing ideas). Finally, students must be able to present their ideas eloquently and persuasively. The last requirement means that they must learn to consider their subject matter and their audience and decide which words and examples are most fitting for both.

Just as the study of formal logic encompasses much more than "critical thinking," the art of rhetoric encompasses much more than the modern study of communication skills.

A colleague at Classical Conversations once taught a freshman-level rhetoric course at a large state university. She was surprised to find that the required syllabus did not assign any speeches! Sadly, too many students are not given the opportunity to practice public speaking. At best, some high schools and universities may require a one-semester course. It's no wonder that so many adults list public speaking as one of their greatest fears. Students (and adults) need practice. They need to start speaking formally in front of their peers at a young age (say 4 or 5) and then continue to speak, debate, lecture, and present throughout their student years.

During the high periods of classical rhetoric in Greece, Rome, and medieval Europe, very young students were first exposed to speech and debate through poetry. They memorized and recited poetry and heard adults recite poetry. This gave them a solid foundation in language. Then, older students would dispute with tutors and one another, taking a position, arguing for it, asking questions, clarifying, and refining their positions. Later, they studied the great speeches of others, paying careful attention to the logical flow of the arguments and to stylistic devices. Finally, they practiced crafting speeches of their own. As contemporary classical educators and parents look back to try to find lost tools for learning and teaching, they often begin with Aristotle.

In *Rhetoric*, Aristotle outlines three kinds of speeches—political, forensic, and ceremonial. In a classical education, students should practice all three kinds of oratory. Students usually practice political oratory through policy debate, forensic oratory through mock trial, and ceremonial oratory at special events such as graduations. Students must master both the five canons of rhetoric and the three types of appeals to the audience—*logos*, *ethos*, and *pathos*. *Pathos*, the emotional appeal, is more likely to be appropriate in a ceremonial speech, while *logos* is more fitting for policy debate. *Ethos* gives speakers credibility in the one-on-one format of Lincoln-Douglas (values) debates.

EXAMPLE 1: POLITICAL SPEECH

Students practice political speeches most often through participating in class debates. Although not all students will become competitive debaters, I believe all classical students should have some exposure to policy debate because it teaches them to craft a persuasive argument. For example, students might propose that the United States change its policy toward its territories or that the United Nations should be significantly reformed or that public schools should be abolished. In order to argue for any of these topics, students must have wide-ranging knowledge. As Aristotle writes, "Whether our argument concerns public affairs or some other subject, we must know some, if not all, of the facts about the subject on which we are to speak and argue" (*Rhetoric* II.22). Political speakers must be aware of the workings of government, particularly in five main categories: ways and means, war and peace, national defense, imports and exports, and legislation (*Rhetoric* I.4). What is the point of introducing students to all of these categories? After all, they won't all be professional politicians or legislators. In a democracy or a democratic republic, all citizens are government leaders. They must understand these issues and practice sound judgment because they all will be voters. Even if they are not called upon to give a political speech in adult life, they certainly will be called upon to evaluate political speeches.

As in literature, parents and teachers can use the five canons of rhetoric to guide their students through speech and debate.

Invention

In a modern speech class, invention would be called brainstorming. Students are trained to throw out a lot of ideas without evaluating them and then to sort them out later. The ancient word "invention" is much richer than "brainstorming" because it connotes a careful attention to detail. Think about the invention of a new technology like the light bulb. Edison considered and rejected many designs before landing on the right one. This should produce copiousness—the goal of invention is to produce more arguments than one will need in the end so that one can choose the best ones. If a student wants to persuade his classmates that English should be declared the national language, he should list as many positive and negative arguments as he can muster. Then, later, he can evaluate them for their persuasive value and begin to arrange them. At this stage, students should draw on their storehouse of memory to think of any pertinent examples from literature, science, history, movies, or famous quotations.

Arrangement

After gathering ideas during invention, students must begin to sift through them and organize their thoughts into a logical flow. For a persuasive speech, they should follow roughly the same outline as for a persuasive essay. They should begin with an *exordium*: a quotation, question, statistic, or story that will draw in their listeners. Then, they should include a *narratio*. The *narratio* allows them to give their listener a brief bit of background information on the issue. Sometimes this will be a definition of the terms or a brief overview of the history of the issue. Next, students should acknowledge both sides of the issue. Then, they announce which side of the argument they will take and why. The statement of their position will allow them to move seamlessly into the proofs for their argument. Here, they will draw upon experts to support their position. At some point, they will need to address the counter-argument. If they suspect a hostile listener, they may want to address and refute the counter-arguments at the beginning of the speech so that the listener will be more favorable toward them. For other audiences, it may be more effective to address the counter-arguments at the end. Finally, the speech should end with a restatement of the speaker's position and a call to action. Students should ask their audience to think or behave differently in response to their speech.

In classical rhetoric, this act of arranging one's speech was not called outlining but rather arrangement or disposition. In *Classical Rhetoric for the Modern Student*, Corbett writes:

> Disposition then becomes something more than the conventional system for organizing a discourse, something more than just a system of outlining the composition; it becomes a discipline that trains writers in the judicious selection and use of available means to the desired end. (292)

In rhetoric, arrangement of ideas is dependent upon the occasion, the subject matter, and the audience. Students should always consider these three factors in evaluating the order of arguments within a speech. Now that we have listed the main parts of a speech, let's look at each of them a little more closely.

Exordium—The exordium is the speaker's attempt to interest their audience, draw them in, and induce them to sympathy or receptive listening. Consider a few examples from history:

> Four score and seven years ago our fathers brought forth on this continent, a new nation, conceived in Liberty, and dedicated to the proposition that all men are created equal. (Abraham Lincoln, "Gettysburg Address")

Here, Lincoln stands looking at the carnage of the Civil War that threatens to undo permanently the union of the states. He calls his audience to remember the Founding Fathers and their goals for the nation. He calls them to consider that they are bound together by their physical geography ("this continent") and by their ideals ("the proposition that all men are created equal"). In one short statement, he draws them together and invites them to listen to the rest of his speech. His exordium was echoed later by Martin Luther King, Jr. during the Civil Rights movement:

> Five score years ago, a great American, in whose symbolic shadow we stand today, signed the Emancipation Proclamation. This momentous decree came as a great beacon light of hope to millions of Negro slaves who had been seared in the flames of withering injustice. It came as a joyous daybreak to end the long night of their captivity. (Martin Luther King, Jr., "I Have a Dream")

Notice how he echoes Lincoln's opening words with his use of the words "five score years ago." Here he asks his listener to consider the great length of time that has elapsed since the Emancipation Proclamation. He builds a crescendo by describing the great hope that the proclamation fostered for his people and then shatters it by describing how none of those hopes have been realized. His *exordium* captured the attention of the audience.

Narratio—Next, the effective speaker will move into narration, sometimes referred to by its Latin name *narratio*. In modern speech and composition classes, this is called background information. Here, the speaker must give the audience enough information about the issue so that they will be engaged and informed listeners. For example, if I wanted to persuade you that every American should have a classical education, I would need to define "classical education" and contrast it with "modern American education."

Divisio—This part of the speech is perhaps the most important for today's speakers and writers. In the division of a speech, the speaker acknowledges both sides of the argument. Too many debates in the public arena today fail to consider the other side. In a dialogue (two-way communication), it is important for each speaker to acknowledge the possibility that the other person is right. In a speech (one-way communication), it is important for the speaker to acknowledge the opposite position. For example, I might be able to give you a fine speech arguing that we should abolish the death penalty in America. Let's suppose for the sake of our example that you are a strong proponent of the death penalty. You may not listen to my arguments because you are forming counter-arguments in your head. Instead, I should acknowledge that some favor the death penalty

In a dialogue (two-way communication), it is important for each speaker to acknowledge the possibility that the other person is right.

and explain why they do. Then, I can directly address your arguments. Two purposes are accomplished. First, I have your attention. Second, you have the ability to respond in a respectful, well-reasoned way because I have acknowledged your argument. High school students are particularly prone to make quick judgments and then argue incessantly over them. Practicing division teaches them to consider their opponent's position and to address it with consideration.

Confirmatio—By this point in the speech, it is time for the speaker to offer proof for the claims they make. If this is forensic oratory, such as mock trial, the attorneys for either side must offer proof of the defendant's guilt or innocence. If students are practicing team policy debate, they must show the benefits that will come from adopting their plan and the harms that will result from rejecting it. For example, let's say students wanted to convince an audience that the United States should stop allowing states to draw their own congressional districts, a process that often results in politicians "gerrymandering" their districts and cherry-picking their voters. The students would need to cite studies to demonstrate that voters have been harmed in this process. They would also need to propose a reasonable alternative plan for drawing Congressional districts and to demonstrate the advantages of their plan. Students must learn to pick sources that will accurately demonstrate their case. In a speech about human nature, an example from literature or history might be adequate proof or "confirmation" of the stated argument. In a science research paper, students must cite research conducted by a reliable scientist or university. The ultimate goal of persuasion is to persuade the audience that one's own position is the one that leads to the common good.

Peroratio—This fancy word is what we moderns call a "conclusion." Here, the student restates the major points of the argument that they have just made and sometimes presents a call to action. For example, a mock trial closing argument will repeat all of the evidence in favor of that team and will call the jury to vote in their favor. A team policy argument will repeat the advantages of adopting that team's plan and will call the judge to vote in that team's favor. Most of us were taught in school to use the conclusion to repeat the major points of the essay. However, modern speech and composition programs seldom include the other piece of the conclusion—the call to action. When students engage in persuasive speech, they should call their listeners to action. The audience should be moved to think, behave, or vote differently.

Once students have gathered ideas (*invention*) and arranged their ideas, including all of the parts of a sound speech (*dispositio*), they are ready to polish their speech.

Elocution

As in arrangement, students who are choosing their style (elocution) must consider their subject matter and audience. If you are speaking to a group of scientists, you may not want to use a lot of flowery, literary language. If you are a scientist speaking to a group of non-scientists, you will want to avoid highly technical terms. Whatever the situation, the language must be appropriate. It must also be persuasive and memorable. A speaker's words should linger in their listeners' minds. Stylistic devices accomplish this. Have you ever wondered why people remember Shakespeare's speeches or why so many of his expressions have entered common usage? He was thoroughly trained in a rhetorical tradition that forced students to over-practice an arsenal of stylistic devices.

By way of example, let us consider Martin Luther King, Jr.'s famous "I Have a Dream" speech. In addition to his booming voice, one of the elements that makes this speech so memorable is his repeated use of the opening phrase, "I have a dream." This is a stylistic device known as *anaphora*. Winston Churchill employed the same device in his speech to rouse the British to press on in WWII: "We shall fight on the beaches, we shall fight on the landing grounds, we shall fight on the fields and in the streets, we shall fight in the hills; we shall never surrender." The repetition both makes the speech memorable and builds the speech to a crescendo. In King's case, the audience cannot help but hope that his dream is fulfilled. In Churchill's case, the audience is fortified by a sense of British bravery and endurance, and they are energized to go forth and fight another day.

Memory

In order for students to deliver speeches that are polished and persuasive, they must learn to memorize. In Classical Conversations, we provide opportunities each year for high school students to speak in front of their class. Some assignments ask them to memorize historical speeches of presidents and other world leaders, while others require them to remember speeches from Shakespeare's plays. The purpose of these assignments is twofold. First, we want students to exercise and train their memories. Second, students must practice all of the skills involved in delivery (eye contact, voice volume, gestures, inflection, etc.). Outside of mock trial and debate, students also give original speeches in several of their courses. Every year I remind students that this is a speaking exercise, not a reading exercise. Memorizing and delivering a speech is very different from reading a paper. Students have opportunities to be so familiar with their arguments that they can present them from memory. All of us have attended speeches or college lectures in which the speaker never looked up from his notes; he made no connection at all with the audience. Students must memorize their speeches so that they can engage their audience through eye contact, dramatic voice changes, and gestures.

Delivery

The final canon of rhetoric is delivery. Once students have brainstormed content (*invention*), organized and arranged their content (*arrangement*), polished their argument so that it is persuasive and stylistically appealing (*elocution*), and memorized their speech (*memory*), they are ready to deliver it to the audience.

If you conduct a survey of the general population asking them about their greatest fears and most frightening experiences, public speaking ranks high on the list. I would argue that lack of preparation, lack of instruction and feedback, and lack of low-stakes practice are the primary culprits. Who ever found comfort in imagining the audience to be wearing nothing but their underwear, anyway?

Fortunately, the five canons of rhetoric provide preparation as you work through invention, arrangement, elocution, and memory before you even get to delivery. From there, conversations allow you to provide instruction and feedback. Watch videos of great speakers and analyze what they do well so that your student has a model to imitate. Pick one goal that your student can realistically achieve, and then allow him to evaluate how well he met his goal. Maybe he struggles to make eye contact. Work on just that one thing. Another time, focus on speaking slowly. Another time, make enunciation your goal. Then, practice, practice, practice in an environment that feels safe.

Start small, with a mirror. Move up to one or two trusted family members. Then invite a friend or two. Take turns reciting something to your children and listening to them recite so that you can laugh together when you make mistakes. Always talk about these habits of good delivery in the context of getting your message to your listener. By asking your student to improve his delivery, you are demonstrating that you think he has something to say that is worth hearing.

EXAMPLE 2: FORENSIC SPEECH

Aristotle's second category of speech was forensic speech, speech that relates to evaluating past actions. Most students practice this through events like mock trial. You may be thinking, "I can understand why everyone needs to be familiar with political speech, but what is the purpose of all students learning forensic speech? After all, they won't all be lawyers, right?" This is certainly true, and some of Aristotle's focus on forensic speech results from the fact that many Athenians were called upon to defend themselves in civil suits. (Like modern-day America, it was a litigious society, so most rhetoric texts offered advice about forensic speech). Aside from preparing students for a career in the law, what is the purpose of mock trial? First, just as all students will be called upon to be informed voters as adults, many of them will be called upon to serve on a jury. This is one of the rights and responsibilities of citizens—to serve on a jury of peers. Second, the activity of mock trial gives students yet another opportunity to practice thinking and speaking skills and to practice exercising judgment.

Picture a group of fourteen-year-old boys and girls gathered to work on a mock trial defense team. At the first practice they read their opening statement, which sounds like a recap of the police report, complete with the mention that the defendant has shot her husband six times. One parent has offered to help lead them through this process and decides to start the conversation.

PARENT: What is your job in this trial?
STUDENT: To prove that the defendant is innocent.
PARENT: Are you sure?
STUDENT: Yes. Absolutely.

PARENT:	Have you ever heard the phrase "innocent until proven guilty?"
STUDENT:	Yes.
PARENT:	Wouldn't that suggest that it is the prosecution's job to prove your client guilty?
STUDENT:	Yes.
PARENT:	Have you ever heard of "providing proof beyond a reasonable doubt?"
STUDENT:	Yes.
PARENT:	Whose job is that?
STUDENT:	I guess the prosecution.
PARENT:	So, now what do you think your job is as the defense team?
STUDENT:	I guess it's to create doubt.
PARENT:	Does your opening statement do that?
STUDENT:	No.
PARENT:	How can you change it so that it does?
STUDENT:	I guess we shouldn't focus on the fact that she shot him six times.

At this point in the conversation the parent realizes exactly how much these young students do not know about mock trial, so she wisely realizes it is time to start further back.

PARENT:	When are you going to deliver your opening statement?
STUDENT:	I don't know. What do you mean?
PARENT:	What's the order of the trial? Look in your notebook.
STUDENT:	The prosecution goes first, then we go, then the prosecution calls their witnesses, then we call our witnesses, then we make our closing statement, and then they make theirs. Hey, this doesn't seem fair, why does the prosecution get to go first and last?
PARENT:	Tell me again. What is the job of the prosecution?
STUDENT:	To prove beyond a reasonable doubt. Oh, I see, they have to work harder, so they get to open and close.
PARENT:	Why are we doing this exercise?
STUDENT:	I guess so that we can see what a trial is like?
PARENT:	Why is that important?

STUDENT:	Because everyone has the right to a trial in this country.
PARENT:	Where do these rights come from?
STUDENT:	I don't know.
PARENT:	What document records most of our rights?
STUDENT:	The Bill of Rights.
PARENT:	How many rights are listed there?
STUDENT:	Ten.
PARENT:	How many of them have to do with trials?
STUDENT:	(beginning to recite) Warrants, cannot testify against self, right to a speedy trial, right to a jury, cruel and unusual punishment. That's five. Wait. . . five out of the ten have to do with trials!
PARENT:	Why do you think those particular rights were so important to the Founding Fathers?

If the student were not preparing to play a role in the mock trial, some of these important life questions may never have surfaced. Often rhetorical events, such as speech, debate, and mock trial, are professionalized like so many other student activities today. Maybe you have considered a professional speech, debate, or mock trial coach for your student. The skills he needs to succeed at mock trial or debate or ceremonial speeches are the same skills he needs to write a successful persuasive essay, so a professional coach is not necessary.

What if we coached the team to think of the mock trial preparation like the crafting of a fine essay? The opening speaker for either the defense or the prosecution parallels the exordium (opening paragraph) of the essay. The speaker must consider how to draw in his audience—the judge and the jury. This opening statement will conclude with the thesis statement or statement of fact: "You should find my client guilty (or innocent) for the following reasons." Then, the lawyer who questions the witnesses must provide the proofs. In an essay, the reasons supporting the thesis would be stated outright. In a courtroom, a skillful questioner will elicit the reasons from the witnesses. This process of offering proof for the argument is known by the Latin name *confirmatio*. Finally, an essay would close with a paragraph that restates the thesis and explains why the audience should care about the conclusion. This portion of the essay, called the *peroratio*, mirrors the closing arguments of both teams. In his writings, the Roman orator Quintilian said that this portion of a speech should include two parts, a summation of the major points already made and the production of the appropriate emotion in the audience. This is what the successful lawyer accomplishes in the closing argument. How do the successful students craft their arguments? They use the canons of rhetoric.

> **"Putting Literary Characters on Trial" by Jen Greenholt**
>
> When I was in high school, my sister and I competed in a national homeschool debate league. During those four years, I traveled around the United States competing and spent my spare time researching topics that ranged from immigration to agriculture to trade policy. One of my favorite debate rounds, however, came in an unusual venue: Shakespeare class.
>
> In eleventh grade, the community I attended one day a week was studying five of Shakespeare's greatest plays in depth. Because the plays were written to be performed on stage, we approached the text as something that was meant to be spoken, not only to be read. We practiced reading the plays aloud. We memorized lines and presented them to each other to practice public speaking. And when we got to *Hamlet*, we tried something altogether different.
>
> Rather than simply writing an essay about whether or not Hamlet was insane, as many high school English students do, we put Hamlet on trial. My peers and I took on the roles of prosecutor, arguing that he was sane and should be held responsible for his murders; defense attorney, arguing that he should be found not-guilty on a plea of insanity; witnesses, including Claudius, Gertrude, Fortinbras, Laertes, and all the rest; and the defendant, Hamlet himself. (Having witnesses who can speak from beyond the grave is one of the advantages of putting a literary character on trial.)
>
> Practicing debate skills with literature as your source material has other, more important benefits as well. As a student, it forces you to dig deeply

> into the text to find clues about your character's identity. You have to practice good reading skills and pay attention to the sequence of events in order to ascertain a character's probable motivations and rule out unrelated incidents.
>
> Furthermore, a lively debate breathes life into older literature that might otherwise seem distant and irrelevant to modern students. Debating the sanity of Hamlet, or the guilt of Hester Prynne, or the leadership of Achilles gives students a vested interest in the material. At the same time, it provides a beneficial context for debate practice because both sides have access to the same, finite information, and the outcome is determined by solid argumentation rather than who can find the most obscure evidence.

Invention

In invention, students must gather all of the information they will need to build their case. What are all the facts of the case? Who are the available witnesses? How reliable are they? Which previous cases are similar? What types of appeals will be most effective with the audience? In previous chapters, we have talked about choosing the types of appeals based on the subject matter and audience. Here, we need to consider those in the context of a forensic speech.

1. *Pathos*, the emotional appeal, is critical to both teams because the jury must be moved to empathize with either the victim or the defendant.
2. *Logos*, the logical appeal, concerns the way in which the speaker crafts a sound, reasonable, and logical account. The lawyers must craft a clear, cohesive argument to present a credible story to the jury.
3. The speaker must also convey *ethos*, the sense that his account is believable because he is a reliable and honest man; therefore, his presentation of the event can be trusted. It is as important to establish the *ethos* of the defender as that of the defendant. As Aristotle argues, "rhetorical persuasion is effected not only by demonstrative but by ethical argument; it helps a speaker to convince us, if we believe that he has certain qualities himself, namely, goodness, or goodwill towards us, or both together" (31).

Arrangement

Which witness has the strongest argument? Perhaps they should go last. Which witness has the second strongest argument? Perhaps they should go first so that we start forcefully. Which witness is weakest? We should place them in the middle so that they don't make a lasting impression.

Elocution

Should the prosecutor sound calm and reasonable or indignant and angry? Should the defense lawyer sound confident and assured or dramatic and wounded? The tone of the speech is critical because he cannot afford to alienate the judge or the jury by sounding slick or condescending. The best way to help students negotiate these decisions is to have them practice in front of a jury of parents before the actual mock trial. After the run-through, students can ask the mock jury and judges if they noted any weaknesses in their case or if they struck the right tone.

Memory

How does the lawyer practice so that their opening and closing arguments are persuasive? The successful trial speaker delivers a polished, memorized speech that still sounds conversational. As I mentioned above, students should practice speeches over and over so that they have mastered the material. Mastery of the material allows them to focus not on their words but on their audience.

Delivery

How does the lawyer draw in the audience? The lawyer must consider hand gestures, voice volume, and eye contact with the jury. At times, they must be solemn, appealing to the jury as reasonable people who will see the obvious logic of their case. At other times, they must be dramatic, appealing to the jury to sympathize with either the victim or the defendant. At times, they should speak quietly and calmly; at other times they should raise their voices to emphasize the importance of a particular point.

According to Aristotle, forensic orators must also be aware of motives, of victims, and of degrees of wrong. The prosecution must demonstrate that the defendant was motivated by an emotion that we consider to be wrong—jealousy, anger, greed, etc. The defendant must demonstrate that the motive is less grievous. The wife who, in our example, murders her husband because she has just learned that he is having an affair is different from the wife who murders him because she fears that he is about to abuse her again. The speakers must also consider the victim of the crime. If the woman's husband has viciously beat her, then the crime does not seem "as wrong" to us. If, however, he is a fine, upstanding citizen who has been falsely accused of beating his wife, his murder will be a double fault against her because she will have killed his character as well as his body.

Of the three types of oratory, forensic rhetoric has the most potential to stray from our definition of rhetoric as "the persuasion of others to truth." How can we continue to say that we are training students in the tools of truth when we are training them to manipulate the facts in favor of the prosecution or defense? There are two answers, one of which concerns the nature of education and the other that concerns the nature of human rights. When students engage in arguments for or against an issue or a person, we are giving them an opportunity to practice discernment. We are not assuming that they have mastered this skill. They are practicing, and they must practice with all kinds of issues, arguments, and styles until they have mastered the tools. Much deeper than the nature of educational practice is the introduction of students to fundamental human rights. Although we may have a jaded view of defense lawyers, they are vitally important to securing our freedoms. John Adams felt so strongly about this that he defended the British soldiers who killed American citizens during the Boston Massacre.

EXAMPLE 3: CEREMONIAL SPEECH

Ceremonial speakers offer praise or blame of an individual, an occasion, or a nation. These types of speeches used to be made in celebration of memorable historical events or figures. Today, citizens rarely engage in public praise or blame (unless they are on the campaign trail). Our students may only encounter ceremonial speech at formal ceremonies, graduations, and funerals. Delivering a ceremonial speech on these occasions indicates the importance of celebrating a life that is just beginning as well as a life that has just drawn to an end. The aim of ceremonial speech is to praise virtue and censure vice. According to Aristotle, the forms of virtue are "justice, courage, temperance, magnificence, magnanimity, liberality, gentleness, prudence, wisdom" (Book I, Chapter 9). These virtues are paralleled in Scripture: "But the fruit of the Spirit is love, joy, peace, longsuffering, gentleness, goodness, faith, meekness, temperance: against such there is no law" (Gal. 5:22–23, KJV).

When our elder sons graduated from homeschooling, we held ceremonies in our backyard in order to thank the men who invested in teaching them virtue. Each time, about fifty people attended, and we had a band play music while everyone feasted and played games. Everything about the tone of the party changed for the actual ceremony. Trumpet music introduced the graduate who had changed into his cap and gown. The sounds and visuals of the event were appropriate for the seriousness of the occasion. Leaving the protection of your parents and the support of your community demands thoughtful reflection. So each of our sons honored four or five men who had impacted their lives. My sons publically thanked the men and asked them to pray that other godly men would be a part of their futures. All of their grandparents attended so the boys could reflect on their heritage and thank their grandparents for raising parents that loved them. The actual ceremony was not a formality but the very heart of the gathering. They both included humor in their speeches, but honor and respect for their elders was the significant theme of the ceremony, so the deliveries were honorable and respectful. If any of the five canons had been neglected, the ceremony would have been less than their mentors and grandparents deserved. Good rhetorical skills matter and make an impact.

Don't you wish that more public figures had an education that forced them to think about temperance, magnanimity, or prudence?

Even though most rhetoricians strictly delineate the three types of speeches, the ceremonial is often contained within the forensic, particularly when it comes to student assignments. For example, one student may wish to argue in an essay or a speech that Brutus is not a good leader in Shakespeare's *Julius Caesar*. This thesis statement would necessarily involve the ceremonial topics of praise or blame. As our students read, listen to, or deliver ceremonial speeches, they engage in another important formative activity—they contemplate virtue. Don't you wish that more public figures had an education that forced them to think about temperance, magnanimity, or prudence?

High school students need many opportunities to practice different kinds of speeches. In fact, when my oldest was in junior high, I decided that it was no longer effective to pursue a classical education at home with our family. He needed a community of peers led by a loving, older mentor in order to engage in discussion, speech, and debate. My firstborn is a confident speaker and exercises good judgment today because he debated with his peers and delivered so many speeches. Looking back, I am so grateful that many families chose to join us for this adventure of forming wise, virtuous citizens.

Speaking eloquently, *using the five canons of rhetoric:*	
Invention	What is your purpose in giving this speech? Who is your audience? What information and facts do you need to gather? What type of testimony will be most reliable?
Arrangement	What is the most logical way to organize this speech? Have you addressed both sides of the issue? Have you provided evidence to support your argument? Have you included a call to action?
Elocution	What kind of language is appropriate for the audience? What tone is suitable for this speech?
Memory	What stylistic devices will make the speech memorable? What tools will help you memorize this speech? What prior knowledge will the audience bring to this speech?
Delivery	Have you practiced your speech in front of family and friends? Are you maintaining eye contact? Is your volume appropriate and your enunciation clear? Are you using the right amount of gestures and movement?

CHAPTER FIVE

WRITING

> "Child, to say the very thing you really mean, the whole of it, nothing more or less or other than what you really mean; that's the whole art and joy of words."
>
> —C. S. Lewis, *Till We Have Faces*

Let me tell you a story about my friend's daughter Abby. During her freshman year in high school, she was given the assignment to write a basic research paper about the life and achievements of Louis Pasteur. She was stumped when she reached the conclusion. She'd learned so much in her time researching and writing that she really wanted to say something beyond simply restating her topic and the facts. So, she went to her mother to talk about the problem.

"I've almost finished my research paper. I just need to finish the conclusion, and I'm not sure what to include. What do you think?"

Her mom asked her to define the purpose of her paper's conclusion, and Abby told her that it was to bring the threads of the paper together and to share something more about Pasteur beyond simply restating the facts. The conversation didn't stop there. Next, my friend asked Abby what she found most interesting about the great scientist.

"Oh, I thought it was very interesting that Pasteur liked art," Abby said. "When he was young he didn't even want to be a scientist. He wasn't a very good student. He wanted to study art."

"To be a good artist, you have to pay attention to details. What other studies require a particular reliance on this skill?"

"Math and science!"

"You're right! And from what I've read in your paper, Pasteur really put those skills to use in his field. What would have happened if he had decided to study painting?"

"Well, we might not have discovered pasteurization or vaccines—including the one for rabies!"

"So it was a good thing for us that Pasteur decided to study chemistry instead of art, wasn't it?" my friend asked.

This conversation helped Abby to realize that her discovery about Pasteur was worth exploring and then sharing with others. Pasteur was fascinated by the complexity and design of what he studied through his microscope. He believed it revealed the artistry of God, so he devoted his life to studying God's creation in his lab. Because of all the time and attention he spent on his studies, he discovered important new things that have helped heal many people. Abby realized that it is beautiful to discover and produce medicines that save people's lives. By the time they finished talking, Abby concluded that Pasteur had become an artist after all, using the medium of the microscope and the scientific method instead of bronze or clay. Her conclusion was not only valuable, but also delightful, and she reached it through the process of writing a paper and then discussing it with her mom.

You can use the five canons of rhetoric to write anything well, but I want to begin with an example about writing research papers. Eloquent words are less of a focus in this style of writing, so students learn to focus on invention and arrangement, the first two canons of rhetoric. This allows them to begin with the bones of writing before they progress to the skin. (Writing a work of fiction, like a novel, short story, or poem, would place more focus on elocution, the third canon.) I begin here to illustrate the point that writing is necessary across the curriculum, not just in the humanities. Then, we will take a look at the canons of rhetoric as applied to a persuasive essay.

EXAMPLE 1: A RESEARCH PAPER

Biographical research papers are suited to rhetorical writing practice, especially the canons of invention and arrangement. The guidelines are clear, and the content generally lends itself to a narrow focus so that the research and the writing are achievable tasks. This is particularly true in the early high school years, when students need to solidify their basic writing skills while they practice asking good questions and seeking answers.

Invention

The invention stage relies heavily on asking questions and seeking answers. There are two questions that will guide everything else about your student's writing assignment: "What is my goal in completing this assignment?" and "Who is my audience?"

Abby's goal was to present the most important information about Louis Pasteur to someone who wanted to learn about this scientist, to do so in a way that was beautiful and appealing, and to make her audience feel the delight of discovery, too. Your student's goals in writing might initially be "to complete the assignment" or "to get a good grade," but as you progress in the rhetoric stage, I hope you will point your children toward more lasting goals such as discovering the truth about a particular subject or finding better ways to convey their ideas with wisdom and grace.

Any conversation about the purpose of writing will lead naturally to a conversation about audience. Once you've determined your audience, what can you do to make sure your paper is speaking to that audience? In Abby's case, the audience included those interested in learning about Pasteur, the teacher who would evaluate her paper, and the audience to whom she might present her paper as a speech. She had to make writing choices based on those audiences' preexisting knowledge about the subject and their expectations for proper and understandable language. As Christian parents, we also point our children to the audience we cannot see: the Lord. This is the essence of the Latin phrase *Coram Deo*, which means, "before the face of God." Classical,

Christian educators teach students to be aware that all we do is under His gaze and should be for His glory.

Once your student has identified his purpose and audience, he can begin the concrete work of invention—gathering the facts and information he needs to write his paper. In the example I used to begin this chapter, Abby spent several weeks doing broad research from print and Internet sources in order to decide what sorts of things she thought would be important to tell others about Louis Pasteur. She knew that she would have to include biographical information. From her research, she also discovered several interesting facts about his character and personality. And, of course, she found a wealth of information about his discoveries and achievements since he was such a prolific and influential scientist.

When my students are writing a research paper, I ask them to record their research on note cards and organize them by subject category. They should also write down the bibliographic information for every piece of information they collect so they can find it later if they need to check facts or flesh out an argument. In our digital age, students may be tempted to do their note taking on the computer. That way they avoid having to type things twice. The problem with the "copy-paste" approach is that students may never synthesize the information in their own brains. The discipline involved in writing notes by hand is a tool of memory: repetition, repetition, repetition is what produces understanding and wisdom.

It is often tempting to think of the research paper as a solitary assignment, involving only the student and the sources. However, conversations with parents and peers are another way to glean information and pursue wisdom during the invention stage. Ask your student to define terms, compare ideas, determine the relationship between events (in scientific writing, the difference between correlation and causation is huge!), consider circumstances, and evaluate testimony. If you look for these question types in the dialogue I re-created at the beginning of the chapter, you should find most of them represented. (For more help with this process, see *The Question*.)

Conversations with parents and peers are another way to glean information and pursue wisdom during the invention stage.

Arrangement

Before it is time to begin writing, your student will need to arrange the information he has gathered into a logical order. Note cards are handy at this stage of the process for kinetic learners because students can arrange the physical cards into different sequences to see which order makes the most sense. Students should arrange them in an order that tells a cohesive story—a story that is both informative and interesting. For example, a biographical research paper might progress chronologically, starting with the individual's birth and ending with his death. Another type of history paper might work backward, starting with a war and backtracking to discover its causes. A scientific research paper might begin with a certain phenomenon and then go on to investigate its source.

Students often have difficulty deciding on the best order for their paper. This is another good place for conversation with you. You can give them these options: "Would it make sense for you to write this essay in chronological order, or would it be more effective to start with the scientist's major discovery and work backward, telling your reader how they arrived at this revelation?" Help your student create a very basic outline once he has arranged his research. Write a single sentence or a few key words to represent each notecard. Main points get a Roman numeral (I, II, III) while subpoints get a letter (A, B, C), as in this simple example:

I. Introduction
II. Demonstration
   A. Argument 1
   B. Argument 2
   C. Argument 3
III. Conclusion

That initial research and rudimentary outline will also tell your student what else he needs to research. As Scott Crider writes in his book *The Office of Assertion*, "Meaning is not only discovered through invention; it is also made through organization. The reader of a work that both discovers and makes will experience something unusual but persuasive"(71). Let's say your student is writing a research paper about the characteristics of planets. He gathers initial research on Mercury, Venus, Earth, Mars, Saturn, Jupiter, Uranus, Neptune, and Pluto. He plans to write one paragraph about each one, progressing outward from the sun. Then, he runs into a problem. Recent sources do not consider Pluto to be a planet. Your student realizes that he needs to do additional research into this debate over definitions. So, the scope of his paper and his initial outline may change as a result of his findings.

Once your student has assembled his research data, he can create a detailed outline of his paper. Most outlines include three major sections:

1. Introduction: a statement identifying the topic of the essay and the reasons why one would want to know about and understand the topic.
2. Demonstration: several paragraphs or sections describing the facts. This section is also called the body of the paper. In addition to building his own case or findings, the student may respond to counter-arguments or alternate interpretations of the facts.
3. Conclusion: a synthesis of all the prior sections, emphasizing important facts and themes and drawing appropriate inferences.

These three sections may vary in length. In a short, 500-word paper, each section may contain only one or two paragraphs. In a longer research paper, the "demonstration" section may contain many paragraphs.

Even on short papers, encourage your student to practice the canon of arrangement thoroughly, alternating between one-word and full-sentence outlines. In *The Office of Assertion*, Scott Crider claims that "All the techniques… should convince your reader that the parts cohere into a complete whole, that the essay's design is not only intelligible but also beautiful. Beauty characterizes all good designs"(67). Think how beautiful the structure of a tree root or a spider web or a turtle shell is. These designs are functional but also aesthetically pleasing. Our students should take their lead from the beauty of creation when they create an outline—a skeleton—for their writing. In doing so, they build *logos*, an appeal to the minds of the readers through clear reasoning and organized arrangement of facts and examples.

If your student is champing at the bit to begin writing, you can also remind him of the practical benefits of outlining. First, it is far easier to identify gaps in logic when you look at an outline than it is when you look at a completed paper. Second, thorough preparatory work cuts down on revision time. Third, having an outline beside you staves off writer's block because it provides a set of directions to keep you from getting lost in the prose.

Elocution

Elocution, the actual step of writing the essay, is a question of what style—or stylistic techniques—to use. This stage includes a number of considerations. Help your student to decide what kind of style is appropriate to the audience and to the subject matter. Should he use technical terms or commonplace words, long descriptive sentences, or short, matter-of-fact ones? This step also includes questions of grammar and editing. What kind of appeals should the writer use, *logos, pathos*, or *ethos*? *Pathos* appeals to the emotions and should be used sparingly in this type of writing. Once a student determines the tone and style, he can begin to write a draft of the paper in prose form with full sentences and rough transitions.

Part of elocution is learning to tailor your writing to your audience's limits. This is especially true of academic writing, which will almost certainly include word or page counts. Someday, I hope your student will have some opportunities to write or speak at whatever length seems best to him, when he can use as many examples as he wants and make his case as complex as he needs. As you probably know, however, those situations will be rare. More often, your student will need to meet a set of requirements. This skill will serve him well for many years to come. Even as an adult, whether writing for a newspaper, a literary magazine, or a website, there are likely to be constraints. Even if no explicit limits are given, the audience's attention span places demands on the writer. The example I have been using, a science research paper, will probably be longer—maybe ten to fifteen pages—in order to cover all the necessary material, while an essay about one character in a novel may be shorter.

The fun of teaching writing to rhetoric-level students is that you do not have to stop with word counts, correct spelling, and subject-verb agreement. You might also discuss the conventions of language and how they change over time. For example, your student might appreciate the question of whether or not abbreviations and emoticons are appropriate outside the context of social media. Or even the nuance between "chomping at the bit" or "champing at the bit." Now, if grammar is difficult for your child, you may still have to spend time reviewing the difference between passive and active voice or the proper use of a semicolon. But be on the lookout for ways to turn even these review lessons into a conversation. Train yourself to talk to your student about the consequences of his choices, not just the correctness of his grammar.

Remind your student that his readers do not have the benefit of hearing the inflections of his voice or seeing the expression on his face. They see only the words he puts on the page. While a speaker might be able to rely on nonverbal cues, a writer must use tools, such as verb form, vocabulary, and sentence structure, to set the tone of a paper. Two papers might be written on the same topic, but if one is written in the passive voice, as is being done in these initial clauses, a different tone will be conveyed than in a paper that your student writes in the active voice, as I am doing now, at the end of this sentence. Do you see the difference? All I did was change the passive verbs "be written" and "is being done" to active verbs: "writes" and "am doing." All of a sudden, the tone of the sentence changed. It went from leisurely and vague to succinct and sharp.

Since a research paper is supposed to present facts, the words your student chooses should be clear and precise rather than fancy, and the sentence structure should be as transparent as possible. Think about the long, complex sentences in a novel by Herman Melville (*Moby Dick*), a poem by John Milton (*Paradise Lost*), or a sermon by George Whitefield ("The Method of Grace"). You can return to those sentences over and over again and always discover something new in them, but it may take several readings before you grasp their full meaning. Ask your student whether he intends his sentences to be simple glass windows through which a reader sees his ideas and discoveries or stained-glass windows that bathe his ideas in colorful light. Writing can be like a photograph or an abstract painting, depending on the choices your young writer makes.

One aspect of writing at the rhetorical level is learning to use rhetorical devices, such as metaphors, similes, and alliteration, to make writing beautiful (see appendix 2 for a list of commonly used devices), but an equally important aspect of this stage is learning when not to use those devices. *The Elements of Style*, by William Strunk and E. B. White, gives this advice:

> Vigorous writing is concise. A sentence should contain no unnecessary words, a paragraph no unnecessary sentences, for the reason that a drawing should have no unnecessary lines and a machine no unnecessary

parts. This requires not that the writer make all his sentences short, or that he avoid detail and treat his subjects only in outline, but that every word tell. (II.13)

Responsibility and self-control are character lessons that apply to writing as well as to finances or employment. We should train our children to be good stewards of words as well as of money and time.

Memory

When we talk about this fourth canon of rhetoric, we are not just talking about memorizing a paper to recite it verbatim, although that is one way to practice *memoria*. First, a good writer draws from his own memory in crafting an argument or a conclusion. Your student should search his memory for other papers, readings, or assignments he has done that are relevant to his current writing topic. Your student should also allot enough time for research so that he can internalize his findings and see the relationships between ideas. The keys to memory are intensity, frequency, and—this is significant—duration. Ideas need to be repeated over periods of time to aid memorization. Trying to cram a paper into one night robs your student of the opportunity to make the connections that only rise to the surface with time, like bubbles in a boiling pot of water.

> *Responsibility and self-control are character lessons that apply to writing as well as to finances or employment.*

Second, a good writer should seek to understand the prior knowledge that his audience will bring to this paper. In a research paper, that might mean choosing sources that will be credible to his audience members: respected scientists, reliable studies, and reputable publications. It might mean acknowledging (remembering) arguments that have already been made about this topic or faulty conclusions that have been drawn in the past and referencing them in the paper. It might also mean following the appropriate style guidelines that his audience would expect such as MLA or APA. All of these decisions help to create the student's *ethos*, the means of persuasion that relies on a person's credibility or character.

Third, a good writer looks for ways to make his writing memorable to himself and to his audience. Ancient bards who presented their tales orally night after night—imagine trying to recite Homer's *The Iliad* from memory—were able to do so because they used conventions, such as meter, alliteration, and other tropes, to aid their memory. The equivalent for a scientific paper may be a striking image or graph. Think of Leonardo da Vinci's diagram of the proportions of a man. He could explain the concept in text, but the image made it ten times more memorable. Three hundred years later, Florence Nightingale, a British nurse who investigated the causes of death in the Crimean War and found that poor sanitation practices were far more deadly than battle wounds, used her "Diagram of the Causes of Mortality in the Army in the East" (1858) to change military medicine for the better.

Students may also make a written work memorable by guiding the reader clearly through it. In the introduction, students should clearly tell the audience what they are about to learn. In the demonstration, or body, students should tell the audience the important points. In the conclusion, students should briefly repeat the major points of the paper so that their audience hears the major ideas three times. After your student has written his essay, you should read it and then have a discussion together. Tell him what you remembered about his essay. Tell him if anything confused you. Tell him if you needed more information in a certain section. You can serve as the first audience for your student's written work.

Delivery

Ideally, if all canons of rhetoric were to be followed in this exercise, your student would now distill his research paper into speech form, memorize it, choose appropriate visual or other media aids to help him explain and illustrate his material, and then present it orally to his audience. If he had a large audience and the technological capability, he could create a PowerPoint presentation or even a video. In a science fair setting, he might create a poster displaying his pictures, tables, and graphs. For a small group presentation, he might create a handout outlining his talk, or other visuals that he could pass around.

In those situations, delivery would focus on his personal presentation skills such as clear speaking, appropriate attire, good eye contact, and connection with the audience. However, even if your student does not have the opportunity to present his findings in public, you can still have a fruitful conversation about the canon of delivery. Why do some teachers ask that a paper be typed in a certain font with specific margins and a cover page, while others are less particular? What difference does it make? Talk with your student about courtesy when it comes to delivering a paper as requested and on time. Appropriate delivery is all about demonstrating personal *ethos* and respect for your audience. Your student can learn lessons from handing you a neatly typed, one-page research paper just as well as from presenting a lecture in front of a hundred people.

EXAMPLE 2: A PERSUASIVE ESSAY

Persuasive essays teach your child to emphasize the all-important questions, "What is my goal in completing this assignment?" and "Who is my audience?" When your goal is to persuade another person of something, you will make all of your decisions with that person's needs, interests, and prior knowledge in mind.

Invention

I use *The Lost Tools of Writing* curriculum by Andrew Kern to teach my students persuasive writing since it uses the five canons to structure student learning, but you can practice these skills no matter which curriculum you use. In the invention stage for a persuasive essay, students begin with a "should" question about their topic. They gather everything they know about the issue and divide these nuggets of information into categories based on whether it supports the "should" or the "should not" answer.

Let's say that you have just completed a reading of *The Hobbit* with your child. You can start thinking together by discussing the choices that Bilbo made. Let's say your student wants to think about whether Bilbo should have gone on the journey with the dwarves. Spend some time with him thinking of all the reasons Bilbo should go and all the reasons he shouldn't go. There are powerful reasons on both sides of this argument, and you must explore fully both sides with your student before beginning to craft the persuasive essay. Then, the student should decide which argument to defend based on which reasons are most convincing to him. Once he assesses the issue, weighs the arguments, and chooses a side, he is ready to begin arranging his personal argument into a logical sequence.

Arrangement

For a persuasive essay, students should follow roughly the same outline as they would follow for a persuasive speech. The introduction of a persuasive essay would start with a quotation, an unexpected statement, or a question; provide the general context of the issue at hand; and present points of agreement, the point of contention, and a claim or thesis. The next sections of the outline should list the proofs (examples, logical reasons, evidence) that confirm the thesis, then refute potential counter-arguments that the audience might raise against the thesis. Finally, the conclusion of the essay would sum up the main arguments and make a closing appeal to the audience's sensibilities.

When your student is outlining this portion of the paper, ask him to think back to his audience and identify the reasons that would be most likely to inspire them to change their actions or beliefs. Questions you can ask are, "Do you want to appeal to your audience's emotions (*pathos*)?" "Do you want to appeal to your audience's rationality (*logos*)?" and "Do you want to appeal based on your own credibility and your audience's sense of virtue (*ethos*)?" Once your student has outlined these elements of the persuasive essay, he is ready to begin writing, and you are ready to begin talking with him about style.

Elocution

Read the two sentences below and compare them:
1: "As long as this gate is closed, as long as this wall is permitted to stand, the German question remains unanswered."
2: "As long as this gate is closed, as long as this scar of a wall is permitted to stand, it is not the German question alone that remains open, but the question of freedom for all mankind."

What changed? The second sentence simply adds a few words. It implicitly compares the wall to a scar in the first sentence, creating a metaphor. Next, it implicitly compares the German situation to a door by using the word "open" to describe the unanswered question. This in turn creates irony, because Germany is like a *closed* door as long as the wall stands. Finally, it makes the concrete problem of the Berlin Wall a physical representation (a metaphor) of mankind's abstract struggle for freedom. These may seem like minor adjustments, but they are all stylistic choices that affect the persuasiveness of the speaker's point.

As you may know, the second sentence comes from former President Ronald Reagan's 1987 remarks at the Brandenburg Gate. Imagine if Reagan had said not, "Mr. Gorbachev, tear down this wall!" but "Mr. Gorbachev, I would like you to set in process the administrative procedure that would eventually result in the deconstruction of this wall." Not very persuasive, is it? Those small changes have a great impact. More words are not always better.

Spend these high school years reading great speeches, articles, and essays with your student and discussing them. The conversations will be richer than you can imagine, and, more importantly, your student will begin to think about writing as a series of interesting decisions rather than a monotonous exercise in meeting a word count requirement.

More words are not always better.

A young lady in my church, a recent high school graduate, is an aspiring writer. I was talking to her one Sunday morning before the worship service and suggested some books and practices she might find useful in developing her writing style and voice. She mentioned to me that she never really learned how to write; her love for writing developed from her love for reading. She had practiced writing in school, but she had never really learned how to do it. Her story reminded me of one of my favorite books, *Carry On, Mr. Bowditch*.

By her own admission, she never really learned grammar or writing techniques. However, she wanted to learn to write well, and because of her love for reading, she knew that grammar and writing techniques mattered. Since she wanted to write well, she had to pay attention to these things. So, whenever she would write, she would open a copy of one of her favorite author's books and imitate what she saw. This enterprising young lady would open a copy of *Harry Potter* and imitate J. K. Rowling's grammar, style, and voice.

Just as Mr. Bowditch taught himself by imitation and comparison, this young lady did the same for her writing. She would imitate the best of J. K. Rowling's sentences, grammar, and descriptions. From the art of imitation, she learned about her own voice and style.

Memory

Memory informs persuasive essays just as much as it does research papers. If an argument is not memorable, it will not inspire someone else to take action or make a lasting change. Students should be challenged to write a persuasive essay and then to memorize it. Remember, the keys to *memoria* are repetition, intensity, and duration. Your student should start by reading his essays aloud multiple times (repetition), discovering the rhythm of the sentences and editing them as needed, paying close attention to their word choices (intensity). Then, he should go back to the outline he created in the arrangement stage. Using those key points, can he recite the essay in full? If not, go back to reading aloud until this step becomes easy. When he can comfortably recite the essay using only the outline, challenge him to set aside props altogether. Allow plenty of time (duration) for the memorization process, although it will get easier with practice.

> *If an argument is not memorable, it will not inspire someone else to take action or make a lasting change.*

The end goal is for students to present the memorized speech to family, classmates, or a group of friends. This last step tests the persuasive power of the essay. If students have trouble remembering the main points, their audience will have the same problem.

Delivery

With this type of memorized assignment, you can then go on to practice the traditional form of delivery: oral address. Students can practice their speech first at home with an audience of parents and siblings. As a parent, you can give feedback on delivery elements: eye contact, voice volume, clarity and speed of speech, gestures, and memorization. You can listen to determine if your student included all of the parts of a speech. As you evaluate him, be sure to give positive, encouraging words about what your student did well and concrete ideas about what he should correct.

> **"The Tough Skin of Words" by Jen Greenholt**
>
> We often think about creative writing as the easiest kind of writing to do, but it is actually the most difficult. A rhetorical student can learn a great deal about elocution by reading and creating poetry.
>
> Poetry is language condensed into a compact, refined shape, the same way that a diamond is carbon that has undergone immense pressure and temperature. Paul Engle, an American poet who was nominated for the Nobel Prize in 1976, said it this way: "Poetry is ordinary language raised to the nth power. Poetry is boned with ideas, nerved and blooded with emotions, all held together by the delicate, tough skin of words" (*New York Times Book Review*, Feb. 17, 1957). Notice how he uses the human body as a metaphor for a poem!
>
> If the goal of a research paper is to discover truth and share it, and the goal of a persuasive essay is to inspire others toward goodness, then the goal of a poem is to uncover beauty and share it with those around you. Consider Robert Frost's famous poem "The Road Not Taken." On the surface, it simply describes a fork in the road. "But what is a fork in the road *like*?" the poem encourages us to ask. Well, choosing one branch of a road is like making a life decision, like choosing between two colleges, or choosing to homeschool through high school. The poet uses the surface meaning of the poem to reveal a deeper truth about choices, consequences, and regrets. By using a metaphor to do so, he gives readers the freedom to discover this truth on their own.

WRITING TO THE N^{TH} DEGREE

Ultimately, the goals of writing are to deliver and expand the reach of truth by informing, persuading, and engaging the imagination. This process should elicit delight in both the writer and the reader, whether the form of writing is a research paper, a persuasive essay, or a poem. Writing is a form of contemplation; it enables the writer to deliberate fruitfully on his topic as he applies the five canons of rhetoric and it enables the reader to meditate on the beautiful results of this contemplation. Contemplation allows us to let our minds dwell at length upon truth, goodness, and beauty. This trains us to be quiet and still and enables us to heed the instruction of the Lord, who invites us to "Be still, and know that I am God" (Psalm 46:10).

As they learn to write, students also learn to exercise discernment. Writing exercises ask them to make important, informed decisions at every step of the journey: what to write about, how to organize it, the manner in which to articulate it best, how to internalize the information and make it memorable, and by what means to communicate it to their audiences. The same thing is true whether your student is writing about literature, science, history, or the neighborhood talent show. David Hicks writes in *Norms & Nobility*:

> The modern school gives the impression that communication skills are merely techniques whose mastery is important for scoring high on tests and doing well on the job. But is there no transcendent value in learning how to speak and write exactly? To what extent can man be a sentient, moral creature without the ability to communicate clearly with others and with his cultural past? Can there be true independence of thought without mastery of language? (12)

By constantly practicing making good decisions throughout the writing process, your student will learn to write more persuasively and reflect truth, goodness, and beauty.

In the *Shema* (a Hebrew prayer, Deut. 6:5), the Lord instructs the Hebrews to love Him with all their hearts, souls, and strength. Jesus later expands this commandment, instructing Christians to love God with all their hearts, souls, strength, and *minds* (Luke 10:27, emphasis added). Practicing rhetoric through writing is one way to achieve this goal. Poet Suzanne Rhodes writes in *The Roar on the Other Side*, "God made our minds to love Him…We love God with our minds by…thinking about excellent, lovely, wholesome things…noticing what God has made is important. In noticing, we name…" (13).

If we think about naming in a broader sense as identifying truths and making assertions about the world, then we can see that writing is really one of the most wonderful actions we can exercise as free human beings. Richard Weaver describes writing in his book *The Ethics of Rhetoric*:

> [T]he right to utter a sentence is one of the very greatest liberties… The liberty to impose this formal unity is a liberty to handle the world, to remake it, if only a little, and to hand it to others in a shape which

may influence their actions…The changes wrought by sentences are changes in the world rather than in the physical earth, but it is to be remembered that changes in the world bring about changes in the earth. (118–119)

What a beautiful incentive to put pen to paper and to learn to write well, all for the glory of God!

Writing essays, *using the five canons of rhetoric:*	
Invention	What is your goal in completing this assignment? Who is your audience? How can you ensure that your paper speaks to that audience? What information do you need to write this paper?
Arrangement	What is the most logical way to organize this information? What kind of outline will help you prepare to write? What else do you need to research to complete your outline?
Elocution	What style is appropriate to the audience and to the subject matter? Should you use technical terms or commonplace words? Should you use long descriptive sentences, or short, matter-of-fact ones? What kind of appeals should you use (*logos*, *pathos*, or *ethos*)?
Memory	What other assignments have you done that might be relevant? What prior knowledge will your audience bring to this paper? How can you make your writing memorable?
Delivery	What is the appropriate way to deliver this paper or essay? If typed, should you use a certain font, specific margins, or a cover page? If oral, what one skill should you practice in your public speaking?

CHAPTER SIX

SCIENCE

"Life at its best is an adventure, a voyage of discovery. What could be more gratifying than to discover, describe and explain some basic principle that no human being has ever understood before? This is the stuff of true science."
—Peter Doherty, *The Beginner's Guide to Winning the Nobel Prize*

"Johnny just has a cold," the doctor says. "He should feel better in about seven to ten days. Make sure he gets plenty of rest and fluids, and he should be fine."

"Aren't you going to give him an antibiotic?"

The doctor looks at the impatient mother standing in front of him and sighs. He is faced with a dilemma. Will he, like many doctors, make his patient happy, ensuring customer satisfaction and the likelihood of a return visit, which in turn makes the hospital happy and provides him with job security? Or, will he make the tough decision his knowledge demands, maintaining that a cold is a virus and cannot be cured with the use of antibiotics?

The doctor in this story is a rhetorician. He encounters ethical and dialectic decisions like the one above every day. When we visit the doctor's office, we expect the medical professionals we encounter to make wise judgments, as they should. Unfortunately, pressures from hospital administrators, insurance companies, and state and federal governments mean that a doctor's choice of treatment may not be based solely on what is best for the patient. At the same time, patients have access to more and more information (or misinformation, as shown in the example above) about our health—websites like WebMD, nutrition blogs, books about fad diets, and TV shows that stage soap operas in a hospital setting. It takes judgment to distinguish opinion from fact and make decisions accordingly. The doctor in my initial example often expresses frustration that his patients lack a basic understanding of science and the ability to discern wisely which information to trust. Meanwhile, politicians and educators bemoan the United States' poor ranking in STEM subjects. A 2012 report from the President's Council of Advisors on Science and Technology proposed that the United States must turn out one million more STEM professionals over the next decade in order to meet the demands of global competition. What are we doing wrong? Why don't we know how to speak the language of science?

First, let me ask you another question: why do we encourage kids to be excited about science in elementary and middle school but then expect high school students to focus on passing a science test for credit? Books like *The Kid Who Invented the Popsicle* and *Mistakes That Worked* may be too simple to challenge a high school student's reading level, but they introduce us to the thousands of innovations and inventions that have come from ordinary people exploring and asking questions about the world around them. They make us think that we too have the ability to be scientists.

If we do not encourage students to use their imaginations when they study science just as much as they do when they study art, it will be difficult to inspire the next generation of innovative scientists and engineers.

When I think about contemporary science education, I can't help but think about the scene in the movie *The Truman Show* when the young Truman tells his teacher that he wants to be an explorer "like the Great Magellan." Pulling down a world map with a sharp snap, the teacher says, "Oh, you're too late! There's nothing left to explore!" Today's sciences are taught by lecture, textbook, and isolated lab work far more often than they are taught through active learning. If we do not encourage students to use their imaginations when they study science just as much as they do when they study art, it will be difficult to inspire the next generation of innovative scientists and engineers.

Instead of focusing all your energy on sterile lab experiments, send your student outside to a lake to come up with his own questions about weather (physical science), water currents (physics), ion balance (chemistry), or algae (biology). Find a veterinarian or a doctor with whom he can chat about the puzzles and challenges of medicine. The questions he asks may be more complex than the ones he asked when he was younger, but he can still move forward with a spirit of inquiry and adventure. Wonder and delight should always be the catalyst behind a rhetorical study of science.

Wonder and delight should always be the catalyst behind a rhetorical study of science.

To model using the five canons in this kind of rhetorical science, we will use several sample assignments.

**"The Many Lessons of Chemistry in Classical Education"
by Jonathan Bartlett**
Originally published in Classical Conversations Writers Circle, July 8, 2013.

Many students question the need to study chemistry in high school. However, key lessons lurking in chemistry will help students pull deeper meaning from it and thus take a deeper interest in it.

To begin with, *chemistry is the study of the invisible*. While chemistry studies things that are material, these things—atoms, molecules, energy, and so on—are all invisible. In chemistry, we learn to examine secondary attributes to gain a deeper understanding of the things we cannot see directly. In life, we will need to probe many visible attributes in order to deduce the invisible truths.

Second, *chemistry is based on philosophy*. Nearly all of science depends on philosophy. With chemistry, this is simple to demonstrate. The philosopher Descartes made this statement: *ex nihilo nihil fit* ("out of nothing, nothing comes.") This principle of sufficient reason also exists in chemistry. Why do we balance chemical equations? Because all of the products must come from the reactants. Why? Because *ex nihilo nihil fit*.

Third, *chemistry utilizes logic*. In chemistry, there are formulas to memorize. However, unlike other subjects, chemistry requires students to link together multiple different equations. Suppose students want to use the ideal gas law to know how much pressure a certain number of gas molecules will exert. Rather than being given the number of molecules, they are given the weight of the solid reactants that form the gaseous molecules. Thus, the student must first use the periodic table to convert weight to number of molecules, use the chemical equation to figure out how many molecules of product were generated from the reactants, and then use the ideal gas law to figure out the pressure. Students must logically sequence these steps to find the right answer.

Fourth, *chemistry is foundational to learning modern scientific thought*. Chemistry introduces students to macro and micro scales, the naming of chemical substances, and the interior of the atom. All of these are concepts that develop scientific literacy. Familiarity with these concepts gives students confidence in public discussion on scientific issues.

Finally, in Classical Conversations, *chemistry reinforces themes from other subjects*. In Challenge III, the focus of the year is on consequences. Reading Shakespeare is all about examining the chain of effects created by the actions of the characters. Sproul's *The Consequences of Ideas* covers the repercussions of various philosophies. Chemistry fits by providing students with tools for predicting and evaluating outcomes in a controlled environment. Thus, chemistry provides a microlaboratory for thinking about, predicting, and evaluating consequences.

EXAMPLE 1: WRITING A SCIENTIFIC RESEARCH PAPER

After your student uncovers mysteries of science that intrigue him, he can begin to suggest answers. In that process, he may need to develop formal hypotheses and test them with the help of others. He should know how to use the scientific method, but he must fuel it with wonder and awe. That's why we read books, both fiction and nonfiction, about scientists like Nathaniel Bowditch (*Carry On, Mr. Bowditch*, by Jean Lee Latham) and doctors like

Ben Carson (*Gifted Hands*) who begin with passion, go on to sharpen their natural gifts with the help of books and mentors, and then use their skills to serve and instruct others. We also read books about the history of science, studying major developments in our culture and other parts of the world.

A key rhetorical task is to take this information and distill it into a research paper about a scientific question or phenomenon. In doing so, your student must learn to make a logical appeal (*logos*) to the reader, but he must also prove himself to be a thorough and meticulous researcher who strives to uncover and present truth (*ethos*). Your student will also need to learn to separate emotional appeals (*pathos*) from arguable facts, both in the authorities he chooses to believe when he is conducting research and also in his style of writing as he considers his audience's sensibilities. We begin with the canon of invention.

Invention

When your child is becoming a dialectic learner, he focuses on asking good questions, using Aristotle's common topics as a starting point. When your older student begins to write a scientific research paper, he should begin in the same way. This time, however, his goal is to discern the answer to one of his questions. I like to give students as much freedom as possible to choose a question that intrigues them so they will be motivated to learn while they are mastering the form of the research paper. Former students have written about nuclear energy, black holes, vibration in stringed instruments, pasteurization, and the flight trajectory of golf balls.

If the student does not enter the process with a specific question in mind, he might gather preliminary research to help decide what kinds of questions to ask. Or better yet, he might have a conversation with someone who loves the topic and can inspire him to ask interesting questions. The nature of the topic will govern the type of sources used to generate and answer questions. While a student might refer to a history book if he or she were writing about the life and contributions to science of Marie Curie, the student might need to use Internet sources to research the work of the National Aeronautics and Space Administration (NASA) in the twenty-first century. As your student learns more about the topic, he should begin to hone in on an interesting question to research further. The topic of nuclear energy might become a question such as, "Is nuclear energy a safe source of fuel for general use?" The topic of pasteurization might become a question such as, "Do the benefits of raw milk outweigh the risks of consuming unpasteurized dairy products?"

Say he chooses the latter question. In order to write a research paper on the subject, he might use Aristotle's five common topics to **define** raw milk and pasteurization, **compare** the end product, determine the **relationship** between pasteurization and healthy or harmful bacteria, weigh **circumstances** related to refrigeration and the "buy local" movement, and consult the **testimony** of doctors, scientists, farmers, and policy-makers on the issue.

The canon of invention does not end here, however. Encourage your rhetorical student to think about his purpose in writing, whether it is to delight, to inform, or to persuade. Aristotle reminds us that the rhetorician should also know his audience: Who are they? What do they know? What do they assume? What do they need to know? Do they require convincing? Once all this information has been gathered, he is ready to move forward. This information will allow him to start developing a loosely-held hypothesis, one that will be tested as he proceeds through rhetoric.

Arrangement

Now is time for the canon of arrangement. One of the reasons a scientist or statistician must be ethical to deserve our respect is that pure data can be rearranged to prove almost anything. Presenting the facts in a different order changes the message of a paper or a graph or chart by giving more importance to some facts than others. Likewise, the impact of a research paper will change if you start out with your conclusion in the form of a thesis, versus if you allow the reader to join you in your journey through the facts and only reach an answer at the end of the project.

In a similar way, when a student is reading a scientific article or watching a scientist share the latest theory of health, technology, or physics, he must learn to arrange the ideas presented, pulling out major points and ordering them to discover the scientist's underlying argument. Only then can he weigh the merits of the argument and decide whether it is worthy of action in response.

Elocution

When students write about science, they face a particular challenge of using specific, precise language to describe their questions, answers, and, later, experiments. Why? So that future scientists can repeat what the students have done and build on or test the validity of that conclusion. Even though a research paper may focus on information that other scientists have already discovered, the rhetorical student should use this opportunity to practice the form of scientific writing. In writing about science, you will not find elaborate metaphors or flowery language, so student writers may need good models to gain familiarity with this style of writing.

Encourage your student to read scientific articles from *The New England Journal of Medicine, Science*, or another peer-reviewed journal. Look at the length of sentences and kinds of words the authors use. Notice the verb tenses, the use of passive or active voice, and the presence or absence of pronouns like "I" and "we." Students should model their own writing on these examples. Writing this way teaches your student to provide his readers with a window into the topic at hand. The student should write transparently enough that his readers see what he has seen and have the opportunity to share in his appreciation for the beauty and complexity of science.

Memory

Just because we do not spend all of our time in high school science studying a textbook does not mean that memory work has no place in upper-level science. Scientists performing complex laboratory experiments also use *memoria* to recall the results of prior tests and experiments so that they can adjust for errors in their own work, or so that they can replicate their previous methods precisely. Accurate science depends on this skill.

Memory also permits your student to evaluate another scientist's work. The basic principles that he learns and commits to memory should be in the back of his mind when he reads an article or a book and considers whether or not to believe its contents. He should be able to judge whether the article violates laws of nature or principles of science, and if so, if it can justify doing so. He should be able to weigh new information against that which he has encountered before, and the only way to do that is to have a storehouse of scientific knowledge that he has mentally sorted, categorized, and filed away for future use.

Delivery

If memory seems to be of secondary importance in science, the canon of delivery may seem even less significant. When we think about science at work, we probably picture a scientist hunched over a notebook with a microscope beside him and reams of data spread across the desk. He is usually alone—like the mad scientists of novels such as *Frankenstein* and *Dr. Jekyll and Mr. Hyde* or cartoons such as *Pinky and the Brain* or *Megamind*. I know a young woman with a master's degree in science who applied for a part-time customer service job and was asked if, being a "science type," she was capable of talking to people without frightening them away. Where do we get the idea that science has nothing to do with communication and delivery skills? Wherever the idea originates, it is a misleading one. The best scientists today are working on teams, reaching across different fields to combine expertise for projects, and using their ability to explain science to ask for grants and support for their studies.

Last summer, the inaugural class of students from the Mandala Fellowship in West End, North Carolina, watched a TED talk about new technologies for light-based transmission of wireless data. The students ranged in age from seventeen to twenty. They listened to a fifteen-minute talk and then spent another fifteen minutes discussing the ideas. I sat back and watched, enjoying the questions that peppered the room in response to a few basic questions that I had asked: "What did you think?" and "Were you persuaded?"

This particular speaker spoke smoothly and confidently to a live audience. His manner was earnest and enthusiastic; his dress, professional; and his body language, relaxed. His delivery was expert, but what about his message? Some of the students knew a great deal about wireless technology, and they took the opportunity to explain micro-transmitters to those less versed in physics and information technology. Other students, even if they did not know the details of the technology, were able to respond by asking more questions about the scientist's methods, his assumptions, and his conclusions. They were learning to set aside the authoritative tone of the speech and evaluate the argument behind it. When scientists speak to the general public, they may attempt to present their conclusions as unbiased information, but they are always informed by their worldviews. They may speak with authority, but rhetorical students should begin to evaluate the content as well as the style of each speaker who stands before them.

In contrast, we watched a second video about the visible constellations in that particular week of July. The speaker looked directly at the camera the entire time. He spoke as if he were reading off a teleprompter, and his tone did not modulate as he moved from topic to topic. While he spoke, the students murmured in the background. His content may have been informative and correct, but his delivery did not capture the attention and respect of the group. As a result, his rhetoric was less persuasive than it might have been. Scientific discoveries that cannot be communicated well will have a very limited reach and influence.

Scientific discoveries that cannot be communicated well will have a very limited reach and influence.

Unfortunately, perhaps because so many scientists fail to communicate the delight of their studies with the broader community, science education has become about following a series of steps to a prescribed end rather than about exploring the world around us. Peter Doherty, 1996 Nobel prizewinner for Physiology or Medicine, laments in *The Beginner's Guide to Winning the Nobel Prize*, "There can be a worm in the shiniest apple and sometimes, of course, the worm is more interesting than the apple. Do kids get bored with school science because they don't see that intriguing worm and, instead, come away with the impression that the whole game is predictable and mechanistic? Nothing, of course, could be further from the truth" (37).

EXAMPLE 2: FINDING CONNECTIONS BETWEEN SCIENCE AND EVERYDAY EXPERIENCES

While our boys were in high school, and then into college and beyond, my husband and I worked hard to give them opportunities to relate science to endeavors that interested them. We could do that because homeschooling allowed us to be flexible rather than demanding that the boys be in a classroom five days a week. William and David took scuba diving lessons, so their lives depended on understanding pressure, depth, and oxygen depletion. William worked to earn his pilot's license, so he had incentive to understand aerodynamics, weather patterns, and geographical terrain. John pursued carpentry, so he needed to know about angles, force, levers, load-bearing capacity, the composition of building materials, and much more. Robert worked with an engineering firm, developing their website and manipulating data. In each case, the boys acquired knowledge because a practical application demanded it. We can follow the five canons of rhetoric as they apply to practical experiences just as well as we can for a formal product like a research paper.

Invention

This stage of rhetorical expression can be one of the most difficult for parents to master with their students. You will notice that practical application often requires you to step outside the home and seek mentors and master craftsmen to teach and advise your children. There were serious consequences should my sons misunderstand or misapply a concept in scuba diving and piloting, so my husband and I looked carefully for trustworthy mentors who could guide their early efforts. We also paid attention to the *ethos* these master rhetoricians exhibited. We considered their character as well as their credentials. Would they teach our sons not just to be skilled but also to be trustworthy masters in their own right? This responsibility is one reason I am so grateful for the growth of community in the homeschooling world over the years I have been homeschooling. Now I have access to thousands of people, in person or virtually, who can advise me about the resources available for scientific learning that occurs outside the home.

Let your high school student's passions drive the kinds of opportunities you provide for him. Remember, though, that practical science does not have to come with a hefty price tag. Look for 4-H clubs or scouting troops near you. They are often in need of volunteers and leaders to work with younger children on projects related to health, exercise science, survival skills, engineering, forestry, and many other branches of science. A leadership role in one of these organizations can give your high school student the chance to practice rhetoric by teaching younger children what he has already learned. Seek out summer camps that give your student the opportunity to meet other like-minded students and learn from mentors in his field of interest. A few examples are the Alaska Summer Research Academy, the National Flight

Academy in Florida, and Outward Bound programs around the country. If finances are an issue, be sure to ask if scholarships are available or if the camp ever hires students to work part-time in exchange for the cost of attendance. There are hundreds of camps around the United States, and many offer this type of work-study program.

Encourage your student to do his own research, so that he is personally invested in the process. Consider the costs of each program, and invite your student to brainstorm ways to raise the money or exchange work for lessons with a craftsman in the community. Consider unpaid internships and apprenticeships as well as paid programs. It is amazing how many opportunities you can uncover, even on a limited budget, when you unleash your student's imagination and creativity on a project that inspires and drives him.

Arrangement

Once you have enrolled your student in a summer camp, found a mentor, set up an apprenticeship, or simply sent him outside to experience and experiment with physics, engineering, and biology, it is the student's job to sort and arrange the information he acquires. A friend of mine loved horses when she was in high school, so she took a part-time job at a stable to pay for riding lessons. The job required her to learn about equine biology (What can horses eat? How often should they eat?), animal psychology (How do you train horses? How do you work safely around them?), and chemistry and physics (How do you stack hay bales in a loft to keep them from spontaneously combusting?).

For example, one day at work, she was loading hay bales into the loft to store for the winter. Her boss, the stable manager, corrected her stacks, telling Jen that she needed to leave room for air between the bales. My friend naturally asked why and was told that the hay bales might explode and set the barn on fire if they were packed too tightly. That type of information immediately triggered her curiosity, and because they did not have time to discuss the reasons in the midst of a hard day's work, she stored the information to look it up later.

When she left her job at the end of the day, she had to take her experience with the hay bales and make sense of the information, committing it to memory in the process. In some cases, arrangement might require nothing more than mentally reviewing what has happened during the day and picking out the lessons to be learned. In this instance, she did not know why hay bales were in danger of spontaneous combustion, so she talked to a few knowledgeable adults, did some research online, and discovered that some hay is not dried properly before it is baled. The trapped moisture, combined with the sugars in the grass itself, produces heat energy through plant respiration. When the heat reaches a critical point, a combination of heat, moisture, and insulation can lead to combustion. If any of the hay around the area is dry, it quickly ignites and can burn down an entire barn.

In some cases, arrangement might require nothing more than mentally reviewing what has happened during the day and picking out the lessons to be learned.

You will notice that practical experience provided a catalyst for the additional research and required my friend to arrange her thoughts clearly so that she could avoid a potentially dangerous mistake in the future. (In your science classroom, be sure to leave room for the discoveries that can come from error.) She had to discern whether the information was folklore or whether it could be explained logically. At the end of this process, she was able to synthesize her experience and research knowledge in order to determine the best way to do her job the next day, which in the practical application of science could be called the *elocution* of an idea.

Elocution

For many practical applications of science, elocution might consist of learning how to articulate what you have observed as part of your experiences. In other instances, students might formalize what they have learned through a science fair project poster, a report, or a homemade "how-to" guide. I know students who have demonstrated their familiarity with a new technology by creating a user manual for less tech-savvy members of their family. The whole family might benefit from that lesson! When I tutor ninth graders in physical science, I ask them to rewrite their textbook in their own words over the course of a semester. They create their own diagrams and design laboratory experiments to demonstrate that they understand the key concepts in the book. At the end of this process, they would presumably be able to teach a younger student about physical science, using the textbook they have created (more on that idea under the canon of delivery).

Memory

Practical application of science demands that you be able to store basic facts and "book learning" and recall it at will. When you are looking at a slab of rock on the side of the Grand Canyon, you probably will not be carrying a textbook that distinguishes between igneous, metamorphic, and sedimentary rocks or names the types of rock you are likely to see there (sandstone, shale, and limestone). Memory enables you to apply what you have learned in contexts where reference books are unavailable. Let me give you another example. When you are scuba diving, you may begin to feel slight pain in your ears from the water pressure squeezing your body inside your gear. When you begin to feel that twinge of pain, you will not be able to look back at the textbook telling you how deep you can go safely or how slowly you need to return from depth to allow your body to stabilize. In this situation, memory ensures that the information you need is readily available to you in situations when you need it quickly and effortlessly. Practically speaking, memory functions two ways. First, your student needs to learn enough information from mentors and other resources to lead to a practical application of his knowledge. When memory work and classroom practice become wearisome, remind your student of the applications toward which he is striving. Second, experiencing something directly rather than just reading about it gives your student an opportunity to remember it personally and to add first-hand experience to his knowledge base. That's the virtue of using real-life experiences as teaching moments and the importance of paying attention to practical experiences as they happen. Encourage your student to keep a journal about his experiences with applied science. That way, by the time he has finished applying the new knowledge, he will have taken care to remember and refine his understanding of what has happened so he will be ready to teach it or deliver it to someone else, or to repeat the application and continue refining his skills.

Delivery

The first four canons of rhetoric, when traced in practical applications of science, open up a world of possibility for our students as they become adults. They may never be brain surgeons, but they will all be teachers and leaders at some point in their lives, whether as parents, professionals, or craftsmen. Delivery might consist of doing a job and doing it well. It might mean taking off and landing a plane safely. It might mean constructing a deck that can withstand the weight of a July Fourth barbecue crowd. It might mean achieving the optimal acid level in the soil to grow a tomato plant. It might mean baking a delicious loaf of bread and adjusting for high elevation or dry air quality.

I know parents grow weary of homeschooling by the time their children reach high school, but I can tell you honestly that few things are more rewarding than seeing the results of your hard work reflected in your adult children as they practice the delivery of their scientific knowledge. As I sit and write this week, I can hear the sound of hammers and men talking about precise measurements. My son John is building an addition onto our house. It is a joy to watch him demonstrate rhetorical leadership as he explains the finer points of carpentry to the men who work with him. That is rhetorical physics and math in action, and it is truly a thing of beauty.

HOPE FOR THE FUTURE OF SCIENCE

The root of the word "science" is the Latin verb *scio / scire*, which means "to know." We should never cease to wonder about this place in which we live: what it is, how it works, and the secrets that it begs us to seek out. My friend Kate says that science calls us to awe at the "relentlessly physical" universe we touch and smell and taste and see every day. All of science should lead our students to know the creation better.

All of science should lead our students to know the creation better.

George Washington Carver once said, "I love to think of nature as an unlimited broadcasting station, through which God speaks to us every hour, if we will only tune in" (George Washington Carver National Monument). It's sad that many scientists, while marveling at the intricacy and complexity of the natural world, show hostility toward Christians, who share their sense of wonder but see in it the handiwork of a Creator. I am grateful for stories of scientists who show us how to respond to scientific discovery with a spirit of wonder and awe.

Dr. Francis S. Collins directed the Human Genome Project and now serves as director of the National Institutes of Health. In 2007, he was awarded the Presidential Medal of Freedom for his work. Persuaded as an adult by the words of C. S. Lewis, Dr. Collins went on to write *The Language of God: A Scientist Presents Evidence for Belief*. In the introduction, he describes the moment when President Clinton presented the findings of the Human Genome Project to the nation. "It is humbling for me, and awe-inspiring, to realize that we have caught the first glimpse of our own instruction book, previously known only to God"(3). Collins baffled many in the science community because he was highly respected for his scientific work yet continued to speak openly about his belief in God.

Dr. Richard A. Swenson is a physician, researcher, and the author of bestsellers *Margin* and *The Overload Syndrome*, which discuss the impact of the hectic American lifestyle on health and wellbeing. His book *More Than Meets the Eye* describes the wonder of even the simplest scientific facts. "As a scientist with training in both medicine and physics, it is easily apparent to me that the majesty of God is revealed in the human body. His fingerprints are, in fact, all over us" (17). He goes on to number the 10^{28} atoms in the human body, ninety percent of which are replaced annually. Even more compelling than his argument is the playful way he writes about the creation: "Science devises new and sophisticated technology to penetrate ever smaller levels, only to find yet another little critter winking mischievously at our machines"(18–19). As this statement suggests, we must hold lightly the discoveries and theories that contemporary science puts forward, but let us not be the kind of people who fear all science. If we believe in a God of truth, then we have nothing to fear from honest examination of His creation. Even Doherty, who is deeply cynical about the relationship between religion and science, concludes, "Knowledge enriches. If beliefs are valid, they will survive" (199).

WHY SHOULD WE STUDY SCIENCE RHETORICALLY?

Whether they are Christian or not, scientists are realizing that something is not working in the way our culture passes on the language and art of scientific inquiry. We are inundated with information, yet we are crippled in our ability to judge that information well. In contrast, look at the stories of men and women who matter most in the history of science: Newton, Curie, Copernicus, Galileo, and Einstein, to name just a few. None of them were prodigies as children. Most of them did not have a STEM-focused education in their teenage years. Several of them struggled with formal schooling. What encouraging news for the average homeschool parent! Instead, what they shared was a love of and dedication to their work. Because of that passion, they were willing to do whatever was necessary to uncover truth.

We are inundated with information, yet we are crippled in our ability to judge that information well.

Leonardo da Vinci is a perfect example of this dedication to scientific knowledge in all its forms. He "had no formal schooling, although he had some private tutoring, what we might call 'home schooling,'" writes Bülent Atalay in *Math and the Mona Lisa: The Art and Science of Leonardo da Vinci* (4–5). Yet as an adult, Leonardo was known not only for artistic masterpieces like the *Mona Lisa* and *The Last Supper*. Atalay writes:

> Among the designs that fill [da Vinci's] notebooks one can see that he prefigured, among other devices, the bicycle, the automobile, the tank, the collapsible bridge, the parachute, the underwater diving mask, the flamethrower, scissors, and the submarine. To satisfy his scientific curiosity he performed ballistic experiments in order to determine projectile trajectories and painstaking dissections to understand anatomical structure. With seamless facility he functioned as anatomist, botanist, geometer, physicist, architect, mechanical engineer, hydraulic engineer, civil engineer, and even aeronautical engineer. (7)

I cannot help but chuckle when I picture the experiments Leonardo must have arranged. I'm not sure if I responded favorably to my sons' "ballistic experiments" over the years. I picture Leonardo as a toddler flinging peas across the table, using a spoon as a catapult, and then illustrating the results of his experiments with a stick in the sand. After all, science can happen anywhere. Homeschooling classically allows you to make science a living, breathing thing rather than something distilled into textbooks and divorced from students' reality.

Even today's scientists acknowledge the important role practical application played in their early training. Doherty writes, "Science cultures differ in many details, but the underlying focus is always on discovery and innovation. The very basis of science is about probing reality"(xiii). "Probing reality" means not only being creative and innovative but also connecting scientific inquiry and creative ideas to your own reality, the world you live in. Although he received a public school education in basic physical science, Doherty first gained a sense of awe and curiosity about science by reading several of Aldous Huxley's novels, which combined fictional characters and plots with contemporary scientific themes. Afterward, Doherty had an opportunity to tour the School of Veterinary Science at the University of Queensland in Brisbane. He watched demonstrations in embryology, anatomy, and pathology. In his biography, he recalls the "permeating smell of hot embedding wax and formalin" that brought science to life (5). Listen to these key words Doherty uses to describe the experience: "real," "interesting," and "doable."

Or, take Collins. As a boy, he learned about science in simple ways. A feature article in *The New Yorker* reports that this future scientist grew up on a farm in Virginia, "collecting eggs, milking the cows, and shucking corn" (Boyer, 2).

> He could set a barn door and knew how to predict weather by reading the sky over the distant Alleghenies. He did not see the inside of a schoolroom until sixth grade, because Margaret taught her boys at home. "There was no schedule," Francis recalls. "The idea of Mother having a lesson plan would be just completely laughable. But she would get us excited about trying to learn about a topic that we didn't know much about. And she would pose a question and basically charge you with it, using whatever resources you had—your mind, exploring nature, reading books—to try to figure out, well, what could you learn about that?" (Boyer, 2)

To parents afraid to teach their children science, I would echo Doherty, who says, "Everyone can achieve at least a measure of scientific literacy and, what is more, people will gain both personal satisfaction and even a sense of wonder and delight from having a better understanding of the natural world around them"(37). When we raise students who act wisely based on their knowledge of the world and who retain their wonder at the creative universe by engaging it scientifically, we will have given our society a great gift indeed.

Investigating science, *using the five canons of rhetoric:*	
Invention	Have you chosen a question that interests you? What sources will aid you in your research? What opportunities will allow you to practice applied science?
Arrangement	Have you ordered the facts in a way that is honest and leads logically to your conclusion? Have you arranged your practical learning to make sense of your experiences?
Elocution	Have you used specific, precise language in your writing? What stylistic techniques do you see in other scientific articles? How does your new learning prepare you to do a better job next time?
Memory	What other similar tests and experiments should inform your work? What basic scientific principles apply to this situation? What knowledge should be memorized to help you practice science?
Delivery	Can you articulate what you have learned? Did you communicate your findings so your audience could understand? Have you done your job and done it well?

CHAPTER SEVEN

MATH

"The mathematician's patterns, like the painter's or the poet's, must be beautiful; the ideas like the colours or the words, must fit together in a harmonious way. Beauty is the first test: there is no permanent place in the world for ugly mathematics."

—G. H. Hardy, *A Mathematician's Apology*

Math is a touchy subject these days, especially when it comes to discussing educational practices. Many news stories about education today seem to emphasize STEM subjects. Because America has not fared well in these areas, compared to other countries, we have poured a lot of time and money into addressing the gap. Though it would be great if all of our students achieved perfect math SAT scores or completed calculus and physics in high school or won STEM scholarships to college, my greatest pleasure is in hearing that they walk with the God of the universe. We need to return to the beginning and ask why we are teaching math before we can address the question of how.

Why do I teach math to students? I teach math so that students might love the Creator of math. But also I teach math so that I will love God and love my children more. To clarify, I believe that the best way to learn anything is to have a conversation with someone interested in the topic. When I can't explain something, I know I am about to learn something new. I have a question that needs to be answered. My happiest moments are when my children have a question for me or can answer my questions about math. When we can't figure something out we have learned to wait. We usually find the answer to our question in a surprising way. We may have to move ahead a few lessons, we may have to back up to an earlier difficulty, or we may have to wait and ponder the question.

To clarify, I believe that the best way to learn anything is to have a conversation with someone interested in the topic.

In the classical world, people like Plato, Aristotle, and Pythagoras studied numbers because they were moved by the wonders they saw in the natural world. They were moved by curiosity. How can we encourage our students to marvel at numbers and to have great conversations about math? I'm fortunate because I spend time every week with students who do just that. One student James pulled together thoughts from math, philosophy, and science to think about the concept of origin. Not only did he integrate these subjects and think deeply, but he knew enough to make a joke about it, declaring himself the center of the universe! If you've studied foreign language, you know you have grasped the language when you can make a joke.

My favorite weekly conversation with high school students centers on the ideas explored by mathematicians. The parents of my students require them to study certain classical subjects whether they delight in the topic or not. Because of this direction, the students are broadly interested in academics. Their previous preparation in grammar and dialectic is producing fruit in the rhetorical stage.

As James' comment above demonstrates, these students can integrate a variety of subjects with a mature sense of both humor and seriousness. They are able to determine when to be serious and when to make one another laugh. They think. They choose their words. They ask questions. They get off topic in interesting ways and then return to the topic with new understanding. Preparing for cultural leadership excites them. No subject is boring, because they know how to ask questions and make the information relevant to their lives.

Can you imagine how privileged I feel—to be challenged by such curious youths? Meeting once a week to discuss math concepts with students who do their work and have parents who provide time and encouragement to complete their work is a very pleasant way to spend the day.

I tell my students that if they knew how wonderful they were, they would bow before one another under the weight of their fellow students' glory. Not because they are idols or demi-gods, but because they are made in the image of the living God, and nothing they do is common. Life is characterized by the wonder that we who are so feeble will live forever. We can think God's thoughts after Him. We can be heirs and judges with the King of Kings. Who wouldn't feel privileged to hang out with such interesting people?

I did not begin parenthood and homeschooling by engaging in high level math conversations. These discussions are a regular part of our children's high school experience because we started with nothing but never gave up. We have been talking math as a family for almost thirty years. We are no smarter than anyone else, but we believe math matters. Thanks to perseverance, my children, their friends, and I can "speak" math. The families who have homeschooled for the last thirty years with us share the same experience.

The main thing I've noticed about all my friends who homeschool through adulthood is that they like talking with their children. I emphasized the kind of questions a parent learns to use to initiate conversation in my previous book *The Question*. As students mature, they begin to ask me questions to initiate conversation. We are becoming intellectual peers through a lifetime of discussion.

> *The main thing I've noticed about all my friends who homeschool through adulthood is that they like talking with their children.*

Let's look at how to use the five canons of rhetoric to guide students through math conversations. As we were working on this book, some of my colleagues were skeptical that these canons could be applied to math. Their questions made me more determined to demonstrate how these canons can be applied to any subject. I believe we use the canons in math just like we use them in literature.

In higher math, students must quickly brainstorm over possible approaches to solving a problem and then choose how they will proceed. This is called "invention." Once they have a strategy, they must arrange the information into a solvable form. This could be equations, charts, or graphs. Then they must act. They must go through the algorithm or procedure. They have to demonstrate they know what they are doing. This is elocution. But there is a little more to it than that. As they proceed through the problem, they must bring all their math memory to bear on the problem: Do I need to work out the square root of 121 on the side of the paper, or can I instantly plug in 11 because I've memorized that the square root of 121 is 11? If I have to recalculate arithmetic on the side, my delivery isn't nearly as elegant. As I proceed through the elocution, I may recognize that a term I struggled with is now easy or that there is a term that requires definition. I may stop and research the term, and I may start again with a more elegant delivery of the solution.

I do not intentionally walk students through each of the five canons for every single math problem, but they do categorize well the process of communication. For example, in the last step of a problem, I may realize there is an easier solution. If I'm studying on my own, I may not redo the problem. But if I am teaching the problem, I will start over and point out different facts (memory), explain the problem more clearly (elocution), and use a simpler delivery.

The beauty of using math for conversations is that the problems are short and sweet. A math conversation can take fifteen seconds or fifteen minutes to complete, compared to a science text, which may take fifteen weeks to study, or a novel, which may take a few days to read. We can practice the five canons quickly with each math problem.

The beauty of using math for conversations is that the problems are short and sweet.

EXAMPLE 1: A LESSON ABOUT CLOTHES SHOPPING

As students progress into higher mathematics, there are multiple ways to solve each problem, and some even have multiple answers. It is a myth that math problems can only have one answer. Think about the square root of 9. The answer is both positive 3 and negative 3. Why? And which one should I use? Should I consider both as correct? I have structured my class as a "math conversation" for this very reason. Students should be as comfortable presenting their solution to a problem and explaining it clearly to the class as they would be discussing a novel or a video game. They become truly rhetorical in math by teaching it to others.

Invention

In writing a persuasive essay, invention is used to gather the materials one will need to form an argument. In math, the student must gather all of the information he needs to solve the problem. This might mean recalling formulas or making a list of the known quantities. Then, it will mean thinking of a way to solve the problem. Let's say after brainstorming with a class you recognize three possible ways to approach a problem. One student makes a pictorial answer (chart), another an abstract answer (algebra equation), and another describes relationships and proportion. Math teachers now face an important choice. They can affirm the student who solved the problem in the way that makes sense to the teacher, or the one who solved it the way that the problem is solved in the answer key, or the one who solved it in the way that made sense to the student. A wise teacher would spend time looking at all three solutions, allowing students to explore and discuss them. The five canons of rhetoric provide a form for conducting the discussion. Let's step inside my weekly math class to see how this process might look.

Tom bought some sweaters for $16 each and some shirts for $10 each. He spent $98. Altogether he bought 8 articles of clothing. How many of each did he buy?

ME: Does it matter that the guy's name is Tom or that the problem is asking about sweaters or shirts?
CLASS: No.
ME: Do you ever go shopping for clothes? When you check out you have a total. Can you imagine you are at the store and you just paid $98?
CHRIS: Yes. But what about the tax?
ME: Do we care about tax for this problem?
CLASS: No.
ME: Now we know that this question relates to something we do regularly, but how are we going to tackle it?
MIKE: I can do it in my head!
SIERRA: I would make a chart.

SALLY: I already wrote the algebra equations—there are two equations and two unknowns.

ME: Everyone try to solve the problem using your method and then explain it to the class.

The students work on their small dry erase boards and hold them up as they complete the problem.

As you can see from this discussion, you may have one student who discusses the three different ways, three who each take a different way, or a large class divided into three groups and assigned an approach. Class size doesn't matter; awareness of strengths and weaknesses and loving your children or students is everything. There are different ways to lead students through the invention process.

Arrangement

Next comes the arrangement stage. How will you arrange your equation, chart, or proportion? For a persuasive essay, students gather the information they brainstormed in the invention stage and organize it into a whole. Similarly, students must outline the math problem in a series of logical steps.

ME: Sally, tell us how you arranged the problem.

SALLY: I saw right away that there were two equations with two unknowns so I arranged the equations like this:
$sw + sh = 8$
$sw(16) + sh(10) = 98.$

ME: Good. Mike, what about you?

MIKE: Well, I'm not very good at algebra, but I like shopping at the sports store. I imagined I had $98 and 8 things in my hand. I tried different numbers until I came up with a reasonable answer that I think is correct.

ME: Thanks, Mike. We'll keep working on the algebra so you can solve really difficult problems later, but I'm glad you have such good number sense. Sierra, how about you?

SIERRA: I can't hold numbers in my head like Mike. I essentially arranged it the same way, but I made a chart so I could keep everything straight.

ME: Ah! Good thinking. Show us your chart.

MATH

Shirts	3	4	5	6
Shirt cost	30	40	50	60
Remainder	68	58	48	38
Divided by 16			3	
			5 + 3 = 8	

ME: Why did you choose shirts over sweaters?

SIERRA: The math was easier. I had to multiply by 10 many times and divide by 16 once.

Even if your student finds math easy, you should train him not to skip steps, because they need to make sure the other students understand the solution too. This is what it means to be rhetorical. If a student masters a subject in a way that only he understands, the knowledge gained stops with him—he can't pass it on! A rhetorician needs to know every step so that he can guide someone else through every step as well.

Elocution

In persuasive writing, elocution means that the student takes his arranged ideas and writes them in full sentences that are clear to the reader. Here, in math class, students must clearly explain their methods to the audience.

ME: So now that each of you has explained your method and arrangement, let's go back and hear your explanation for the solution. Sally?

SALLY: Well, since I had two equations and two unknowns, I chose to use substitution to solve the problem.

ME: What else could you have used?

SALLY: Elimination, but substitution is easier, so I used the identity law and rebalanced the equation using subtraction and came up with this equivalent statement:

$sh = 8 - sw.$

Then I applied the properties of equality and substituted for sh in my next equation like this:

$sw(16) + (8 - sw)(10) = 98.$

Now that I have one equation and one unknown, I can solve this equation.

	First I distributed and got $sw(16) + 80 - sw(10) = 98$. Then I rebalanced the equation using addition on the left side of the equal sign and got $6sw + 80 = 98$. Then I used the identity law for subtraction and gathered the 80 and 98 to have $6sw = 18$. From there I used the identity law for division and divided by 6 on both sides of the equation. Of course, that gave me $sw = 3$. So if I have 3 sweaters and I bought 8 objects, I must have 5 shirts.
ME:	Great explanation. I appreciate how well you used the proper math terms. Your turn, Mike.
MIKE:	Well, all I know is that 16 times 3 is 48, which ends in 8, and I had $98, which also ends in 8. So I thought I'd start with 3 sweaters. 8 items minus 3 is 5. 5 times $10 is $50. $50 and $48 make $98, so I knew I was correct. I think I was lucky to get the first guess right. It just seems like common sense.
ME:	Especially if you are really familiar with numbers. Nice elocution. It's often hard to see what is in your head, but that was a pretty clear explanation. Thanks. Sierra?
SIERRA:	Well, I think my chart shows what my brain was doing.

Shirts	3	4	5	6
Shirt cost	30	40	50	60
Remainder	68	58	48	38
Divided by 16			3	
			5 + 3 = 8	

I wasn't sure what number to begin with so I established a pattern. As soon as I saw the 48, I was pretty sure that was where I needed to look more carefully because then I remembered that 3 times 16 is 48. Then I realized that 5 and 3 make 8, and I was finished.

Remember, students should demonstrate the problem so clearly that all students in the room can understand the method they used. Students should ask themselves these questions: How am I going to tell the story of my solution? As I think about this story, what ideas need explanation or context? The student's math memory will provide answers to these questions.

Memory

As we have discussed in previous chapters, memory involves several skills—bringing previous knowledge to bear on the current situation and having a storehouse of memorized information. Both of these come into play in mathematics. The first involves recognizing similar math problems the student has encountered that function like the one they are currently working. The second involves remembering math information stored for years such as multiplication tables, formulas, and laws.

Memory involves several skills—bringing previous knowledge to bear on the current situation and having a storehouse of memorized information.

ME: Let's talk about the *memoria* involved in solving this problem. What previous knowledge did you bring to bear on the solution to this problem? You all seemed to notice that 3 and 5 were related to 8, and 3 and 16 were related to 48. Why?

MIKE: Because you keep making us practice our multiplication tables. We just see solutions now.

ME: Good! Sierra, how did you think to use a chart?

SIERRA: Well, we just discussed one in physical science, so it was fresh.

ME: Good. Mike, what were you seeing as you did your problem in your head?

MIKE: I just kept picturing the teller at Wal-Mart as I checked out.

ME: Ha! How about you Sally?

SALLY: I've written so many equations from word problems that I just write symbolically what I see.

If solving math problems is difficult for your student, it may mean that he needs to go back to the basics (multiplication tables, squares, cubes, laws, etc.) to add to his math memory.

Delivery

Finally, there is the delivery itself. We've all been frustrated by a teacher who knew too much or too little to explain just what we needed to know. We all know students who write so sloppily that we can't read it or others who won't (or can't) write down their thoughts, and so their delivery is incomprehensible. Everyone in the class should understand the delivery of the solution.

ME: Sally, could you have used Mike's or Sierra's method?

SALLY: I don't see numbers like Mike does, but I could have used a chart like Sierra did. I probably wouldn't have used the remainder to reduce my need to plug and chug. That was quite eloquent, Sierra.

ME: Mike, can you see the benefit of Sally's delivery?

MIKE: For a simple problem, it seems like too much work. Same as the chart. But I know that when there are three or four unknowns with lots of relationships, I need to be able to use algebra. I just like short cuts.

SIERRA: The more we talk about simple problems, the more I appreciate Mike's gift for number sense, and I wish I were as good at algebra as Sally. I'm just glad we talk about alternative solutions to problems. I like that I can "see" what is being asked of me.

MIKE: Sierra's right. I like how I can just see numbers, but I wish I knew the vocabulary as well as Sally. I get so frustrated when I see how to solve a problem but can't explain it.

ME: Good insights! Let's do another problem. As I write it on the board, I want you to know how much I appreciate how much you enjoy one another's methods. Mike could be arrogant because he sees the answers so easily and might not be willing to learn how to write down the steps. Sally could be boastful that she can use algebra when you two can't. And Sierra is willing to apply her organization skills to harder problems. I just love learning from the three of you.

"What If the Art Teacher Taught Math?" by Courtney Sanford
Originally published in Classical Conversations Writers Circle

When my daughter was thirteen, she was preparing for a mock trial competition, so we took a field trip, along with several moms and teenagers, to visit a courthouse and watch a real trial. As we waited for the trial to begin, the sheriff talked with the students and moms. At one point, he turned to the moms and asked us if we had been teachers before we started homeschooling our children. (This did not feel like small talk anymore. It felt as though he was checking our qualifications.) At the time, I did not want to say that I had been an art teacher. I assumed the sheriff would think that an art teacher ought not to be teaching government, literature, and, especially, math!

Since then, I have given this some thought, and I have come to the conclusion that perhaps more art teachers should teach math. I do have to read the lessons carefully, and sometimes I have to work an equation before I remember the rule. I used to need flash cards with the answers on them in order to drill the multiplication tables. (Don't worry; I know them quite well now.)

I am not coming into math class with only art information in my head, however. I come to math class, or any class, knowing how to learn, and I learn with my children. It is great fun to learn something new together. I sometimes struggle with my student over a long equation, and then we both get really excited when one of us finds the solution. My oldest son often experiences the joy of figuring out the solution before his teacher.

I am currently reading a beautiful book about math titled *Mathematics: Is God Silent?* The author, James Nickel, might like the idea that the art teacher is teaching math. He explains that the reason many students dislike math is because it is taught so abstractly that we do not see the relationship of math to creation. Math, he explains, is the language that describes and explains creation and helps us to understand and know the Creator a bit better.

As the art teacher, I can see this easily. The leaves on a branch either follow an alternating or opposite pattern. Flowers have radial symmetry. I can show and explain to my students the golden rectangle and its spiral, and how the ratio of one side of the rectangle to its other side is the same ratio in a pinecone, a sunflower seed, and a nautilus shell. These elements found in creation beautifully demonstrate math concepts: pattern, symmetry, geometry, and ratios.

Once I start to see math in creation, not only can I see the existence of the Creator but also I can see His great wisdom. He arranged things we cannot even see in complex and beautiful patterns (e.g., the double helix of DNA). He instructs flowers and pinecones to grow, following these patterns. The pinecone grows in a ratio that I have trouble calculating. This does not mean the pinecone is smarter than I am; it means that God is smarter than I am. He has hidden mysteries in biology, chemistry, and physics, and when we learn math, we can understand the complexities behind something that seems simple at first glance.

I believe that human beings have only scratched the surface of the mathematics in creation. That is why we should study math. We need to know the language of math in order to discover and appreciate more of the beauty, complexity, and greatness of God.

I never had a math teacher who showed me this, but a homeschool mom did. Imagine that! Therefore, the question asked of us by so many—"Are you qualified?"—is not really relevant. The question is, "Can God equip you to do this?" If you know anything about pinecones or sea shells, then you know that, yes, God is more than (>) capable of equipping us to teach math or art, or more importantly, to raise a child who is completely in awe of God.

EXAMPLE 2: A LESSON ABOUT TERMS

Because talking about math can be more intimidating than talking about other subjects, let me give you another example of a math conversation that progresses through the five canons of rhetoric. This time, I won't give as much explanation for each canon. See if you can follow the progression of the conversation and identify the kinds of questions that prompt each part of the conversation.

What are the 20th and 50th terms of this series? 8, 13, 18, 23, …

Invention

In this example, a large part of the invention involves looking at the problem itself. Too often, students don't really think about the questions they are given. Instead, they rush headlong into solving something that they don't understand. In college, a wise math tutor once told me to spend far less time trying to figure out the solution and far more time trying to understand the question. So, for this question, I want to use the invention stage to train my students to be keen observers of the problem. They need to list all of the things they see before we can begin the solution.

ME: So class, what do we see in this problem?
SIERRA: A number series.
SALLY: An integer series.
MIKE: They are all 5 apart.
CHRIS: They continue indefinitely.
AMY: We see the first four terms.
JAMES: We need to find the 20th term.
CLASS: We need to find the 50th term.

Arrangement

Again, there are multiple ways to approach this problem, so I want to give the students a chance to share these different approaches.

ME: Take a few minutes and let me know how you will arrange this problem.
Sally?
SALLY: $8 + (t - 1)5$ is what I see algebraically, but that reduces to $5t + 3$.
ME: Great. Mike?
MIKE: Well, this is a little too long to hold in my head. So I would write down a few more numbers in the sequence, like 28, 33, 38, and see if I can find a pattern.
ME: OK. I'm curious to see where that gets you. How about you Sierra?
SIERRA: I'm with Mike in that I'd write out the sequence and see if I can see the pattern and then come up with a formula like Sally has.

Elocution

ME: OK. Work the problem and explain to the class how you did it.
SALLY: Well, it was easy for me to plug in any term because I wrote the information out as a formula. $5t + 3$. So the 20th term is $5(20) + 3$ or 103 and the 50th term is $5(50) + 3$, which is 253.

THE CONVERSATION

SIERRA: Sally's way is so easy because I can even tell you the 1000th term is 5003. My problem is that I can't see how she comes up with the equation. I wrote out the sequence and could see I started with 8 and kept increasing the number by 5, but I am confused as to how to write out the formula, and how did she come up with 3?

ME: What do you think Mike?

MIKE: I understand what Sally did, now that she explained it. And I even see why she has a 3. But I couldn't see it when you first showed me the problem. I have a hard time writing the relationships into math symbols.

ME: OK, Sally, explain a little more to us.

SALLY: Well, I think I see the algebra for the same reason Mike sees the number patterns. He's always thinking about numbers in a practical sense while I'm always practicing formulas in an academic sense. I need to try to be more like him as I live life, and he needs to practice writing out more problems. We're both smart enough to learn each other's methods if we would just work.

What I noticed that helped me with the algebra was that I started with 8 so I wrote 8. Then I saw that the next number was 5 more, so I wrote 8 + 5. But that only helped me with the second term of 13. The third term, 18, is the same as 8 + 5 + 5, which is the same as 8 + 2(5). The 8 + 2(5) gave me the third term, but I wrote the number 2. So how do I make a 3 a 2? I subtract one. So I knew each term would be $t - 1$ + my original first term, which was 8. So 8 + (term − 1) × 5 or 8 + $(t - 1)$ × 5. But this isn't as compact as possible. Using the distributive law, the equation becomes 8 + $t5$ − 1(5). Well, 8 minus 5 is 3. So the equation is simplified to $5t + 3$. I can switch the 5 and t around, thanks to the commutative law of multiplication.

Memory

ME: So Sierra, what did you already know that helped you understand Sally's solution?

SIERRA:	Well, I knew what the 20th term meant, and I knew I would have to find a relationship in the sequence. And I knew that it would need to have a 5.
ME:	Mike, what didn't you know?
MIKE:	I could follow Sally's explanation, and I can see how elegant the solution is for infinite terms. But I just struggle with setting up the problem.

Delivery

When you and I were in school, I would guess that we had similar math experiences. We had an assignment each day that we handed in the next day. The teacher graded it and returned it. We either filed it or threw it away and promptly forgot about it. That's why, at home with my boys, I require them to correct every missed math problem. I don't want them to remain in error. In class, I want to use the delivery time to encourage students to reflect on gaps in their education and to formulate a plan for filling in those gaps. In this example, I had two students who really needed to work on their ability to translate problems into algebraic equations. I want them to recognize that this is a math gap for them and to form their own plan for filling the gap.

ME:	What could you do to help yourself improve?
MIKE:	Download Sally's brain into mine?
ME:	Ha… Seriously.
MIKE:	Well, I know in the beginning of the algebra text, I was frustrated at one point because I couldn't do the problems in my head. I think I should go back there and work those problems. They were easy like these, and I can probably put them into formulas, now that Sally has shown us how.
ME:	I agree. I think that would be helpful. We often have to back up to simpler problems to master a concept. How about you, Sierra?
SIERRA:	I think I need to do the same thing. I remember doodling around lesson 30—that is where I began to get confused.
ME:	Sally? What do you want to work on?

SALLY: Well, I'd be happy to do a brain exchange with Mike. I need to pay attention to mechanics and investing and science like he does.

ME: I think your brains are just fine, and I'm glad we get to spend an hour talking about math together.

A WORD ABOUT HIGHER MATH

The examples I gave above come from Algebra I. Many homeschooling parents believe they can hang in with their high school students through Algebra I, but they balk at teaching anything higher. Let me encourage you to focus on really solidifying the concepts in arithmetic and algebra using the method I outlined above. Studying calculus will come naturally to your children if they thoroughly master arithmetic while developing curious minds, good study habits, and effective communication skills. I'm in my fifties and have an engineering degree, and I'm still studying arithmetic. I make mistakes, improve speed and accuracy, invent math laws, and discover new ideas in arithmetic almost daily. People think I am good at math, but really I am fascinated by arithmetic. The more I study arithmetic, the more I understand why arithmetic is fundamental to everything else you study. Higher math is just longer arithmetic problems with more variables or unknowns.

Many people have misconstrued my comments to mean that I would only have parents and students learn arithmetic and not the higher maths. By no means! But when I am working with young people in the higher maths, I focus on their arithmetic skills. Then the problems are easier to solve. I try to bring the five canons of rhetoric to bear on a few problems at a time. It is very important to solve a lot of math problems with speed and accuracy, but it is equally important to discuss math step-by-step, strategy-by-strategy. One of the things that frustrates good math students in high school is the number of choices they must make with each problem. It takes just as much nuance to solve an algebra problem as it does to write a good poem. As students progress from one way to solve a problem to other ways, the solutions and answers take many forms. The calculus student who knows arithmetic well is like the poetry student who knows sentence structure well.

The beauty of classical education comes from its universal application to the human mind. Since skills that are common to man are emphasized, both teachers and students can help one another define their weaknesses and then strengthen their skills. Someone who doesn't know how to start a problem needs to tackle invention through solving lots of easy problems. Someone who can do the problem in his head but can't write it down needs help in elocution. Someone who sees solutions easily needs to work on recognizing the audience's prior knowledge (memory) before delivering a solution. Someone prone to careless errors needs to work on arrangement. The five canons of rhetoric defined, practiced, and internalized will make better storytellers of us all, no matter the subject.

Investigating math, *using the five canons of rhetoric:*	
Invention	What do you see when you look at this problem?
	Have you gathered all the information you will need to solve the problem?
	What possible approaches will help you solve the problem?
Arrangement	How will you arrange your equation, chart, or proportion?
	Have you completed all the steps?
Elocution	How are you going to tell the story of your solution?
	As you think about this story, what ideas need explanation or context?
Memory	What similar math problems have you encountered?
	What math tables, formulas, and laws apply to this problem?
Delivery	Have you written out your solution neatly and legibly?
	Can you clearly explain your methods to the audience?
	Have you corrected your mistakes? What did you learn from them?

THE CONVERSATION

CHAPTER EIGHT

GOVERNMENT AND ECONOMICS

"It is often sadly remarked that the bad economists present their errors to the public better than the good economists present their truths."
—Henry Hazlitt, *Economics in One Lesson*

"Are choices always a good thing? I mean, is it always a good thing to have many choices: flavors of soda, presidential candidates, or health care?" one student asked. I wasn't sure what he meant.

"Are you asking if having choices is bad, if specific choices can be bad, or something else?" We were studying American documents and economics, which always leads to fascinating discussions about the types of government and economic systems a particular culture and nation may have. In America, we tend to associate freedom with a multitude of choices. We frequently interchange the terms "freedom" and "choice" as if they have the same meaning. Our class discussion of different kinds of governments led this particular student to think about whether a multitude of choices is always a good thing. This student had moved on from our discussion of particular governments and economic systems to the idea of choice itself. In other words, he had

If we allow our children to think about important ideas, discussing them becomes natural.

moved from observing the particulars to attempting discovery of a universal truth about choice. If we allow our children to think about important ideas, discussing them becomes natural. People are wired to seek truth. We can use the canons of rhetoric to guide these conversations and to deepen our understanding of the topic. We can start by learning how to apply the modes of persuasion to a particular field of study such as government or economics. (Some of this will be a review from chapter 2.)

Logos is the use of propositional truth to communicate truth, goodness, and beauty. It is what we are asking our students to discover through the questions in invention, and it is what we are asking them to communicate in elocution and delivery. They must recognize that what they are pursuing is truth: good, old-fashioned, objective truth. They are not in pursuit of relativism or opinions, but truth. At the same time, they must apply truth to certain circumstances. While a principle is universal, its practical application will not always be the same. Once students uncover *logos*, they will communicate it to others, including their family, their classmates, or their youth group at church. They must go beyond knowing the *logos* to persuading others that it is true.

Ethos refers to the ethical reputation of the communicator of truth, goodness, and beauty. Our students must consider the *ethos* of the authorities on whom they depend as they build a case for truth in government and economics. For example, appealing to Thomas Jefferson's authority on equality in the Constitution may be problematic in light of his position on slavery. To reject the principle of equality in the Constitution because Thomas Jefferson may have been hypocritical, however, is to commit the logical fallacy *ad hominem*. Our students must not confuse the two.

Pathos is the use of an emotional appeal to move the audience toward an understanding of truth, goodness, and beauty. Students today (and parents, too) are often wary of the emotional appeal. They associate it with manipulation. Like all modes of persuasion, *pathos* must be used appropriately and fittingly. History affords many examples of emotional appeals that have moved people to act on behalf of others. During the Victorian era, two writers used *pathos* to move entire nations. Dickens used emotional appeals to stir the nation of Britain to do something about orphans and the poor. Harriet Beecher Stowe used emotional appeal in *Uncle Tom's Cabin* to arouse a nation to the evils of slavery. In both of these cases, the writers used stories to move their audience to righteous action. Years of pamphlets and meetings did not move people like these stories. The incorporation of stories to analogously communicate truth, goodness, and beauty is important to effective communication and persuasive argumentation. Our students should be immersed both in good stories and in the science of the world around them so they will be able to use nature and literature analogously. To begin, they must establish the principle—the *logos*—they are learning. To do that, they must begin with a series of questions.

> *The incorporation of stories to analogously communicate truth, goodness, and beauty is important to effective communication and persuasive argumentation.*

EXAMPLE 1: AMERICAN GOVERNMENT AND THE VOTING PROCESS

It is often helpful, here, to ask your student to imagine a specific scenario through which he can think more deeply about government and economics. You might ask him to think through the process of starting a business or running for office. You might ask him to simply consider his own participation in the voting process.

Invention

Invention begins with questions from the five common topics (see my previous book *The Question* for more on how to use these questions with geography and current events). We want to define our terms, compare governments and economic systems, consider the circumstances and relationship of events, and evaluate what testimony or authorities may have to say on the matter.

While students are in the invention stage, they need to discover as much information as they can about the topic at hand. In order to discover new ideas, they must set aside preconceived opinions. The students should not assume that the particular economic and political system practiced in the

United States is necessarily the best, although they may come to that conclusion. They should begin by defining capitalism and comparing that economic system to socialism, communism, nationalism, feudalism, monarchism, and others. They should define different forms of government such as republic, democracy, monarchy, aristocracy, and military dictatorship.

At some point, however, they will need to interact with the particular system we live in: a free market republic. By defining and comparing different economic systems, they will discover that what we call a free market has been somewhat socialized by government legislation and regulation, and that our republic has been somewhat democratized. To notice these nuances, though, they have gone through the invention process and discovered similarities between the American economic system and a socialized or nationalized system. They will also have noticed similarities between the American republic and a democracy.

When students vote, are they participating in a republican process or a democratic process? Are they electing someone to represent them or someone to defend the Constitution? As a voter, is it more important to be informed about local elections or national elections? The common topic questions provide answers for these questions as well. Define the American system. Compare it to other systems. What are the circumstances affecting this particular election, office, and candidate? What has happened before that might cause certain issues to be important to this specific election? What might happen as a result of the election? (These latter two questions are related to relationship.) What does the testimony of authorities say about the candidate? Who or what serves as an authority: your pastor, your parents, the Bible, the Constitution, your worldview, your political affiliation? Why? Finally, how can we organize these answers into a coherent thought that informs our decisions?

Arrangement

As the students think through these questions, they must pick a side and defend it. As David Hicks points out in his book *Norms & Nobility*, "Dialectic begins with acceptance, not negation," and "dialectical learning requires that [a student] accept a dogma before he rejects it" (69). Once the students have picked a side, based on the information learned in the invention process, they can test it against the other canons and either correct, modify, or replace it.

We do this all the time. Most of us started classical education or homeschooling with one curriculum and style of teaching and have changed over the years. This is part of the process of learning and maturation we both undergo and model to our students so that they might understand they are learning in the same way. We allow students to go through the process themselves, even if we don't always like their conclusions. For instance, I may believe strongly that the United States has a republican form of government and that voters should elect representatives who will defend the Constitution. My students, though, may come to a different conclusion initially, and they may accept a different principle to be tested. We must give them the time and freedom to test their ideas.

Let's assume my students determined that when they vote, they will operate as if the United States is a democracy and will elect someone to represent them and their desires. Determining and assuming the democratic nature of the U.S. government, my students then apply that understanding to their lives, recognizing and asking additional questions. In this example, having arranged their understanding of the voting process around the upcoming election, they will assess their voting options against it. They will then be able to consider how best to state their position.

Elocution

Once they've arrived at the canon of elocution, they will need to explain—even defend—their decisions. They can articulate what they believe the American system of government to be: Democratic. They can explain why they believe that: We participate in popular elections. They can explain why they are going to practice voting a particular way in line with this understanding.

When we think of elocution from the perspective of writing, we imagine the author making specific judgments about which words to use and which turns of phrase to use that will make the essay or story as persuasive and beautiful as possible. When we think of elocution from the perspective of argumentation and debate, we imagine the speaker making judgments about which words to use in an effort to make the speech as persuasive as possible.

As your student articulates his understanding of government and voting, he will be practicing a similar skill. Determining which arguments explain his position best and which words to use to communicate that position is a skill quite similar to that used in creative writing, persuasive writing, and formal debate. As parents and teachers, we can ask questions that help students to see areas in need of correction or modification. However, these conversations also become opportunities for us to learn and have our presuppositions and standards tested and then corrected or modified. Through these scenarios we are learning together with our students. In fact, it may be better to consider ourselves as lead learners rather than teachers.

It may be better to consider ourselves as lead learners rather than teachers.

Elocution, then, is a stage in which we can develop and strengthen one another in our views and positions. It can help to reveal weaknesses, misunderstandings, and straw man arguments. Through this process, the students correct, modify, or replace their principles. We don't hear their explanations and respond by demanding they go back to the invention stage until they satisfy our demands or agreed with us. Rather, we continue the questioning that will help them to correct, modify, or strengthen their position, or we continue the questioning that will ultimately lead them back to invention of their own accord. Whichever route they take to arrive at their final conclusion, it will ultimately be informed by the knowledge they have.

Memory

When we think of memory, generally, we think of the students memorizing their speech or written work in order to present it publicly. Memory, though, is much more than this. In the study of government and economics, memory may include committing quotations, laws, or statistics to memory for the sake of one's argument. These, then, can be used in the exordium, proofs, or elsewhere. We also want to consider, however, how previously memorized information may be used to inform our students and their position. Your student may recall, for example, that George Washington refused to become king of the United States because he remembered what had happened to Oliver Cromwell and his revolution in Britain. It was Washington's memory of Oliver Cromwell's history that informed his own decisions. Likewise, it may be your student's memory of Washington's history that will inform his decisions. The key is to ask questions and start conversations about history that encourage your student to draw lessons from the past into his present decision-making.

History and literature are always prescriptive. In other words, they can always be used to prescribe to us how we should or should not live. Whether a specific example from history or literature is prescribing how we should live or not live may be difficult to determine, but it is doing so. In fact, we could say history is begging to be judged. It wants us to ask questions that will allow it to inform us. This is part of the reason why we ask our grammar-aged students to memorize grammatical information for each subject (see my earlier book *The Core*). Those facts not only become the pegs that help us to organize later information, but they also become the information that will help us to answer questions of invention and to pass judgment on history. In other words, the act of passing judgment on history is the act of determining what history is prescribing for us so that we may undergo the challenge of pursuing truth, wisdom, and the virtuous life.

History and literature are always prescriptive.

Reimagining memory in this way allows us to see how our students can be informed so that they learn to ask not only "*Can* I vote this way?" but also "*Should* I vote this way?" Does voting the way I am intending to vote emphasize the individual to the neglect of the community? Does it emphasize the community to the neglect of the individual? Does it strike a proper balance—tension even—between the individual and the community? They may answer these questions with the information they have committed to memory, the stories they have read, and the historical events that have become prescriptive for them—positively or negatively. At this point they are ready to apply what they have learned in wisdom and virtue.

Delivery

In its plainest sense, the fifth rhetorical canon of delivery focuses on how your student presents the words he has chosen. At this point, students would focus on hand gestures, eye contact, speed, volume, and other elements of presentation. However, there is a deeper sense in which we can understand this canon when it comes to the study of government and economics. As your student has considered the process of voting, he has engaged in invention by developing his understanding of voting and the government system in which he lives. He has engaged in arrangement by applying his understanding of the system and making some assumptions about how he should vote. He has engaged in elocution by presenting, explaining, defending, and refining that position. He has engaged in memory by applying memorized language to their presentation and by applying historical and literary events to his final understanding. It is now time for him to deliver what he has concluded: to act on it and to live it.

Delivery changes with the conclusions of previous canons. It may look different from one student to the next. One student may, after a study of the specific example we've considered, find it affects how he votes. Another student, after the same study, may find it disaffects her, and she won't vote. A third student may find that voting isn't enough, so she will not only vote but also become engaged in the election process. This student, and others with her, may find they reach out to local candidates and join their campaign teams as paid employees or volunteers.

I've had several students regularly join in the activities of organizations like TeenPact. My youngest son, David, participated in a state TeenPact event in Raleigh, North Carolina, where he served as a campaign manager. Later, he participated in a national TeenPact event in Dayton, Tennessee. Another of my Challenge I students, James, was with David at the state event in Raleigh and ran for TeenPact Senate, where he was elected. He and David both participated as campaign staff for a candidate at the national event. There are a variety of ways your student can express or deliver his conclusions. We do a disservice to our students when we ask or expect them to all look the same in their delivery.

EXAMPLE 2: ECONOMICS OF PRODUCTION

In the government example, you asked your student to imagine himself voting. Let's now turn to an example that specifically deals with economics. Ask your student to imagine he is involved in production of a product such as milk. Ask him to work through the process to determine how much milk he will produce weekly. The point is to get him to think through these economic or governmental principles.

Invention

To know how much milk to produce, your student will ask some invention questions. He will need to know under which economic system he is operating. Does the government or some other agency tell him how much milk to produce? Does the government have laws, as North Carolina does, establishing a state minimum price for a gallon of milk? Which figures might be helpful from previous production numbers and sales?

Arrangement

Once he has that information, how does the arrangement of it affect his decision? As he arranges that information, he may discover he needs more information and has to ask additional questions from the invention process. He should also consider who cares about the thesis (how much milk is produced) and why.

Elocution

Next, your student will articulate his decision, test it, and defend it. Ask him questions he might not have thought to ask, and provoke him to think of the question from different perspectives. As you help him to test his conclusions, you are not answering questions he has not asked. You want to provoke him to ask questions he has not asked, and then you can help him to discover the answers. For example, he might not purchase milk often enough to know that some states have state minimum milk prices. You should ask questions that will give rise to that thought. You might ask him, "Who determines prices for a product?" You will most likely hear that supply and demand sets the prices. To that, you can follow up by asking if supply and demand always sets prices, and if not, who does. Your goal is to help him think more thoroughly, not to think like you.

Your goal is to help him think more thoroughly, not to think like you.

Memory

Memory requires students to remember their argument, make it memorable for others, and apply what they know and have previously memorized to their argument. From there, your student can make a final decision about milk production. Here, additional testing of his decision takes place. How much of his milk is purchased? Did he produce too much, too little, or just the right amount? Was the price set appropriately? Here, adjustments are made and he starts the process again.

Delivery

Asking these questions and refining the answers guides students toward a stronger understanding of their relationship to their own communities. These discussions demonstrate our students' need to study these two subjects. A practical reason to study them is to raise up a generation of leaders who will participate well in government and economics. The way we organize our economic and governmental systems both reveals what we believe about humans and also affects what we believe about humans. It reminds us to consider who is more important, the individual or the community. Does this question have an either-or answer? Why do some believe the government needs to legislate everything and others believe the government should legislate nothing? What does each belief imply about humanity? What do we believe, and does our view of government consistently reflect that belief? How does our understanding of government and economics affect us individually and as we relate to our communities? Asking these questions can help guide students to make wise decisions as citizens and, more importantly, as humans.

"Spontaneous Integration: Jazz Music, Playwrights, and the Cold War" by Jennifer Courtney
Originally published in Classical Conversations Writers Circle

What do Shakespeare, actors, newspapers, jazz, and communism all have in common? One Challenge III [eleventh grade] class was able to weave together these seemingly disconnected ideas in a moment of spontaneous subject integration.

First, we discussed the surprising role of jazz music during the Cold War. We then talked about how rock music played a large role in the fall of the Berlin Wall. From the rise of communism to its fall, there was an ongoing connection to music.

We started with the simple question, "What in the world could jazz music have to do with politics?" The students looked at me somewhat blankly, so I asked them to think about jazz music and jazz players. "Do jazz musicians usually follow the notes on the page?" One student noted that jazz musicians are known for improvising. I followed up with, "Does this quality make them more likely to follow the crowd or to live like distinctive individuals?" This one was easy—clearly, jazz musicians like to go their own way. We kept going: "In communism, do you want people to follow a uniform path or to improvise?" Art reminds people that they are uniquely created individuals, that they are not designed to be state-controlled robots.

It would have been fun to camp out on this topic for the whole hour, but we had to move on to McCarthyism, which provided another opportunity to consider the connection between fine arts and government. In an effort to pinpoint the origins of McCarthy's bad reputation, we harkened back to Challenge II when the students had read Arthur Miller's play *The Crucible* in which he compares the McCarthy era to the Salem witch trials. We talked about the impact of Miller's pen on McCarthy's legacy.

After U.S. history, we turned our attention to the Shakespeare seminar. We happened to be reading the scene in which Hamlet devises his famous mouse trap to catch his murderous uncle. As Hamlet turns the players over to the hospitality of Polonius he warns, "Do you hear, let them be well used, for they are the abstract and brief chronicles of the time. After your death, you were better have a bad epitaph than their ill report while you live"(act 2, scene 2). McCarthy could have benefited from these words. Hamlet's words led us to discuss Common Core reduction of fiction texts in favor of non-fiction texts. The students concluded that the plays provided a richer understanding of human nature. It was a great day of making connections between seemingly disconnected subjects.

DEVELOPING LEADERS

In the Classical Conversations communities that I founded, we have worked hard to design our curriculum for the dialectic and rhetoric years (the Challenge program) around a central idea that students should understand by the end of the year. In each of the Challenge levels, there is a theme that binds them internally and in relation to one another. In Challenge A, which is loosely comparable to seventh grade, the curriculum is bound around the theme of ownership. The theme is to engage them in taking ownership of their own education, but the curriculum takes them through ownership of everything: education, life, faith, and more. In Challenge B, the theme of ownership proceeds into the theme of discipline. With ownership, students must learn to be disciplined to own their responsibilities well. In Challenge I, the equivalent of ninth grade, discipline leads to freedom. Freedom, then, leads to choices, the theme for Challenge II. As we wrestle with freedom and choices, we must learn to identify the consequences of our choices, the theme for Challenge III. As we learn to accept the consequences of our choices, we learn to exercise duty, the theme of Challenge IV. Ultimately, those who exercise ownership with discipline and can live freely understanding choices, consequences, and duty are trained to be leaders—the very thing we hope our Challenge graduates will be.

Learning the art of rhetoric through the study of various subjects, such as government and economics, helps us to develop these leaders. They are learning to think well, to participate well in life and community, to be virtuous and to be wise. They are also learning to see the beauty in order, the freedom in form, and the grace in law.

We often think of form as being restrictive and controlling, but it provides us with the confidence to operate with freedom.

Beauty in order may be the easiest to see initially. The Fibonacci spiral in a pinecone is ordered beauty. Being able to live a harmonious life is beautiful because of the order that society and cultural institutions provide. The ordered thinking that helps us to arrive at truth and to therefore to live wisely and virtuously is beautiful.

Freedom in form may come across as antithetical. We often think of form as being restrictive and controlling, but it provides us with the confidence to operate with freedom. When William was in Challenge III, his tutor, Matt, took the group to dinner and then to see Shakespeare's *Much Ado About Nothing*. Before the event, the young men and women were instructed in formal protocol and manners. The young men really enjoyed the lessons! They felt empowered and confident in knowing exactly what they were supposed to do in specific situations: holding the door for a lady, standing, sitting, and silverware use, among others. What seemed formal and restrictive gave them great freedom in conversation and other interactions because they weren't distracted with other concerns.

Grace in the law may be the least likely to come to mind, especially if we limit our understanding of those terms to theology. Even there, however, the two need not be antithetical. The Law of Christ—to love God and to love your neighbor—is not antithetical to grace. In fact, the more we love God and the more we love our neighbor, the more we see, experience, and offer grace. When we love the cultural norms and institutions of which we are heirs through education, we love and honor our parents. There is, moreover, a grace that is received and experienced in that inheritance. Some of that grace is known only through the gift of beauty that accompanies order and the gift of freedom that accompanies form.

The study of government and economics is neither solely utilitarian nor solely beautiful, but rather a harmonious combination of the two. When these subjects are learned, not as a series of propositional truths we must accept or a series of laws we must obey, but rather as the cultural norms and institutions of which we are heirs, they carry with them the beauty, freedom, and grace we desire.

Were we to only study them didactically, they would be nothing more to us than a series of propositions or laws. This might lead our students to reject them because this form suggests legalism. Propositions joined with cultural heritage prevent such legalism.

Studying government and economics by way of the five canons of rhetoric trains students to ask certain questions, teaches them to test what they are receiving, and helps them to receive the inheritance well.

Practicing citizenship, *using the five canons of rhetoric:*	
Invention	Have you defined your terms for clear discussion? Have you compared several possible answers or solutions? What is the historical context of this particular issue or policy? What qualifies as an authority in this situation, and why? What biases and preconceived ideas influence your thinking?
Arrangement	Have you picked a side of the issue? Can you defend it? What happens when you apply this opinion to real-life situations? Do you need to adjust your position or gather additional information?
Elocution	Which arguments best support your position? Which words and phrases most effectively communicate your position? Which words and phrases are likely to cause confusion or frustration?
Memory	Do you need to memorize quotations, laws, or statistics in order to defend your position? How do history and literature inform your thinking?
Delivery	How should you present the decisions you have made? What action should you take based on your decisions? How do your decisions affect your community?

CHAPTER NINE

HISTORY

"It could be said that our country was invented with a fine sentence."
—Scott F. Crider, *The Office of Assertion*

History is powerful. Remember how students made connections between art and government, music and freedom, as they considered the relationship between jazz music and history? As with government and economics, history helps students understand what it means to be human, and it informs their identity as a member of a particular history. Furthermore, it demands that they ask certain questions and make certain judgments. As with its application to any subject, we must consider rhetoric's modes of persuasion in the study of history. When we study history, we are attempting to identify the facts of our past while sorting through the appeals that others have made about the facts of history, using *logos*, *ethos*, and *pathos*.

With *logos*, we want our students to learn to identify the real principle, concept, or truth of the event. History is filled with particulars and circumstances that may not always apply to every other situation, and yet the principles will. In our modern education paradigm, history can often be rejected as able to teach us anything of value if one points to the particulars, identifies them as dissimilar to our own situation, and then ignores the principle.

Moderns do this with the Bible, philosophers, scientists, and artists all of the time: Paul was a misogynist, Moses was a homophobe, or Plato was a pagan. They do this with circumstantial particulars as well. One might be considering, for example, the importance of an agrarian element to a nation's economy and seek to draw arguments from the lessons of the antebellum South in the United States. Upon considering the particulars, though, moderns may reject learning anything from that history because—among the particulars—the southern economy was a slave economy. The United States today is not a slave economy, so the lessons of the antebellum South, they reason, cannot be applied. This kind of thinking effectively eliminates learning anything—with the exception of some interesting trivia—from the study of history.

With *ethos*, we want our students to learn to identify and determine the value of certain authorities—to recognize their ethical reputation. With the study of history, this includes, among other things, recognizing bias. Don't be fooled into looking for a history that is unbiased. Such a thing does not exist! Some Christian philosophers refer to this as the "myth of neutrality." To describe the history of a people, even at the most basic level, requires bias. Why is it, for example, that few if any histories tell you what the price of socks were? Each historian has determined that the cost of socks is not important enough to include, but that does not make their decision correct. Historians always make decisions about what to include.

Don't be fooled into looking for a history that is unbiased.

Not only do historians face selection bias, but they also write history in the midst of political bias. Many historians attempt or claim to be unbiased in their presentation of material, yet conservatives are often appalled at what they see as a progressive bias, and progressives are often appalled at what they see as a conservative bias. We are all biased.

What would serve us better is if the bias were naturally accepted and included. Then, at least, our students would have the opportunity to accept or reject the bias and would be able to approach it with the academic honesty of knowing it is there. In eleventh grade, my sons and the students I tutor use a book called *A Patriot's History of the United States*, by Larry Schweikart. These students have the luxury of studying American history knowing the author's bias; in fact, he announces it in his introduction. The next year, my students give a rhetorical presentation identifying the bias in a world history book and defending its presence. I also love to teach history through R. C. Sproul's book *The Consequences of Ideas*, which presents philosophers throughout history. Many students have been inspired to study the philosophers more thoroughly and directly because they have learned to recognize that R. C. Sproul can't help but have been biased in his presentation. Teaching them to identify and judge the *ethos* of the authority helps them to practice ferreting out bias.

With *pathos*, we want our students to recognize emotional appeals and to use them rightly. *Pathos* is generally communicated through stories, parables, metaphors, and analogies. Students must learn the art of using these tools accurately and identifying when they have been used inaccurately. How often have you heard, or used yourself, an analogy that can be rejected because it fails to take into account some aspect of truth in the argument?

For example, I have often heard students compared to machines. This analogy, while it may offer various elements that can be helpful, conjures up the idea that education is like programming. If we just give the students the right information, they will operate as expected. But this analogy fails to take into account time and nurture. Students are more like plants in a garden that require regular input and habitual practices to help them grow. I've also heard the plant analogy criticized because it does not consider the individuality of the students. In my garden, I treat all of my tomato plants the same way, but I don't treat all students the same. Maybe students are still like the plants in a garden, but one is a tomato plant, another a carrot, another a cucumber, and another an herb. As students study history pathetically—with regards to *pathos*—they reflect on the stories, parables, metaphors, and analogies they are encountering to ensure their emotional appeal is genuine and true. And truth, as we know, begins with invention and the proper understanding of definitions, comparison, circumstances, relationships, and authority.

"History Integrates with Language Studies" by Jen Greenholt

You cannot study language without studying history. Likewise, you cannot study history without studying language. Integration occurs naturally between these two subjects. Whether you study Latin, French, Mandarin, or Māori, you are studying the interaction between events of history and the words used to describe them.

Let me give you a practical example. In college, I took an elective course on the history and culture of the Māori people in New Zealand. A major event in the island nation's history took place in 1840, when British representatives negotiated the Treaty of Waitangi with Māori leaders. Unfortunately, when the treaty was translated, it missed an important subtlety of the Māori language:

> In the Māori text of article 1, Māori gave the British a right of governance, *kawanatanga*, whereas in the English text, Māori ceded 'sovereignty'.
>
> One of the problems that faced the original translators of the English draft of the Treaty was that 'sovereignty' in the British understanding of the word had no direct translation in the context of Māori society. *Rangatira* (chiefs) held the autonomy and authority, '*rangatiratanga*', over their own domains but there was no supreme ruler of the whole country. In the Māori version, the translators used the inadequate term '*kawanatanga*', a transliteration of the word 'governance', which was then in current use.
>
> Māori understanding of this word came from familiar use in the New Testament of the Bible when refering to the likes of Pontious [sic] Pilate, and from their knowledge of the role of the '*Kawana*', or Governor of New South Wales, whose jurisdiction then extended to British subjects in New Zealand.
>
> As a result, in this article, Māori believe they ceded to the Queen a right of governance in return for the promise of protection, while retaining the authority they always had to manage their own affairs. (New Zealand Ministry of Justice, 2014)

> Language, in this instance, changed history and not for the first or last time.
>
> When President Jimmy Carter visited Poland in 1977 to hold a press conference in the midst of Cold War tensions, his translator mistranslated the simple phrase, "I left the United States this morning" as "When I abandoned the United States." That simple phrase, along with other translation errors, made the president the recipient of laughter rather than respect (*The Evening News*, Dec. 30, 1977).
>
> There are many ways you can enrich your history studies with language study. Here are just a few to get you started:
> - Talk about why the early Church banned or discouraged translations of the Bible in the Middle Ages.
> - Discuss the contribution of Bible translators such as Jerome, John Wycliffe, and William Tyndale.
> - Discuss the importance of designated translators in the Age of Exploration.
> - Ask your student to research the Latin mottos used by various states.
> - Consider why some people were offended by a 2014 Super Bowl commercial featuring the national anthem sung in languages other than English.
> - Talk about the influence of Latin phrases, such as *carpe diem* and *e pluribus unum,* in contemporary culture.
> - Research the mottos of prestigious universities and consider why those particular phrases were chosen.
>
> Through these and other activities, invite your student to see the many ways that history and language intersect. Both language and history will be enriched by this rhetorical exercise.

As we've studied history through grammar and dialectic in the early years, we've learned historical facts (people, places, and dates) and we've discussed them with respect to one another and the other subjects we've learned. We want to be able to take the truths we glean and apply them to life in wisdom. As we ask questions about an individual topic, whether war, leadership, democracy, or civil rights, we can find the prescriptive claim of historical events and learn from it. To do this, we must be willing to ask prescriptive questions about history: What *should* Benedict Arnold have done? When *should* the United States have entered World War II? After all, we accept the maxim that those who do not understand history are bound to repeat it. C. S. Lewis might add that we learn not only from the positive examples of history but from the negative examples as well. Thus, we ask our students to begin with the prescriptive question.

EXAMPLE 1: THE 17TH AMENDMENT AND THE FEDERAL RESERVE

In a study of American history, students learn that three interesting and related events occurred in 1913: passage of the Federal Reserve Act, ratification of the 16th Amendment, and ratification of the 17th Amendment. The first created the Federal Reserve. The second allowed the Federal government to directly tax the income of citizens of the United States. The last changed the election process for senators; they were no longer to be appointed by their state governments in accord with their state's laws, but were to be elected popularly within their state.

Let's begin, just as an example, to teach our students to ask prescriptive questions. Their first step is to identify an event they are studying. In our case, they have identified three events from the year 1913. Asking a prescriptive question can be as simple as changing the event into a question using the word "should." Should the United States have ratified the 17th Amendment?

Invention

Now we enter the specifics of invention. Students ask the invention questions (definition, comparison, circumstance, relationship, and authority) about the terms in the issue. Start with definition. What does the 17th Amendment say?

> The Senate of the United States shall be composed of two Senators from each State, elected by the people thereof, for six years; and each Senator shall have one vote. The electors in each State shall have the qualifications requisite for electors of the most numerous branch of the State legislatures.

> When vacancies happen in the representation of any State in the Senate, the executive authority of such State shall issue writs of election to fill such vacancies: *Provided*, That the legislature of any State may empower the executive thereof to make temporary appointments until the people fill the vacancies by election as the legislature may direct.
>
> This amendment shall not be so construed as to affect the election or term of any Senator chosen before it becomes valid as part of the Constitution.

What does the 17th Amendment do? It establishes the popular election of senators. Go on to ask your student to make comparisons. What does the 17th Amendment have in common with the other amendments? How is it different? Next, ask about the circumstances surrounding the main event and the relationships between events. When was the 17th Amendment first proposed? How were senators elected before the 17th Amendment? What events caused the states to believe that the 17th Amendment had become necessary? Finally, what do the different authorities say on the matter? Remembering that authorities don't necessarily have to be humans, students might ask what the Constitution says, what the Bible says, what various proverbs and maxims say, and what scholars and political figures have to say. After working through the invention questions, your student should be able to decide for himself whether the United States should have ratified the 17th Amendment.

Arrangement

Once your student has made a decision about his issue, he needs to arrange the facts in order to make a claim that is coherent and orderly. In a study of history, moreover, his argument should make sense chronologically. It would make little sense to say, for example, that the passage of the 17th Amendment caused the War Between the States, something that happened over fifty years before the amendment was ratified!

In arrangement, particularly if students are writing a formal essay about a historical issue, they are also adding certain elements to their understanding of the issue. For example, an *exordium* helps them to think through quotations, statistics, jokes, or stories that develop their argument. *Divisio* helps them to be clear about what everyone agrees with and where they actually disagree.

Your student might find that he must go back to the National Archives to see which states petitioned for direct election, which ones opposed the motion, and for what reasons. *Narratio* helps students to remember the historical circumstances of the event. Listing proofs (*confirmatio*) teaches your student to judge which arguments are his strongest. *Refutatio* encourages him to engage his opponent's strongest argument—which means he has to know all of the arguments and then determine which is the strongest.

All of these steps help students to develop the argument and its presentation in a logical, orderly, and coherent fashion. Students think through both sides of the argument to ensure they understand it from different perspectives and continue to refine their understanding.

Elocution

In elocution, we normally think about the words used to present an argument or position. Students consider what words, schemes, and tropes will communicate their position most effectively. (See appendix 2.) Point your student back to history to discover how others explained their position on the issue and which appeals those individuals emphasized. For example, in 1897, the Utah State Legislature and Governor crafted a resolution that said, "The Legislature of the several States are often unable to make a choice of Senators without long and continued balloting, resulting in 'deadlock', to the detriment of legislation and injury of the people of the State…" (Resolutions). Which appeal(s) does this quotation contain (*logos*, *ethos*, *pathos*)? Does it contain any rhetorical devices? Ask your student what associations the word "deadlock" might have been intended to produce.

The goal may be to create an essay or speech about their history lesson, but another goal is to develop virtuous people who understand their history-shaped identity.

In all of this, we want students to think more abstractly through elocution and their study and understanding of history. The goal may be to create an essay or speech about their history lesson, but another goal is to develop virtuous people who understand their history-shaped identity.

Memory

As students practice the canon of memory, they will memorize statistics, quotations, and anecdotes to help them understand and explain their argument. One easily overlooked tool is repetition. It is natural for us to provide repetition to young children learning the grammar of a subject, and we ask our children to repeat the alphabet song over and over again until they know it so well they can sing it without thinking. We do it with all kinds of information: John 3:16, "Twinkle, Twinkle, Little Star," the books of the Bible, and others.

Somehow, though, we move away from repetition in the dialectic and rhetoric stages of learning a subject. I tend to think that because a student has read *Hamlet* once, he doesn't need to read it again the following year. I imagine that because a student has been through her Algebra I text once, she doesn't need to do it again. It is an item on a checklist that once checked need not be repeated. We think the same way about history.

Where we don't think this way, however, is with the Bible. Every Christian knows that Scripture is, as St. Gregory the Great described, "like a river again, broad and deep, shallow enough here for the lamb to go wading, but deep enough there for the elephant to swim" (*Moralia in Job*). We expect our pastors and children—even ourselves—to read and reread the Bible, each time learning something new and fresh.

Of course, your student's American history book is not the Bible. Does that mean, though, that we study it differently? What if the way we study the Bible is a model for how we are to study all things? We may learn to read and contemplate all things over and over again by learning to read and study the Bible in that way.

Either way, one pass through a book rarely gives us a rhetorical understanding of what it is communicating. Teaching our students to exercise *memoria* in engaging a book or idea several times only helps them to understand the material more deeply. Studying material more than once helps students to remember statistics, quotations, anecdotes, and analogies they will use for the presentation of their idea.

For these reasons, at the same time as we dig deeply into a subject like the 17th Amendment, I ask my high school students to memorize broadly the order of the Constitution, the Constitutional amendments, and the U.S.

presidents. I ask them to rewrite in their own words famous documents like the Constitution and the Constitutional amendments so that they will imbue the words with meaning and make informed, contextually rich judgments.

Delivery

Your study of the 17th Amendment might culminate in a speech or debate about the topic. For oral delivery, your student should practice body language, eye contact, and voice in presentation. Your student might also conclude his study by writing a persuasive essay defending his answer to the question, "Should the United States have ratified the 17th Amendment?" For written delivery, your student should practice appropriate language, good grammar, varied sentences, and strong paragraphs. Both of these delivery methods are valuable in your study of history; however, we want the ultimate "presentation" to be the students themselves: the way they choose to live based on the lessons they learn from history. Historically literate and articulate students practice the canon of delivery every day. Through a rhetorical study of history, they learn how to act with wisdom and virtue in what often feels like an otherwise unwise and dishonest world.

Historically literate and articulate students practice the canon of delivery every day.

WHY HISTORY MATTERS

A brief overview of a second example might help us to see this model in practice. In August 1945, the United States dropped atomic bombs on two Japanese cities, Hiroshima and Nagasaki, forcing Japan to surrender and ending World War II. Studying this phase of World War II, your student would first convert the event into a prescriptive question: "Should the United States have dropped atomic bombs on Japan?" Then they would ask questions from the common topics of invention. What characterized the United States? What characterized Japan? What is an atomic bomb? What events led up to that day? Building a coherent argument and engaging the opposing view in arrangement would strengthen your student's position and refine the application of his argument. Elocution would provide the words and thoughts to test the appropriateness of his view, and *memoria* would situate his argument in historical perspective. Delivery would be the application of the argument to your student's and the audience's lives.

Think of the implications of these kinds of questions. Regarding this specific question, think of the conclusions our students would draw about justice, just war, retribution, self-defense, offensive war, casualties of war, collateral damage, and more. Does the prevention of possible deaths justify the causation of actual deaths? Their conclusions have implications for personal justice, family justice, community justice, ecclesial (church) justice, civil (state) justice, and international justice. If our students study history rhetorically, we may just end up with leaders who have thought more carefully about these issues than many current leaders.

If our students study history rhetorically, we may just end up with leaders who have thought more carefully about these issues than many current leaders.

The purpose of education in general—and history, in particular—is to raise children who are fully human, embodying the truth they have discovered and their history-shaped identities. Americans have an identity bound up in their history. They are a people who fight for freedom: the War for Independence, the War Between the States, World Wars I and II, the Korean War, the Vietnam War, the Gulf War, the Iraq War, and the War in Afghanistan. All of these wars speak to us about our commitment to freedom and human rights. Documents and speeches, such as the Declaration of Independence, the U.S. Constitution, the Gettysburg Address, and the Emancipation Proclamation, also emphasize freedom.

Christians have an identity of their own bound up in the history of the people of God. The Bible, hymns, prayers, liturgies, the church calendar, church history, the creeds, and the historic faith are all part of the heritage common to Christians.

When students study history, they learn something about who they are and who they should be. History teaches them how to behave and how not to behave precisely because they identify with Americans throughout history, or Christians throughout history, or Romans throughout history—whichever the case or cases may be.

The purpose of history, or any subject for that matter, will never be so mundane as to win a game of trivia or to know how to make change at a cash register. These things, of course, may result from the study of a given subject, but they are not the purpose of that study. In all things, we educate our children so that they may use knowledge and understanding to perceive wisdom, pursue virtue, and proclaim truth.

Remember the conversation with which we began? The students recognized that an appreciation of jazz informed how people lived. It led to rebellion against the communist culture. This rebellion was the embodiment of the principle jazz communicated. Students too can be informed by history, as they find the principle within the particulars that history lessons communicate.

Evaluating history, *using the five canons of rhetoric:*	
Invention	Have you defined your terms for clear discussion? Have you compared historical events and people? Are you dealing with cause and effect or simply correlation? What is the context of this historical event or individual? What do different authorities say on the matter? What biases and preconceived ideas influence your thinking?
Arrangement	Can you form a cohesive argument based on your research? Does your judgment make sense chronologically? Have you considered more than one perspective in forming your opinion?
Elocution	What words will most effectively and persuasively communicate your position? How does history help you to understand and express your identity?
Memory	What statistics, quotations, or anecdotes will help you explain history? Have you re-read your sources sufficiently to understand them well?
Delivery	How can the things you have learned about history teach you to act with wisdom and virtue? How does your study of history prepare you to be a better leader?

CHAPTER TEN

LATIN AND FOREIGN LANGUAGES

> "The foundational ideas of Western civilization are originally Greek and Roman; these ideas arise from texts written in Greek and Latin; translations of these texts offer access to the original meaning, but with diminished access to original associations, beauty, and context; therefore to engage fully with this tradition—which is our tradition—one must return to Greek and Latin…Words in their original language expressed something irreducible which was not as meaningful when translated."
> —Kevin Clark and Ravi Jain, *The Liberal Arts Tradition*

Like advanced science and mathematics, foreign languages can be a stumbling block for parents who are considering centering their students' education at home through high school. If you are like many parents (i.e., infrequent world travelers, not bilingual, not working in diplomacy or translation or as a foreign language teacher), you probably have a dim memory of high school Spanish, French, or German classes—enough to put on a transcript, but not enough to use in conversation. The mere idea of teaching a language to your student might be frightening. We must reassess some of our assumptions about studying foreign languages.

The first myth is that *only an expert can teach a foreign language effectively*. While immersion is an invaluable experience, once your student reaches a certain level of mastery—and I fully support finding outside mentors who can take your student to the next level of reading and speaking a foreign language fluently—the premise that only a fluent speaker can teach the fundamentals of language is false. We teach foreign languages not just for speaking ability (although in our global society that is a fine skill to have) but also for understanding of the structure of language. As a parent, you first taught your child to speak your native language (or languages) by modeling while your child parroted after you; next by prompting and correcting as your child learned to speak and read on his own; and then by encouraging your child to "Use your words!" effectively in conversation. You practiced the arts of the Trivium (grammar, dialectic, and rhetoric) without knowing it. You can do the same with a foreign language if you are willing to embrace a few more paradigm shifts.

> *We teach foreign languages not just for speaking ability ... but also for understanding of the structure of language.*

The next myth is that *language study can be completed in a short time*. We need to commit to consistency, sticking with the same language for multiple years. In modern education, we expect two years of study in a modern language to suffice for college admissions. In that duration, students barely surpass the grammatical elements of memorizing vocabulary and forming basic, perfunctory sentences like "I can read," "My name is Leigh," and "Where is the bank?" Imagine if we stopped teaching reading or speaking in our native language after that sparse taste! We would likely find the subject tedious and fruitless. Only after diligent study will our students be able to move from the grammar of the language (the vocabulary, sentence structure, and parts of speech) to the dialectic and rhetoric stages, when the language comes alive. That means starting early, memorizing vocabulary and word endings in the elementary years, which lays the groundwork for a more intensive study in middle school and high school.

No matter when you start, you will need to give your family time to master the basics. We often refer to elementary-aged children as in the grammar stage, but all we really mean by that is that the art of grammar is the art they are most comfortable with at that age. The same is true of children in the dialectic and rhetoric stages. They are in that stage because they prefer to learn using that art more than the others. What we sometimes fail to see is the impact that has on their willingness to learn something. A student in the rhetoric stage, for example, prefers to learn using the art of rhetoric the most and prefers to learn using the art of grammar the least.

Thus, we often find that children in the rhetoric stage dislike learning foreign languages and will often beg Mom and Dad to let them learn a different language for a variety of reasons. What these students don't realize is that their dislike is more properly attributed to the fact that it requires so much emphasis on the art of grammar. It has to, by the very nature of it being a language. If they switch to the new language, whether it is Spanish, French, German, Italian, Russian, Japanese, or any other language, the primary tool they must use to learn that language is grammar—the very thing they dislike.

Encourage your student to have patience since the best part comes when he enters the rhetoric stage in his study of language. If your student begins a foreign language when he is already in high school, look for ways to give him tastes of what is to come, whether by letting him sit in on a class with students who are more advanced or by attending a public performance of something read aloud in that language. Here, he will taste the fruits of his labors. That nibble will give him a sense of accomplishment and success that will carry him through the pains of grammatical study of any language.

WHY STUDY LATIN? (PART 1)

The third myth is that *learning Latin is not useful*. This myth deserves its own section because it requires a greater shift for those brought up in the modern education system. Classical education teaches that ancient languages, particularly Latin, provide the best soil for cultivating the skill of learning a language. As a parent, you may be wincing, thinking, "Latin? Why Latin? Isn't that a dead language? Won't my child's college of choice reject that?" (This is a common tale and often untrue. Check with the college before accepting someone else's claim on this point.) There are practical reasons to study Latin, including improved vocabulary, higher SAT test scores, and a better grasp of English and English grammar. Those are not the only reasons, however. The student who masters Latin is better at learning other foreign languages not only because it contains the roots of so many other foreign languages (although it does) but also because his mastering Latin will give him the contentment to know that mastering a language can be done, to know how it can be done, and to know that struggling through the grammar stage is worth it.

Furthermore, studying Latin gives us access to the literature, philosophy, and theology of Roman thinkers in their original writings, opening the door to a better understanding of Western civilization. Families read and are familiar with certain books because they have become an accepted part of our cultural heritage. We know who Shakespeare and Bach are for the same reason. There are certain fairy tales, songs, traditions, customs, and even behaviors that we are all familiar with and accustomed to because they make up the Western civilization of which we are a part. We are shocked, even, when we encounter someone who doesn't know these things.

I was talking to a homeschooling father and his son one time about the Jim Carrey movie *The Truman Show*. The father was surprised to find out that his son, who had recently graduated from high school, had never seen the film. The son, suddenly aware of his own ignorance, immediately responded, "That's your fault, Dad! You're the one who is supposed to introduce me to the best books, movies, and music!" While *The Truman Show* may not qualify as a linchpin of Western cultural history, it was seen as such by this homeschooling father. Imagine if he had discovered that his son had never heard of Humpty Dumpty and what happened when he sat on a wall. In fact, this same person expressed dismay after discovering that his children's familiarity with all of the best fairy tales was limited solely to Disney's version of them. At once, he sought out opinions from respected authorities on which translation and version was the best for *Grimm's Fairy Tales*, purchased that copy, and began reading it aloud with his teenage children. How many of us are in a similar situation with our own families?

Because we live as members of Western civilization, we are bound up in a rich cultural heritage that demands our study of it.

Because we live as members of Western civilization, we are bound up in a rich cultural heritage that demands our study of it. This does not mean that we only study people and events of Western civilization. But when I study Western cultural history, I study it as a member participating in it. I come to it with certain assumptions that are acceptable to its study. I come, furthermore, expecting to be formed by it and to engage in forming it.

If we are to be formed by Western civilization, we need to embrace the entire cultural heritage that has been passed down to us and has formed the very culture we now live in. This means embracing the study of Latin. We cannot expect to understand and fully participate in the great, classical conversation of Western civilization without a background in or even mastery of a language so formative of that cultural heritage. One graduate of a classical education summed it up this way, "Learning Latin awakens our minds. It opens the door to a whole new realm of knowledge and opportunities. It helps us know the world around us, understand the struggles we face today, and recognize the beauty in all that surrounds us."

"History, Culture, and the Latin Language" by Matt Bianco

I once spent two years in full-time study of the Chinese language, culture, and history in a school setting. During that time, I learned that the Chinese emperor used to climb a mountain once a year to offer sacrifices to heaven. Halfway up the mountain, the emperor would stop to offer sacrifices on behalf of his own sin, and then at the top of the mountain he would offer sacrifices on behalf of the sins of his people. This practice fascinated me in its similarity to the practice of the high priest in the Old Testament temple. The high priest would offer sacrifices for his own sins, then enter the Holy of Holies to offer sacrifices for the sins of people of Israel.

I later met a man who had lived in China for ten years and I asked him about this practice. He acknowledged the similarities between the two stories but cautioned that it would be wrong to assume the Chinese would have the same conception of sin that Western Christians would have. The emperor may have been doing something very similar to the high priest, but his conception of sin may not have been similar at all. I had studied the Chinese language and culture as an outsider but had neither been formed

> by it nor participated in forming it. This other gentleman, however, had lived among the Chinese, had embraced their culture as his own, had begun to be formed by it, and had begun to participate in forming it. He could see past the cultural assumptions of the outsider in ways I could not.
>
> We can and should study people, events, and cultures outside of our own Western cultural heritage, but when we do, we must recognize our limitations. Whoever we are, wherever we are, we must embrace the cultural tradition God chose for us, and that means learning it, being formed by it, and participating in the continued forming of it. We need to enter the great conversation of our tradition. And for most of us, that means the Western tradition.

Long before Christ, the ancient Hebrews used these same methods to seek knowledge, understanding, and wisdom; the book of Proverbs is full of references to these three goals of education. Likewise, the ancient Greeks were practicing the pedagogical arts of grammar, dialectic, and rhetoric, each of which leads to the corresponding ends: knowledge, understanding, and wisdom. After Christ, the Romans, as well as medieval society, followed in the same educational traditions. It wasn't until the advent of modern education in America that these methods of education were pushed aside.

Your high school-aged child, whether he is just beginning or is continuing in the study of Latin, will use these same arts to study Latin. As he practices the art of grammar, he will need to memorize the vocabulary, grammar rules, and syntax of the Latin language. As he practices the art of dialectic, he will need to work through the questions that will help him to translate large portions of Latin text. As he practices the art of rhetoric, he will need to present, create, and translate Latin to others in conversation.

EXAMPLE: LATIN TRANSLATION

Author David Hicks writes in *Norms & Nobility*, "The teacher's true competence is not in his mastery of a subject, but in his ability to provoke the right questions and get into a new subject quickly and incisively"(129). That is good news for the homeschooling parent, teacher, or tutor because it means you have all the tools you need to teach a foreign language, including Latin, to a student in the rhetoric stage. Let's walk together through the five canons, and I think you will see what I mean.

Invention

Any attempt to engage in the art of rhetoric must begin with the canon of invention. This canon relies heavily on categories of questions. To review, it focuses on the common topics (or categories of questions) that are common to the study of any subject: definition, comparison, circumstance, relationship, and testimony.

Invention and its common topics give you the tools to provoke the right questions. With every question we ask we are doing two things: First, we are asking questions that will provoke a dialogue that will engage students in their own inquiry. Second, we are asking questions that will become models for questions the students will ask in the future.

For the practically minded parent, invention also gives you the tools you need to get into the subject quickly and incisively.

As you are working through a Latin translation, for example, *Veni, vidi, vici*, you will begin with common topics of invention. Ask your student to define what he sees, to compare the words to one another and to other vocabulary and grammar charts, to look at the circumstances of the Latin sentence (endings and its context within a paragraph or chapter), to find relationships (word order, what comes first, and why), and to seek out the testimony of trustworthy authorities (grammar books and dictionaries).

Students new to the study of Latin may use these tools at the level of knowledge they have, even in the rhetoric stage. For example, newer students might seek out derivatives to help them answer questions about a word. If they were looking at the sentence *Christus erat verbum*, they might recognize that *Christus* is much like the words Christ, Christian, and Christianity. Likewise, they might recognize that the word *verbum* is much like verb, a kind of word. Even in making these simple connections, these students are exercising the art of dialectic; they are using the canon of invention and answering the kinds of questions we find in the common topics.

Asking questions from the common topics allows the students to be more conversational in their study of Latin. This helps them in several ways. First, they get a temporary reprieve from the boredom, monotony, and tedium of a solely grammatical approach to the language. What used to be a great joy to them when they were in the grammar stage can become a source of anxiety and frustration. Working through the common topics brings in a conversational element that is more satisfying to your child at this age.

Working through the common topics brings in a conversational element that is more satisfying to your child at this age.

Second, it turns them into discoverers. In a grammatical study of Latin, the students are constantly being told what to know by their parents, tutors, or the textbook. Learn this declension, memorize these vocabulary words, and practice these grammatical constructs. Working through the common topics of invention, however, allows them to ask and answer questions through which they discover new understandings of the Latin language, whether it be the impact a particular ending has for a declension or conjugation, the meaning of a particular vocabulary word, or the way a particular grammatical construct works. Still, for your student to become rhetorical with Latin, simply being able to answer questions about different words and endings in a Latin translation will not be enough. He'll need to do something with those answers.

Arrangement

As your student comes up with a collection of answers to various questions about a Latin translation, he will notice that the English answers put together don't make a whole lot of sense. When my son William was a twelfth grader in our Classical Conversations Challenge IV program, he and his classmates were assigned to translate Book I of Virgil's *The Aeneid*. His tutor provided him with a document that had a passage from the book written out with several blank spaces between each line of Latin text. William would print out the document, then write beneath each word its literal translation. To do that, he would use the common topics to engage with the material, but what appeared in the space immediately beneath that line of text was not a Latin translation.

So William and his classmates would then skip down to the next line and re-order their translations so that they made good sense in English.

They needed to arrange the words, with the appropriate beginning, middle, and end so that they became meaningful and coherent. The exercise looked something like this:

| Tantaene animīs caelestibus īrae? |
| Such great + question marker (-*ne*) | mind/soul | heavenly | wrath |
| Can heavenly minds have so great a wrath? |

In the first row, William was provided the Latin text. In the second row, William translated each Latin word literally beneath it. In the third row, he arranged the English translation so that it made more sense.

Arrangement is an important and necessary canon of rhetoric, as can be seen here. We naturally arrange ideas and things anyway, but without structured intention, the cogency of our arrangement isn't always as sensible as we think it is. Teaching our children to slow down and carefully exercise this canon trains them to think through the order and structure of their translation. Even more important, it trains them to think through the order and structure of all that they do. This is the power, again, of the study of Latin. It trains the learner to think better and more harmoniously about everything. By applying the canon of arrangement to their study of Latin, students improve their orderly thinking in all of their studies.

This step is not the last for our Latin student—there is more that can and should be done. Does William's concluding translation make sense, "Can heavenly minds have so great a wrath?" Certainly, it does. Yet we are moving our students, in the rhetoric stage, to a deeper understanding of and desire for beauty. We need to introduce them to the canon of elocution that they may aspire to beauty in their study of Latin.

Elocution

As our students progress into the next canon, elocution, what we are asking of them is a greater attention to the words they use in communicating. In the translation of Latin, this means choosing words that not only reflect the meaning of what they have translated but also choosing words that communicate that meaning beautifully or poetically. There is a flow to the language that is important in good translation.

In an article I read recently, the author was comparing translations of *The Iliad* by Homer. Although Homer wrote in ancient Greek, the author's observations are fitting to our discussion of elocution. He compared four translations of a section in which Homer was comparing the Trojan army approaching the Greek ships to the waves of the sea as they approach the beach, noting whether the translators conveyed merely the meaning of Homer's words or if they also communicated the effects of his language on the hearer. He argued that some translators made clear the beating of the waves (and the Trojans) by their choice of words. He even demonstrated how one translator made the event feel faster than Homer did with his choice of words. Consider this example I've made up below:

The dark clouds hung heavily overhead, bearing down on the hunched shoulders of the humans below.

The sentence communicates a couple of different things as we read it aloud. The sounds made by the letters *d*, *b*, and *h* have a heavy feeling themselves. The sentence tells us the clouds were heavy with words and shows us the heaviness with sounds. The final consonant sounds made by the *g* in *hung* and in *bearing*, as well as the *–ily* in *heavily* force the mouth to slow down as it vocalizes the sentence. This helps the reader feel the heaviness even more.

As our children study Latin, they will encounter writers who were masters of this use of language and sounds, and they will develop a feel for that particular use of language themselves. This is a skill they will develop as they ask good questions about the text being translated and their own translation.

As we look back at William's original translation of the line from Virgil's *Aeneid*, we want him to ask questions about the original Latin and his own English to see if he is communicating the meaning, the feel, and the beauty of line. William wrote, "Can heavenly minds have so great a wrath?" Another translator of Virgil's text, Robert Fitzgerald, wrote it this way, "Can anger black as this prey on the minds of heaven?" In John Dryden's translation, he writes, "Can heav'nly minds such high resentment show, Or exercise their spite in human woe?" Both of these translators were trying to communicate not just the meaning of Virgil's Latin, but also the emotional weight of it and the poetic feel of it.

Now, it would be difficult to ask William or any student to do the same with just one line of text, but it would be important for us, in exercising the canon of elocution, to ask them to begin to do so with larger passages of translated text. And imagine the beauty of the language our students will master, in the Latin and English, as they even begin to notice these things. It is the asking of these questions that will bring awareness that such beauty is possible. At first, we are interested in teaching them to be aware of it and to begin practicing it. The next canon, memory, is the canon that is most helpful to their catching it.

Memory

In the canon of memory, we traditionally—from the perspective of writing a rhetorical speech—memorize what we have written through the first three canons. It might not seem immediately obvious how the canon of memory works in the study of Latin, but it does. Memory provides practical help with the previous canon, elocution.

When we are practicing elocution, we note that the words communicate a poetic feel through their sounds as much as they do their connotative and denotative meanings. Today, we don't sit in a tavern listening to a bard recount the story of an epic hero but rather read silently. Even when we do listen to audio books, we are often distracted from noting the sounds of the language as we multi-task. To memorize, though, it often helps to vocalize the words. Thus, even if we don't ask our children to memorize their translations, we may still find it helpful to use the vocalizing aspect of memorizing so that they can hear what they have translated and pay more attention to the meaning of those sounds. As our children hear the sounds and their poetic feel, they can go back to the elocution canon and revise their translations.

There are two more benefits to using the canon of memory: First, consider the role that memory plays in teaching our children to catch the skill of writing and translating with words that convey poetic beauty. Latin students need to know what Latin feels like, lest they simply continue to think in an English word order that is not inherent to traditional Latin speaking and writing. To do so, our students need to read Latin aloud, to hear it read aloud by others, and to memorize it. Just as we can feel that a certain way of saying something in English is the right way—even when we cannot explain the grammatical reason—our students will be able to do the same with Latin.

Second, reading aloud and hearing Latin read aloud gets it into our subconscious minds. We can develop that feel for the language and just know whether something is right or wrong, even as we work through a grammatical understanding of the rules. In fact, we will be able to think less about which grammar rule applies because the right way of saying it will be the way that comes to mind the quickest. This is also true with the act of memorizing Latin text.

We tend to ask students to memorize Latin texts from the best of the Latin writers. This means we don't ask them to memorize a Dr. Seuss book translated into Latin but rather the Vulgate, Virgil's *Aeneid*, or passages from Cicero or Caesar. Through memorization, our children learn to feel what the best of Latin sounds like. This feel for good Latin actually helps students with invention and arrangement. It is almost as if they perform elocution while inventing and arranging. The best way of saying something becomes the standard way of saying something. Beautiful prose becomes natural to them.

The best way of saying something becomes the standard way of saying something.

Delivery

What role does delivery play in the study of Latin? In my chapter on science, I discussed how students cultivate their own love for science by experiencing another's love for science. This love is most often communicated to students through the scientist's delivery of his discoveries. Students recognize that love, and that love is further cultivated in them. The same is true of Latin. As we explain the reasons for studying Latin to our students, and demonstrate the beauty of Latin as we encounter and translate it, we cultivate a love for the language in our students. We want them to deliver Latin to others with the same fervor.

A student's delivery of Latin will depend on his audience. He may be delivering the reasons to study Latin, as one of my former students did (mentioned above). He may be delivering a lesson on some grammatical concept or Latin translation. A third way a child delivers Latin might be through the recitation or presentation of a Latin text. In each of these ways, your child will need to be aware of his demeanor, appearance, vocabulary, enunciation, speed, hand gestures, eye contact, and more. The presentation of Latin, whether it is the reasons for studying it, a lesson in Latin, or a recitation of Latin, can be a moving experience for all involved.

WHY STUDY LATIN? (PART 2)

At this point, I hope we have moved beyond the purely practical reasons for Latin. I've expressed above how important it is for our students to see the beauty in their studies, and it seems misguided and inconsistent for me to encourage such thinking only to rely on the practical. There are practical reasons, but they are not the end goal of studying Latin.

There is more to life than the physical. Students study subjects like physics and metaphysics because the world is both physical and metaphysical. When we study metaphysics, we are in search of that which is not purely physical. Scientific laws, like gravity, govern the physical world, and we rightly pursue their study. There are, however, categories of metaphysical principles that govern the metaphysical world. These are truth, goodness, and beauty.

There is more to life than the physical.

As our children study this world, they must also study the metaphysical world. That means encountering the true, the good, and the beautiful, but it also means wrestling with them as principles that govern the metaphysical world. What is truth, and how do I understand it? How do I know whether something is beautiful or good?

We study Latin because it embodies truth, goodness, and beauty, not only in the language itself, but also in the literature, poetry, philosophy, and theology written in Latin. Consider the lengths we went to in our discussion of elocution in studying Latin. Do you see the inherent difficulties in translating, difficulties your student will not have to overcome if he can read these texts in the original?

Look at how difficult it was, for example, to communicate the poetic feeling, the emotion, the sounds, and the speed of the language. To translate the text into English with those characteristics requires adding words that are not in the Latin. Yet, to limit the translation to a literal one is to lose those

Your child will encounter truth, goodness, and beauty simply because he was given the opportunity and time to study Latin.

qualities. In either case, the translation suffers. Not so, if the student can read the text in the original language. Your child will encounter truth, goodness, and beauty simply because he was given the opportunity and time to study Latin.

It is not only the texts written in Latin that embody these three metaphysical concepts but also the language itself. Consider two brief examples, brought to my attention by the *Visual Latin* videos. Whenever I go on a business trip or a family vacation, I often hear people ask one another, "How much stuff did you bring?" I like the word "stuff" as it is used to describe our possessions because it has such a friendly connotation. Stuff is what is found inside of teddy bears, pillows, and cushions. It is soft and inviting. Most of us are familiar with the saying, "He who dies with the most toys wins!" Our toys are our stuff.

If I were to go on a business trip or vacation with Latin speaking people, however, I would find that they would ask the question quite differently. Rather than ask me about my stuff, they would ask me about my *impedimentum*. (This Latin word is also spelled *inpedimentum*, but has the same meaning: "baggage," "hindrance," or "obstruction.") The Latin word *impedimentum* is the word from which we derive the English "impediment." An "impediment" is something that slows us down and keeps us from completing our task. Paul writes in his first letter to the Corinthians, "And this I speak for your own profit; not that I may cast a snare upon you, but for that which is comely, and that ye may attend upon the Lord without distraction" (1 Cor. 7:35). The Latin Vulgate uses the same word, *impedimento*, for "distraction": literally, "stuff that keeps us from attending upon the Lord."

Studying Latin helps us to think of our stuff differently than how our own language describes it. As we consider our stuff, we may find a truth, goodness, or beauty that arises out of the two different languages that we might not have encountered before. A second example will help us see this point. When I meet someone, I often ask, "What do you do for a living?" If I were to ask someone the same question in Latin, I would not ask what he does for a living but what his *vocatio* is. In English, the question carries the connotation of individualism. What do you—the individual—do to survive in this world? The answer is always what the person's job is. The Latin phrasing of the question is so much better than the English phrasing. To ask about someone's *vocatio* is to ask about his or her calling. There isn't a hint of individualism in the question, and there isn't a hint of utility in the question. The question asks what God has called me to be. It asks me to see something true, good, and beautiful in what I do for a living, rather than just how I meet the demands of a modern society.

When we study Latin, we know what we're studying and we know how we're studying it. Now, we know why we're studying it. I hope that you are inspired to more than improved vocabulary, grammar, and SAT scores. I hope that you are inspired to pursue the true, the good, and the beautiful.

Translating Latin, *using the five canons of rhetoric:*	
Invention	What do you see when you look at this sentence? What do you learn by comparing these unfamiliar words to familiar vocabulary and grammar? Does context help you to understand this word / sentence / paragraph? What does word order indicate in this sentence? What resources (e.g., grammar books and dictionaries) can help you understand this material?
Arrangement	Can you translate the sentence one word at a time? How should you reorder your word-for-word translation so that it makes sense in English?
Elocution	How have others translated this passage? Does the translation you have chosen reflect the meaning of the original? Does your translation communicate that meaning beautifully?
Memory	Have you read your translation aloud to test its quality? Have you listened to others read it aloud? What else have you read that will help you understand this passage?
Delivery	What is the best way to recite or present this Latin text? What lessons can you share with others from your study of Latin?

CHAPTER ELEVEN

FINE ARTS

"'Beauty is truth, truth beauty,' —that is all
Ye know on earth, and all ye need to know."

—"Ode on a Grecian Urn" by John Keats

"Tell me why I should like this painting," a student challenged me, pointing to a picture in an art book.

"May I tell you what is wrong with what you just said, first?" I replied.

"Just tell me why I should like it. It sold for $86,882,500 in 2012. I can't imagine why anyone would pay that much for two blue blocks on a red block. I could have done that!"

"It is not wallpaper."

"What do you mean?"

"I mean that the artist created this *art*ifact in order to communicate something to you. If he wanted to be in the business of creating something that you would like to hang on your wall, he would have made wallpaper.

Your response to art shouldn't be limited to whether you like it or not. There is so much more! This artist is trying to engage you and make you think. Some artists may even want you to think about things you don't like or things that aren't pretty."

This student was looking at a modern painting, "Blue, Orange, Red" by Rothko (1961). Like many people, he was unaware that art is a language. In fact, I think we might be born knowing this language, but we are taught, inadvertently, to forget it. Art education is a rediscovery of the language of shape, color, light, composition, unity, and harmony. If we are listening to music we are communicating through the language of notes, rhythm, pitch, time, chords, and audible harmony.

Art education is a rediscovery of the language of shape, color, light, composition, unity, and harmony.

In his famous poem, "Ode on a Grecian Urn," John Keats refers to this language of art. He speaks to the urn, saying "Thou silent form dost tease us out of thought, As doth eternity…" He is saying that the urn "speaks" to him through its silent language, and it is able to do so "eternally," outside of time; it doesn't die. Artifacts outlive the artist. In the same poem, Keats also makes the profound statement, "Beauty is truth, truth beauty." This statement helps us redefine "beauty" from meaning, "I like it, but I don't know (or care) why." We should say, "This artifact speaks to me about a truth or about *The Truth*; therefore, it is beautiful." Through discussion with others we come to see truth and beauty in things we might not have initially understood.

If we learn some vocabulary to help us name what we see and hear, we will begin to understand how elements of art work together. With some practice, we will learn to comprehend what the artist is saying or at least enjoy discussing what the artist might have been trying to communicate. The rhetoric of art, therefore, is engaging in conversation using the language of art either as a creator of artifacts or as a beholder of artifacts.

Some students are destined to be creators of fine arts, and they need to spend time practicing their skills and learning from masters. If one of your children has an interest in art or music or any craft, I hope you will encourage him or her to pursue that interest through instructional and theoretical books, classes, private lessons, and spending time with others who love the arts. As a society, though, we tend to ignore the art education of the other 99% of students. The result is an artistically illiterate society. We all look at things, but how much do we see?

As educators, we need to give our students experiences in both creating and beholding (apprehending with more than our senses) art so that they can delight in the communication that is possible. If we are intentional, our students can also enhance their rhetorical skills through art experiences as well. You do not need to be an expert in art to initiate and participate in art experiences with your student. Rather, you must be willing to experiment and discuss.

EXAMPLE 1: *THE PHANTOM TOLLBOOTH*

In order to communicate an idea through art, you must start with an idea that you want to communicate. A great way to get a student inspired is to begin with something they are familiar with, like a novel they enjoy, and ask them to communicate an idea (or several) through some kind of visual art. Their art becomes a response to or reflection of the writer's ideas. We are all comfortable reading and discussing books, so I have my students read a book and we discuss its metaphors and similes. A metaphor is a thing that represents an idea, and a simile works the same way. We can then draw a picture of that thing (or find a picture of it or paint it) to represent that idea, which moves us into the world of art. If you have several students read the same novel, they will easily understand the metaphors their peers are using and they can have meaningful conversations about their art.

Invention

For example, when my students are about thirteen years old, we read *The Phantom Tollbooth* by Norton Jester. This book is similar to *Alice in Wonderland* in its use of colorful spins on language and lots of delightful metaphors, many of which refer to art and music. The language and ideas in this selection awaken imaginations and prepare students for a creative experience. We make a list of all the metaphors and similes and images that come to mind when reading the book. For example, a watchdog named Tock helps us learn to make the most of time. We can imagine together what Tock might look like. What kind of dog makes a good watchdog? How big do you think he is? What colors? What is his nature? Have your student create a detailed image in his mind of how he would like Tock to be. Two Princesses named Rhyme and Reason represent wisdom and common sense. Imagine what these two princesses would look like in detail. What color is their hair? What would they wear? How do their voices sound? Would they be warm and friendly to you? When the princesses are separated and imprisoned, nonsense reigns. Numbers battle letters. What would that battle look like? Would the numbers line up on the field like British Redcoats? Would letters arrange themselves and form the battle differently? Would they wear uniforms? What would the battle sound like? "The Doldrums" is an actual place. What would it look like? Would it be a colorless, foggy swamp? What would you see, smell, or hear there? Try to engage all five senses when discussing the imagery and setting in order to spur imagination.

Your student now has a wealth of ideas for images that already have an idea associated with them. Your discussion follows the dialectic format we are familiar with. You might ask, "How do you define rhyme and reason? How are they alike? How are they different? What circumstances affected these princesses?" The only difference when dealing with art as compared to dealing with writing a paper is that you will ask questions that help him give form to the ideas. You might ask, "What do you think the princesses looked like?" or "Do you think they looked alike or different?" or "What do you think their prison looked like?" and "What do you think the landscape might have looked like?" Most students love to use their imagination, but feel free to share what you imagine as a way to inspire creativity. Remember this is practice, not a quiz. It is okay to give your student ideas until he can do it independently. In this phase, your student decides which symbols (princess, watchdog, numbers and letters, etc.) he will include in the artwork; he can find images in magazines or through Internet searches and choose colors appropriate to the idea.

Arrangement

Composition is the arrangement of elements in artwork. The first step in arrangement is to decide which element is the most important, then order the other elements from that one down to the least important. There are many techniques students can use to make one element the most prominent item in a composition. The artist may use size, color, or position to give the most important item the most prominence. This is called "establishing a visual hierarchy." Artists keep this in mind as they compose. Students should do "thumbnail" sketches (small, quick pencil sketches) to try out different arrangements. I may do ten to fifteen small sketches of possible arrangements in order to decide what arrangement works best. Some students enjoy trial and error, and some prefer more structure. An easy structure to work with is the "rule of thirds." To do this, have your student divide the canvas into nine equal boxes by drawing two vertical lines and two horizontal lines equally spaced. The intersections of the lines are excellent points on which to place the most prominent items. Centering the largest item may be the first option he tries, but it is not the only option. Students often sketch a centered composition first, but encourage your student to try the rule of thirds since it will hold the viewer's attention longer.

Elocution

The medium and technique the artist chooses are his elocution. Your student needs to decide which medium will be best to represent the symbols he has chosen to work with and which medium he can work with comfortably. Collage on canvas is a good choice for this project. This allows your student to use some existing images and also to add color using paint or colored papers. It offers lots of flexibility in arrangement. If he is comfortable with drawing in pencil or charcoal or painting with acrylics or watercolors, those are good choices, too. The technique the artist chooses carries its own message. For example, in *The Phantom Tollbooth*, there is a land of Chaos. I had one student use the technique of splatter paint to convey chaos, which was very appropriate. Another student decided that the style of Monet conveyed peacefulness. These are thoughtful choices. Try to get your student to be purposeful and thoughtful in the decisions he makes while creating his artifact.

The medium and technique the artist chooses are his elocution.

In elocution, the artist has the ability to appeal to the beholder's emotions and use the rhetorical technique of *pathos*. Color choice can affect the mood of a painting. For example, dark browns with black and dark red create a somber, sad mood, whereas bright green and yellow or powder blue may create a happy mood. The common experiences in nature with color, the fall leaves of gold, brown, and red or the light yellow-green of spring leaves, facilitate those associations in artwork. Artists, of course, can go against common associations, but they keep them in mind. Another element that helps create the mood of the painting is line. If an artist uses very smooth, wavy lines, he may create a peaceful mood, whereas sharp angles in a variety of sizes create an angry or chaotic mood. Keeping these in mind helps the artist inspire an emotion in the viewer that is a persuasive technique.

Memory

In creating their artwork, students benefit from any knowledge they may have learned about art history, art techniques, or artwork they have seen in books and museums. The more they have seen, the broader bank of knowledge they'll have from which to draw. If they do not have a basic art vocabulary or appreciate great artists, it is not too late to learn some words and look at art history books. An excellent source is *The Annotated Mona Lisa* by Carol Strickland. While your student is planning his artwork, you may want to look at some paintings together and discuss them. My artistic friend Courtney had a mother who loved art and always kept art books out on the coffee table so she could often flip through the pages. Courtney says those images have stayed in her mind all her life and that she can draw on them for inspiration when she is ready to create something of her own. She does not need to know the artist's name or significance of the work to benefit from having the images in her head. She remembers vividly a girl in a field of red flowers and loves that she can still see the brush strokes in the flowers. Building a bank of artwork for *memoria* is as simple as putting an art book on the coffee table. For *memoria*, I recommend visiting the bargain section of a bookstore, purchasing large collections of artwork, and letting students flip through them without instruction or discussion. This helps them see art as a conversation—not just between the artists and the viewer, but between artists themselves.

Delivery

Since the focus of this particular project is the concept, not the product, your student needs to complete the experience by presenting it. (A written alternative might be an artist's statement about his influences and why he made the choices he did.) He should prepare a short speech in which he explains his choices of arrangement and elocution and how memory influenced his decisions. He should then ask for questions and comments from his audience and be prepared to discuss the artwork and let the artwork launch further discussion of ideas. What often happens is that the artwork will make the audience think about the ideas in a new and more profound way. Let the artwork be a launch pad and allow the conversations to go wherever the imaginations lead.

EXAMPLE 2: BEHOLDING A MASTERPIECE

Once students have had an experience like the one with *The Phantom Tollbooth* they will believe in art's ability to communicate. You can then move on to art appreciation, or studying artwork of the masters. Following the canons of rhetoric will help your student "hear" the artwork speak as Keats heard from the Grecian urn. For additional rhetorical art experience, choose an artifact from one of the masters and plan a group discussion of the piece, then ask your student to research the painting and deliver a speech about it. Discuss the following ideas as you lead your student through an art project.

Invention

When you first behold a painting, sculpture, or any artifact, ask the questions we've associated with invention. Consider Leonardo da Vinci's painting *The Last Supper*, for example. Ask your student to **define** the topic and theme of the painting. What do you see? You see men sitting at a table doing something all humans do: eating and talking to each other. We further define what we see by saying that we know specifically who these men are. The central figure is Christ. The other men are His disciples. If you **compare** the men to each other, you could probably identify each disciple by their expression and gestures. Under what **circumstance** is this moment happening? This is in an upper room of a home in Jerusalem. Jesus had planned this gathering and invited his twelve disciples. What is the **relationship** to other events? This is the moment right after Jesus has announced that someone in this room will betray him. It is also the evening before Christ's crucifixion. Also encourage your student to find out how this painting fits into the history of art. *The*

Last Supper (c. 1495) is a Renaissance painting. Characteristics of Renaissance paintings are depth, use of light and shadow, and the use of a pyramid shape in composition. Help your student see all three of these elements in *The Last Supper*. Renaissance painters strived for perfection and harmony, and *The Last Supper* certainly fits that description. Consider what **authorities** say about the painting through reference books or Internet searches or seek out a docent at the art museum and find out what they know about it. *The Last Supper* has been considered the most revered religious painting in all of history. Can you find out why experts say this? Do you agree?

Arrangement

How did the artist arrange the elements in his composition? In *The Last Supper*, the table is perfectly centered horizontally, and Christ is positioned in the exact center of the canvas. The lines of the walls and the ceiling all point to Christ. The disciples are arranged equally on either side. Everything is balanced and stable. It is hard to imagine another way to arrange this scene, but if you look at another painting of the same scene, you can see what impact arrangement has on a composition. Look at an image of *The Last Supper* by Tintoretto (painted in 1594) and compare the arrangement of each. In Tintoretto's version the line of the table plunges diagonally across the canvas, there is a cat in the foreground, and heavenly beings are swirling above. There is disorder instead of order. Leonardo's scene is perfect, harmonious, and balanced, and the other is chaotic. What does this say about the artists? What do you think the artists might have been saying to you?

Elocution

If you look closely at Leonardo's painting, you will not be able to distinguish any brush strokes or imperfections. Every man was perfectly proportioned. Every detail executed perfectly. Perfection was the goal of the Renaissance man. Use this time to discuss *pathos*, the awakening of emotion. What emotions do you think the artist was trying to awaken in the viewer? Look closely at the faces and gestures of the men. Their emotions are clear: some are angry and seem to be shouting, some seem heartbroken, and some seem confused. Christ seems thoughtful and sad. He is looking down and his face is turned slightly aside, but his posture is perfectly straight; he is in control. The postures of the other men are curved over, hands flailing, bodies in motion, but Christ is still. The viewer, if he looks long enough, can feel what the men feel. Art in this manner works like a mirror. The viewer can look at it and imagine himself in the painting. Another effective element in this painting is light. The dark corners of the room and darkness under the table are mysterious and may make the viewer feel sad or scared because there is darkness. Yet, if you look behind Christ, through the back windows, there is light. It is distant, but it is light, and there is a beautiful landscape. This may evoke hopefulness in the viewer.

Memory

Take a moment to draw on your own memories as you look at the painting. Do you remember any other accomplishments of Leonardo da Vinci? You probably remember *Mona Lisa* and designs of flying machines. Do you know any other artists who were Renaissance men? Michelangelo was also one of the great Renaissance artists. What do they have in common? You might remember that Michelangelo was sometimes called "Michelangelo, the Divine." Both loved harmony and perfection and sought it in their art and in their lives. Do you remember anything else about the biblical account of the last supper? You may remember hearing the story and taking communion at church. You may remember the taste of the drink and the bread. Let that association come to your mind as you view the painting. Do you remember the yeasty smell of bread and how it feels and tastes in your mouth? Have you been seated at a similar table with lots of discussions going on at the same time? Remember the sound. In our culture, we only sit in this seating arrangement at very formal dinners such as the head table at a wedding feast. This arrangement is reserved for very important moments. This dinner may have been the most important dinner in all of history, so the formal seating arrangement that Leonardo has chosen is communicating the importance of the event rather than historical accuracy.

Delivery

After your student has engaged in this great conversation with the painting, be sure he has the opportunity to present his findings to his peers. Ask your student to deliver a speech describing his discoveries. This is an important part of the

After your student has engaged in this great conversation with the painting, be sure he has the opportunity to present his findings to his peers.

process—please don't skip it! Ideas come to fruition when students must put them into words. If we stop before this point, the emotions and thoughts will just be floating around in the mind without structure or purpose. Asking for a paper or written speech requires students to order their thoughts. Be sure that your student follows the topics of invention and is aware of the canons of rhetoric as he organizes his thoughts so that they are solidified in his thinking. This will help him appreciate the art more deeply and help him remember. It is then stored in his mind so that he can draw upon the memory later.

We follow the canons of rhetoric with other arts, like music. Many parents require their children to learn an instrument—piano and violin are the top choices. Benefits to playing music are great: increased ability to remember new information, enhanced hand-eye coordination, improved ability to do math calculations, sharpened concentration, and perhaps even an increased capacity for joy. The relationship between joy and music is uniquely human and is completely cross-cultural. Confucius (551–479 BC) is reported to have said, "Music produces a kind of pleasure which human nature cannot do without."

EXAMPLE 3: MUSICAL PERFORMANCE

Students must work hard in the grammar and dialectic stages of learning an instrument: they must learn the names of the notes and the sounds they make, the proper handling of instruments, time signatures, and techniques. But the joy of music can be experienced as soon as a simple tune is played on a tin whistle. That joy will motivate the hard work required. That joy is the language and the rhetoric of music. A highly skilled rhetorician in music can move his audience with the passion he pours into the music. Music evokes the emotions of the listener without the study of keys and notes and time signatures. It is universal. It speaks directly to the soul. Let's first walk through the canons of rhetoric for the composer or performer of music, then we will consider the five canons for a listener of music.

Joy is the language and the rhetoric of music.

Invention

The composer asks, "What piece of music shall I play or what music will I write?" The composer may have a message in mind and so chooses the instruments that would communicate that best. An orchestra piece might be the fullest sound and have the ability to inspire a large crowd, whereas a trio may be the choice for an intimate, small group. A march may be needed to inspire a nation to patriotic duty, whereas a jazz quartet may be chosen to set the mood for a different occasion. The artist may be commissioned with a specific message, or he may be free to invent music that comes from his own passion. Definition, comparison, circumstance, relationship, and authority may all be considered in this phase.

Arrangement

The job of the music writer is to arrange notes in time. There are infinite combinations of notes and infinite combinations of divisions of time. How they are combined and timed is an art of arrangement. You may be familiar with the different forms of poetry: the sonnet, haiku, or ode. Within the genre of classical music, some forms are sonata, concerto, suites, serenades, fantasias, rhapsodies, opera, and ballet. These forms give the composer some structure to follow and also allow for creativity within form, which will make the creative process easier for the conductor. The composer also chooses which instruments will play which parts within a form. Some instruments will carry the melody, and different instruments will provide harmonies. Will the same instrument continue in the same part all the time, or will it change?

Elocution

A composer writes on sheet music with a language that indicates how the music should be played. Your student will need to learn the symbols that indicate dynamics and musical expression, which include *crescendo* (growing louder), *decrescendo* (gradually softer), *tempo* (speed), *forte* (loud), *fortissimo* (very loud), *piano* (quiet), *pianissimo* (very quiet), *presto* (very fast), *glissando* (gliding), *largo* (broadly), *lento* (slowly), *maestoso* (majestically), *or vivace* (vivacious). To write music well, your student will also need to study the language and mathematics of music so that he can translate his musical ideas into a form that others can play and enjoy as well.

Memory

The best music is performed from memory, either memorized precisely as written by a composer, or music that swells up from a general musical *memoria* (knowledge of chords, musical phrasing, rhythms, etc.) as an impromptu performance. The key to playing from memory, like the key to memorizing a speech, is practice: practice with intensity and focus, practice with repetition, and practice over a sufficiently long duration. Composers also help future musicians by employing repetition in their writing, including variations on the same theme throughout the piece (a "refrain").

Delivery

The delivery is the communication from composer to musician and from musician to listener. The composer may indicate *decrescendo* (grow quieter) over several measures of music, but the musician must interpret how much quieter, or how loud he is to begin with. The actual performance of the piece comes from the heart of the musician in combination with other musicians and sometimes a conductor. The musician fully focuses on the music and the moment and allows his whole body and soul to express the music. The performance is the direct conduit of communication from composer to listener.

The performance is the direct conduit of communication from composer to listener.

The playing of music should be a part of every child's education. If finances are tight, get creative. Consider buying used instruments or inexpensive instruments like a tin whistle. I have a student with an extraordinary violin on loan from a retired professional. Maybe there is an older student who could give your child beginning lessons. Internet searches can help you find videos that demonstrate techniques. If space is a problem, consider the violin instead of the piano.

In addition to playing music, students should listen to and learn about classical music. Following the same canons of rhetoric, you can study a piece of music with your student. If you have a music background, you may have already listened to and discussed music together. If you are learning along with your student, I recommend the book *Classical Music for Dummies*. Listen to a selection while studying the music outlines in chapter 5. Then discuss the accuracy of the outline or ask questions such as, "What did you hear? Did you notice how the elements are arranged?" Talk about the elocution, or the style of music and instrument choices. Talk about the delivery. Did the musicians and conductor deliver the piece with passion? Use the listening guide to learn music vocabulary and enrich your understanding of the message the artist is conveying through the language of music. Learn more about the period of the piece and the composer through research and compare the piece to other compositions. Attend concerts whenever possible and seek out musicians to talk to. Before long, you and your student will be appreciating the language of music and the truth conveyed therein.

EXAMPLE 4: HANDEL'S *WATER MUSIC*

Let's walk together through the five canons of rhetoric listening to Handel's *Water Music*. If you are near your computer, you can listen along or you can use this as a guide to how you would listen to and study a piece of classical music. First, listen to the piece just to get an overview. I would choose "Suite Number 2." (*Water Music* is divided into three suites; I'll just refer to the second suite here.)

Invention

Why was this piece of music invented? Handel was asked by King George I to write some music for a spectacular pageant. King George did not normally like big pageants, but this one time he wanted to throw a grand boat party on the River Thames. He asked Handel to write something impressive for musicians to play on a barge as they floated down the river. People gathered on the banks of the river to hear the music as it floated across the water and to catch a glimpse of the royals as they floated by on a separate barge. Handel wanted to make a big impression, so he wrote the piece for fifty musicians, with majestic melodies and triumphant loud moments. He used horns with strings and woodwinds, which was revolutionary for his time. It was like nothing that had been heard before. The king loved it, as did the public.

Arrangement

Handel arranged the sections of music in a new form that was so popular it was copied thousands and thousands of times over during his time and is still followed today. It has come to be known as the sonata. It begins with a melody that is played with horns and woodwinds together in different variations and then repeated. What follows is a different slower and softer section, and then the original melody is repeated in variations. The structure of the sonata is simply indicated as "A-A-B-A".

Elocution

Handel would have indicated in his written music instructions for how he would have liked the music to be interpreted. He would have indicated loud, staccato, lively playing in the A sections. The B section would have had indications to play smoothly and quietly, creating a noticeable contrast to the A section. Students can study Handel's elocution by learning how to read sheet music and, as they study it, talking about the kind of choices the composer made: Why did he choose *staccato*? How would the music have been different if he had written it to be played *legato* throughout? To articulate their responses to music, students will need to acquire a musical vocabulary and practice using the terms correctly, just as learning to name and correctly identify metaphors and similes makes a student a better writer.

Memory

If you see this piece performed by a symphony today, you will see the musicians reading sheet music as they play, but much of their music will have been memorized. Memorization of music is a bit different than the memorization of a speech. Their body and fingers learn the patterns of the music as muscle memory for many sections, and the whole body is involved. The conductor will often have the entire piece, every part, memorized and conduct completely from memory.

Delivery

The delivery of this piece of music is best appreciated in a live concert, but watching a video also gives you a sense of the live experience. You can appreciate the musician's total body involvement when you watch him. You also experience the emotion (*pathos*) of the music more when you see the expressiveness of the musicians as they play. If you watch Handel's *Water Music* performed, the conductor will probably use large hand motions and movements to help the orchestra give a grand performance. The musicians will sway with their instruments in the smooth sections and they will lean forward and move with the lively sections. The musicians feel the music as they play it, and you will hear and feel the music differently when you are there with them.

> **"There Is Intelligence There" by Kate Deddens**
>
> Recently, our youth choir did a workshop with an internationally acclaimed choral conductor. The conductor spent several hours working with the youth chorale to demonstrate his conducting principles and techniques to music teachers and directors. Many of these were classical methods, including modeling, repetition, and allowing the young singers to develop an innate musical sense and feel a deep ownership of their singing. In fact, he quoted a maxim by the ancient biographer Plutarch, which is much quoted by classical educators: "The mind is not a vessel to be filled but a fire to be kindled." He applied it to music, drawing out the parallel truth that children cannot be filled with musicality from an outside source: humanity has within itself the gift of music, and this sense of music must be ignited from within.
>
> The choir practiced a round by Telemann, a German composer from the Baroque period, called "I Want to Praise the Lord All of My Life." The piece had a great deal of inherent structure and form, which the children were independently capable of perceiving accurately. All the children had to do was be given the opportunity to recognize it and implement it on their own. The acclaimed conductor—as opposed to another who might not have understood that the children could hear it and do it on their own beautifully and who might have tried to exert too much control over the performance—allowed the children the time and the freedom to explore this without dictating to them.
>
> Instead of trying to force them to see the ordered musicality of the piece in a certain way, and to sing it by following his specific instructions, he simply asked them to listen carefully to the piece and to one another as they sang; he asked them to pay careful attention to when they thought other sections should be more prominently heard and when they should be quiet, as well as when their own sections should be dominant and

> other sections quiet. Then he set the piece in motion and quietly walked off the stage. Without any director or active conducting, all the sections of the choir produced a gorgeous performance. You could feel the wonder and the appreciation from the audience in the deep silence that followed the performance and preceded a burst of enthusiastic applause. He then stepped back to the center of the stage. He said, "See. There is intelligence there."

Studying art rhetorically allows us to learn the language of art, both to read it and to speak it. In classical education, art is not an add-on. Contemporary Christian artist Makoto Fujimura said it well:

> The assumption behind utilitarian pragmatism is that human endeavors are only deemed worthwhile if they are useful to the whole, whether that be a company, family or community. In such a world, those who are disabled, those who are oppressed, or those who are without voice are seen as "useless" and disposable. We have a disposable culture that has made usefulness the sole measure of value. This metric declares that the arts are useless. No—the reverse is true. The arts are completely indispensable precisely because they are useless in the utilitarian sense. (Lecture, "Art, Love and Beauty: Introduction")

In the fine arts, we see how someone who learns eagerly, practices diligently, and performs joyfully brings joy to all observers. Simply put, the fine arts prepare entire families to resound in celebration.

Studying fine arts, *using the five canons of rhetoric:*	
Invention	What idea do you want to communicate through art? What images, metaphors, and symbols convey this idea? What do you notice in other artists' works? What do you hear in other musicians' works? What piece of music shall you play or what music shall you write?
Arrangement	What tools will highlight the most important element in your art? How have other artists arranged the elements in their compositions? What form of music will best represent your concept? How are the elements arranged in other pieces of music?
Elocution	Which artistic medium and techniques will best represent your symbols? How should you use line and color to evoke emotion? What musical techniques help you express your idea? How do other artists and musicians convey emotion through their work?
Memory	What artworks stand out in your memory? Why? What musical compositions stand out in your memory? What other information can you remember that will help you interpret the artwork or composition? Have you practiced your craft with intensity, repetition, and duration?
Delivery	What is the appropriate way to present your artwork? What is the best way to express your discoveries about an artwork? Did you deliver your musical performance using your whole body? Did the musicians deliver their piece expressively?

CHAPTER TWELVE

A GRADUATION CONVERSATION

> "At its best, schooling can be about how to make a life, which is quite different from how to make a living."
> —Neil Postman, *The End of Education: Redefining the Value of School*

What is the end goal of education? Is it a diploma? Is it college admissions? Is it employment? As our boys grew older, I was forced to ask myself these questions again and again. I now see that I want two things for them: First, I want them to be lifelong learners, eager to try new things and equipped with the skills to do so. Second, I want them to be capable of governing themselves and others well, to live a life of virtue. A democratic republic depends upon an educated populace. All of us are expected to lead either by serving in office or by voting. The more I considered the questions about education, the more my short-term questions of college admissions faded into the background, and the more these larger questions came into the forefront.

However, I understand that two main questions remain for parents who consider homeschooling through high school. Parents want to know if students who are homeschooled through high school have gained admission into colleges and if they have found employment. In this chapter, we will look at these two practical questions: "Can my children get into college?" and "Will they be able to find jobs?" We will consider the questions in terms of homeschooling through high school. Then, I will close the chapter with the larger and much more important question that many of us forget: "How can my children live a life of virtue?" We will consider how a classical education leads students and parents to contemplate important questions of justice, courage, loyalty, truth, goodness, and beauty.

HOW DO HOMESCHOOLED STUDENTS PERFORM?

We cannot accurately measure our students by standardized tests or by numbers. Tests are a poor way to measure the creative thoughts of unique individuals who all have different gifts. These tests cannot measure the character qualities of our children. However, statistics often provide us with a place to start. Dr. Brian Ray, researcher with the National Home Education Research Center, reported these findings in a 2003 article:

- Over 74% of homeschooled students take college-level courses compared to 46% of the general U.S. population.
- 71% of homeschooled students participate in an ongoing community service activity, such as coaching a sports team or volunteering with a neighborhood association, compared to 50% of the general U.S. population.
- Only 4.2% considered politics and government too complicated compared to 35% of adults in the general population.

As you can see, homeschooled students excel both in the short-term goal of college admissions and the more long-term goals of participating in government and community.

Since this book is about giving your children a classical education as well as homeschooling through high school, let's take a look at some measures of classically educated students. A study conducted by the Association of Classical Christian Schools in 2012 reported the following findings:

- The average ACT score for their students was 26.1 compared to a score of 21.1 for all students nationwide.
- The average SAT reading score was 621 for ACCS schools compared to 496 for all students nationwide.
- The average SAT math score was 597 for ACCS students compared to 514 for all students nationwide.
- The average SAT writing score was 604 for ACCS students compared to 488 for all students nationwide.
- Looking at average SAT scores by type of education yields the following results:
  - Classical school students—274 points above average
  - Independent Schools—117 points above average
  - Homeschoolers—72 points above average
  - Religious schools—44 points above average
  - Public schools—73 points BELOW average

No matter what type of private education students received, whether homeschool, classical school, or religious school, these students performed above the average.

THE SECRET TO COLLEGE ADMISSIONS

In the first chapter, we talked about reasons why parents are concerned about homeschooling their children in high school. We often express concern that we will be inadequate to teach them basic subjects such as foreign languages and advanced math and science. However, it would seem from these statistics that homeschooled students are outperforming public school students. If we are worried about homeschooling our children because we are not subject experts, these statistics should give us pause. After all, the students with the lowest scores are attending institutions that strive to hire subject matter experts for each class.

It would be difficult to uncover the reasons that homeschooled students are outperforming their publicly educated peers, but I can hazard some guesses. First, parents who homeschool are deeply invested in the education of their children. Education is a priority in the home. These parents are committed to finding educational resources for their students. If children see their parents valuing education, they will value it, too. Second, I would suspect that many of these parents have trained their students in the habits of hard work and study skills.

Think about "non-academic" things you want your children to learn. You would never expect your children to be dependent on you to balance their checkbooks or clean their homes once they are grown adults. Similarly, homeschooling parents train their children for independence in education. You don't have to be a subject matter expert in all things in order to give your children a good education. The homeschooling parents in my community train their children to prioritize their work and to devote their full attention to it for several hours a day. Most of the time, high school students can learn through conversations with authors both dead and alive, with occasional input and encouragement from the adults in the family. Holding a difficult thought in your head while weeding through a long argument trains you to be both diligent and patient while listening to others. The lead in the conversation reverses when the student shares what she has learned from others with her parents rather than the other way around. A goal of a classical education is to develop students who can teach themselves.

In addition to worrying about complex subjects, parents may also be concerned about the maze of college admissions. Parents are correct in thinking that the path a child takes in high school makes a big difference. The final years of high school do require a lot of work on the part of both student and parent. This is true whether students are at home or in a public or private school. Too often, parents think that a dedicated person at the school will help their children navigate standardized testing, financial aid forms, and college admissions essays. However, committed parents and students do this work at home no matter where the students spend their school days.

Preparation for Advanced Placement tests and SATs requires a lot of dedication. Learning how to fill out a FAFSA form and navigate the college application process is time-consuming. Writing college essays may require working weekends right when "senioritis" kicks in. Notice the words used above: *prepare, dedicate, navigate,* and *write.* There is only one foundational thing needed to prepare high school students for college and careers: time. Many schools have teachers and guidance counselors who will help students prepare for college, but they don't have time to prepare all of them, and they don't do the work for them. They prepare the students and parents who have the character to work hard and prioritize their time.

In other words, there is no secret formula known only to guidance counselors. Hard work and perseverance remain the answers. In college prep, as in everything else, those who prepare far in advance and work like they are running a marathon are the ones who succeed. The college admission process is just another thing to learn to do as a family.

THE SECRET TO LIFE AFTER COLLEGE

As a business owner, I often research best practices for hiring. If you do an online search, you can find all kinds of advice about what kind of person to hire. I acknowledge that some jobs at large institutions require a degree to get through the gate. Following, everyone acknowledges that integrity, work ethic, and communication skills are the hallmarks of the best employees. Consider this November 2013 excerpt from *Time* magazine:

> A survey by the Workforce Solutions Group at St. Louis Community College finds that more than 60% of employers say applicants lack 'communication and interpersonal skills' — a jump of about 10 percentage points in just two years. A wide margin of managers also say today's applicants can't think critically and creatively, solve problems or write well. (Martha C. White, "The Real Reason New College Grads Can't Get Hired")

Additionally, a May 2013 article in *Forbes* magazine claims, "Eighty-nine percent of employers say they want colleges to place more emphasis on oral and written communication" (Carmine Gallo, "The #1 Skill College Grads Should Have Learned in the 5th Grade"). These are the very skills that we work to perfect in classical education: thinking well, solving problems, and writing well.

Home education (classical or not) also addresses many of these issues. When children spend all day with only their peers, they can only learn to think and speak like their peers. When they spend all day with adults, they learn to act like adults. Over and over again, I have heard professors and employers state that they can recognize homeschooled students by the way they make eye contact and communicate comfortably with adults.

THE SECRET TO LIFE BEYOND BOTH COLLEGE AND CAREERS

Should we be worried about anything besides college admissions and job opportunities? Parents want their children to be happy, loving, and wise. I want my children to have a rich, full life with good friends and good conversations about ideas that really matter. I want them to serve others sacrificially. In *The Abolition of Man*, C. S. Lewis addresses the problems of modern education, saying, "We make men without chests and expect from them virtue and enterprise. We laugh at honor and are shocked to find traitors in our midst" (26). Advocates of modern education claim to be neutral and value-free. By their own claims, they thus admit that modern education is also empty. We don't want to create adults with no values. We want to educate the hearts of our children by providing them examples of perseverance, loyalty, and courage. Classical education serves this purpose since its main goal is to form "men with chests": men who know right from wrong and who are wise and brave enough to act on their knowledge. Teaching algebra and physics and Latin is easy compared to teaching virtue and enterprise.

Wisdom is a popular word in the media as pundits with a philosophical bent see the impotence of men without chests. The classics are also experiencing a revival in popularity. Classical music radio stations and PBS *Masterpiece Classics* are as popular as ever and there is a growing genre of movies on modern mythology, that of comic superheroes. People are looking for big ideas. Classical schools, educational services, and support groups are expanding across the country. Will these movements translate into better academics? What did the classical societies do to produce so many gifted thinkers, orators, soldiers, and political leaders?

Teaching algebra and physics and Latin is easy compared to teaching virtue and enterprise.

They focused on ideals more than on paying the bills. Much of their conversation (passed down to us in writing) reflects their preoccupation with courage, temperance, and beauty. Beautiful words, beautiful ideas, and beautiful actions create beautiful people. "How do we make our children hungry for beauty?" seems like a silly question unless you are used to an ugly world. My friend Jennifer Courtney shared how she and her children embarked on a long study of the tabernacle in the wilderness. Their original plan was just to read through the Old Testament together, but they couldn't get over the detailed descriptions of the craftsmanship in the tabernacle. She said, "For the first time in my life, it occurred to me how important beauty is to the Lord. He didn't just say, 'Stick some wooden poles in the ground, throw goat skins over them, and worship me there.' Instead, He oversaw the creation of beautiful fabrics and beautiful furnishings. Only in that space could they truly worship Him."

Beautiful words, beautiful ideas, and beautiful actions create beautiful people.

If we inculcate beauty into our children's lives, truth and goodness won't abandon us. To study truth, goodness, and beauty, read anything by Hans Urs von Balthasar, a Swiss theologian and priest. He argues that an educated society must recognize that beauty rules alongside truth and goodness. Classical educators know the importance of placing beautiful words, beautiful ideas, and beautiful actions in front of their students.

Quotations from the classics should pepper our conversations because they are beautiful ways to position truth and goodness. Imagine spending time with young people who want not just to be intellectually honest but also to be kind and convincing as they speak. That they have been trained to love learning, respect others, and sacrifice their own wants for the needs of others gives me tremendous hope. I have been privileged to spend the last twenty years with such young people as I tutor through a Classical Conversations program for high school students and as I direct the Mandala Fellowship, a residential program for college-aged students.

Of course, all of these students have exasperated their parents at one time or another. Yet, they rise above their own selfish interests as they mature, and they eventually thank their parents by acknowledging a need for virtue and its application in their studies, careers, and family life.

Many young adults are questioning their purpose in life since the promised employment and salaries didn't arrive to pay off their college loans. They want to do good with their lives, find intangible beauty, and find an unchanging truth to guide them. Some try purchasing Tom's shoes, Sevenly shirts, and organic foods. Imagine how much more prepared they would be to meet the modern demands of society as well as to pursue social justice if they had been raised on the classics. Instead of reinventing the practical application of human nature, they would know what to expect. Instead of relying on a specialized degree, they could look employers in the eye, confidently knowing their degree proves they can learn anything, not just one thing. Instead of feeling like failures for living at home too long, they could work together with older generations to build family wealth, relying on family and church for support instead of government services.

In times past, fathers often built businesses to pass on to their sons. In more recent times, we've lost the idea of a family business. Classical education teaches men to embrace the past while improving upon it—not to disdain and disregard it. Much of our current cultural malaise comes from one generation disconnecting from the wisdom of the previous one.

I recently took some students to an art gallery owned by a respected art collector who had been in the business for over 40 years in multiple major cities. Her gallery was impressive. Before she even introduced herself, she said, "I want you to know that no matter what I think about the art, it's up to you to determine if you like it or not." She might as well have said, "Even though I've given my life in service of great art I have nothing to teach young people about beauty and its expression." Of course, she then contradicted the idea that art has no inherent beauty unless the beholder likes it as she led the students on a wonderful tour. She introduced them to the measures of beauty in abstract art and all that she has learned from her intensive studies. When the conversation was over, we had learned some techniques, some science, some economics, and some analysis of art pieces. Her conversation was both concrete and stimulating. We learned to love abstract art because she could clearly describe the beauty in the works she loved and her disappointment in the pieces that fell short of their potential. She explained how our opinions could be informed by artistic features. Because the students had been studying art and were familiar with the grammar she used, they were able to ask her many questions.

What if students expected to be confronted by wisdom and virtue when they met adults rather than to be told their opinions were as good as those of an older, more experienced person? What if adults knew they were responsible for imparting wisdom each time they conversed with youth? What if the classical ideas of truth, goodness, and beauty were foremost in our minds rather than personal relevance, Facebook friendships, or career absorption?

Most people, when meeting someone new, immediately ask the question, "Where do you work?" or "What do you do for a living?" When I meet young people, I am tempted as much as any other adult to ask them what they want to do for a career. Our society loves to measure people by doing instead of by being. Now, I ask instead about their passions, hobbies, and joys in life.

Imagine if we had legislators who valued and studied the thoughts of great thinkers like classically educated students do. I sometimes wonder how many of our leaders have actually read the Constitution, let alone Aristotle or Jefferson, Cicero or Blackstone. Leaders of our great nation should know the authors whose ideas made it into the documents. Since we are all responsible for our democracy, we are all governors of ourselves. Shouldn't all of us read these authors?

AM I TOO LATE?

I want to take a moment to encourage those of you who are already homeschooling in the high school years. Like me, you probably learn something new about home education every week. Like me, you probably wish you could have applied that knowledge to your child's education when they were small. It is never too late for those students who are willing to set a goal and work hard to achieve it.

One of the first students I worked with was "delight directed" in her education, which meant she was a voracious reader with never a math text in sight. She was introduced to the classical model at sixteen years old. By the time she was eighteen, she received a full scholarship to a selective university and to multiple graduate schools. She devoted the last two years of high school to intensive studies and standardized tests rather than to sports and parties. She navigated these years by herself—her brain was filled with copious ideas on how to get things done from all that she had read. Getting into college is an idea. Acting on it takes work.

I also worked with a student who spent most of his life in hospitals due to health challenges. His "medically directed" education also included voracious reading. Due to the delay in "normal" activity, he didn't graduate until he was

Getting into college is an idea. Acting on it takes work.

nineteen and is taking two years off before going to college. One year is to prepare himself academically and the other year is to travel and make up for lost social experiences. Eighteen years old and twelfth grade are not deadlines for him. Because he almost lost his life, he values it and won't be rushed through it.

One of the editors of this book has parents who valued education for the long haul. Classically trained and academically prepared, she took a fairly normal course through high school while participating in Classical Conversations. Her parents made time for our rigorous requirements as well as for additional courses at home in preparation for multiple SAT subject tests and AP exams. Besides riding horses, ballroom dancing, and participating in an active church life, her family serves the greater community. They play, worship, study, and work.

We have a saying in our family: work hard, play hard, and sleep hard. It is a privilege to go to bed tired at night. It is never too late for someone who is willing to work hard.

It's never too late for any of us. I received what the world would have considered to be a good, solid education. I went to a large school with lots of opportunities for advanced classes. I went to a good university and earned a degree in engineering. Yet, I was ignorant of so much basic information. Homeschooling allowed me to study the fundamentals. Just as it was not too late for me, it is not too late for you.

EPILOGUE

LOOKING BACK, LOOKING AHEAD

I began this book encouraging parents to be confident in three areas in order to homeschool through the rhetorical years of high school: authority, habits, and content. Parents have the God-given authority to lead their children into adulthood; they are responsible for inculcating study habits that make self-learning possible and also for determining the academic content their children need to become virtuous adults. For Rob and me, it has taken thirty-one years to realize that homeschooling taught us to be parents more than it taught our children to be educated young adults.

So how do we measure up? Did we do what we said we would do? No. Our credenda rarely matched our agenda. Our beliefs didn't match our actions. We plead for mercy along with Paul, for we, too, do that which we do not want to do. Thank God that He is our greatest Resource. Christ-confidence, not self-confidence, has allowed us to homeschool through high school. Knowing that He is our ultimate authority, that He equips families for Christian habit formation, and that He has created all of the academic content has made the whole journey blessed.

I have learned two things that renew my confidence in Christ for my elder years: First, Christ is not finished with me yet. Spending more than thirty years on such an intense endeavor must have a greater purpose, so with much joy and fear, I look forward to serving the next generation, following God's lead as He renews my purpose, and growing old with my husband. Now that we no longer have young children, I wonder what dangers we will encounter as we spread the gospel.

Second, our sons know that they are servant-kings. That doesn't mean they will always act consistently with what they believe. They are new adults, so who knows how they are going to mess things up. They are going to be broken in ways that will hurt, but they also know that service is hard, the responsibilities of being an ambassador for Christ are enormous, and His grace is abundant. They are no longer sons but brothers to our King. I look forward to serving with them even though I know my contributions to their weaknesses.

I could give you a list of things I could have done better, but I already have, by writing these three books (*The Core*, *The Question*, and now *The Conversation*)! I regret not implementing the things I have described as well as I could have. If you want to avoid my mistakes, don't just read this book, but take action as well! Homeschool for Christ as you inculcate study habits that will last a lifetime. The feast is rich, the methodology is natural, and the rewards are eternal.

The feast is rich, the methodology is natural, and the rewards are eternal.

CONVERSATIONS AROUND THE FIVE CANONS OF RHETORIC

Any time a message is clear, you can count on the presence of the five canons of rhetoric. When we look someone in the eye, touch them on the hand, hear the questions of their soul, and speak eternal words, harmony expands in the universe. The speaker and the listener become one, and Christ's prayer for us in John 17 is fulfilled. Communion is the point of education and it requires more than just connecting to a man's mind. For an unbeliever, his mind may be the way to his soul, so we must educate using the true, the good, and the beautiful, for we never know who is attending to our manners.

I am only beginning to learn how to commune with my family, as we have never all been adults before. I know that every human is "a word, never seen before or ever repeated" (Michael O'Brien, *Island of the World*). Therefore, every communication is unique. Each of us is different moment by moment. The medium and the message of our communications are like the present—words spoken become our history and cannot be taken back. We all want fewer moments of misspoken words and more moments of encouraging words. Quality comes from well-practiced quantities. So we must practice the methods of communication with our young adults who are mature enough to study the forms of rhetoric.

The five canons of rhetoric give us the form of communication. I would argue that this same form was created before the beginning of the universe when it was still a void. The ultimate void is an empty stable, an empty heart, an empty soul. And so God was good and filled it with words He deemed good. As creatures made in His image, we use the five canons to form good ideas because we believe ideas have consequences. We use the five canons to form beautiful structures because the structures cradle the good ideas. We use the five canons to form truth in a way that leads the observer to attend to Truth. By practicing the five canons, we learn to attend to the babe in the manger. God is good to give us our own babes with whom to practice.

GRADUATED STUDENTS

As our youngest sons have neared graduation, I have spent the last two years in intense studies with more than twenty students, most of whom have studied classically at home all of their lives. This was an opportunity to assess my schooling efforts in high school compared with that of some other excellent families. We know that we are known by our fruit. So how was my fruit? And how was the fruit of these other families? Tension came in deciding how to assess the fruit.

The tensions were heightened for me as the assessment came while writing this book on homeschooling through high school. I don't want to look back at more than thirty years of homeschooling, promoting curriculum, and writing books and articles on the subject, only to see that it failed. What exactly was I to assess? Two years gave me opportunities to be both disappointed and triumphant. I want to evaluate honestly. I interviewed many students and had lengthy discussions with others.

Now for the results: If you want your children to do well at academics, homeschooling results are equal to any other system for the top ten percent of students. The academic students who love AP classes and can't read fast enough will do well anywhere. A scholar is a scholar is a scholar. For a while, I was disappointed in the academic abilities of some students, until I remembered that it's not fair to compare a random group of students with the best at Ivy League schools. The group I was working with had average SAT scores of 220 points higher than the average in the United States as well as 100 points higher than average homeschoolers in the United States. They had not been raised with a "teach-to-the-test environment" so their testing success was surprising to me since they were missing some basic academics. It turns out that it is possible to have gaps in education and still do well on standardized tests.

If you want your children to do well at academics, homeschooling results are equal to any other system for the top ten percent of students.

I wanted an answer to these questions: "If I homeschool classically, is there a general statement you can say about my graduates? Are they better at service work? Do they work harder? Do they get more scholarships? Is there anything universally true about these students?" Because we are unique human beings "never before seen and never to be repeated," I realized that these are not the right questions. Yet, I kept asking them. Why was I asking? Because I have spent my life convincing other parents to give this educational model a fair shot and they, like all good parents, want an answer about the finished product. But no child is ever a finished product, and what I was asking is unfair. Is a student really defined by an SAT score or his job earnings? We say no but then act like the answer is yes. Yet, I still wanted an answer to these questions. It is hard to be a pioneer, a fool in the world's eyes, if you are not confident about the results. So is there an answer? There is.

THE CHRISTIAN, CLASSICAL HOMESCHOOL LEGACY

Recently, I was speaking at a Parent Practicum run exclusively by homeschooled, classically educated graduates. Everyone on the Practicum team was under twenty-one years old. Many adults there were thankful that their children could hang out with such responsible, lovely young adults. The adults saw the fruit, and it was pleasing. This is the general response of adults who get to know homeschool graduates. But why is it pleasing? What makes them so admirable? I found my answers as I was speaking.

As I went over the scope and sequence in the Classical Conversations catalog, six little words describing the scope of the Challenge program stood out, and I knew my answer. Even though Classical Conversations explains our seminars much like a school system so parents can understand what we are trying to achieve, our scope actually has different titles than expected. We may list content like Latin and physics and algebra, but our students actually spend these years studying the skills, or arts, of grammar, logic, rhetoric, research, debate, and exposition and composition. Without a doubt, all of the graduates I was working with were competent in these areas.

In other words, they may not be able to give the mathematical equation for the angle of incidence compared to the angle of reflection of light (a few could do that), but every one of them knew that it was a fact (grammar) important to the universe (logic), could research and explain how light works, and write a paper on how this kind of information is relevant to things like product development (rhetoric). They think in a way that integrates broad realms of knowledge. They respect knowledge, not because it is useful to their lives, but because they love the Creator of knowledge and enjoy creating alongside Him.

> *They respect knowledge, not because it is useful to their lives, but because they love the Creator of knowledge and enjoy creating alongside Him.*

I also noticed six other words that describe our academic sequence. Classical Conversations academics emphasize a different theme each year, starting in seventh grade (Challenge A). Ownership, discipline, freedom, choices, consequences, and leadership define our Christian sequence. Every student I worked with understood that they must own their education, which requires strict discipline, in order to be free to make choices and accept the consequences of leadership.

Classical education embodies the study of grammar, logic, rhetoric, research, debate, and exposition and composition. Christian education embodies the development of ownership, discipline, freedom, choices, consequences, and leadership. If you want your child to be an incarnation of these ideals, I confidently submit that homeschooling affords the greatest chance of achieving a truly Christian, classical education.

CONCLUSION

As our youngest son prepares for college, our first grandbaby has arrived. And you can be sure my interest in developing the best of classical, Christian training will continue. The Lord seems to have planned my life so that every fifteen years my devotion to His purposes is renewed by the birth of babies! It is with much joy that I watch as our son Robert and his lovely wife, April, prepare to teach my beautiful grandchild. And I greatly hope that our legacy as a Christian family will continue.

After all, isn't that the real test? Will the legacy continue? Will the next generation want to homeschool? Will they want to raise a generation that respects the past while living in the present? If Robert and April asked me why they should homeschool their children, I would tell them to do so because it is difficult and therefore it will make them into better people. They will spend a large portion of their time on earth learning to die to their own needs and will face the responsibility of their children's waywardness. They will learn self-control, sacrifice, humility, and patience as well as math, language, writing, history, and science. They will become better educated than they thought possible and will learn that they can overcome anything. They will become good grandparents to my great-grandchildren. Education is not about the individual but about the family of God building His kingdom on earth. It is about legacy and heritage.

I would ask our children to homeschool my grandchildren because they will learn that school and education are not synonyms. They will see what it takes to train a young mind to work hard for the sake of hard work. They will struggle with shaping a will without killing it. They will weep at the times they have caged imagination rather than emboldened it. They will rejoice when one of their clumsy children wins MVP for his attitude on the field. They will repent for their failures and keep the mission in mind. They will become compassionate citizens who will trust other parents to rise above their inadequacies rather than look for ways to mitigate them.

Parents who have worked with their children in high school will agree: we have failed, we have won, we have died, and we have grown. We realize homeschooling classically as Christians had little to do with our children and much to do with our own sanctification, and we are grateful for all of it.

PART THREE
APPENDICES

APPENDIX ONE
CONVERSATION GAMES

The art of conversation is no longer learned primarily through imitation, as not all parents pass this art down to their children. Learning how to converse and enjoy the company of your family does not have to be boring, stilted, or forced. You will be amazed how fun it can be to spend time with each other! This appendix is full of games that you can play with your family, your young adults' friends, or your own friends to reclaim this lost art. Feel free to modify the game, rules, or point accruals to fit your family's or your class's needs. Many variations of these games exist.

RHETORIGO

This is a variation on the classic games Bingo, Tic-Tac-Toe, and the alphabet game, designed to be played in the car, while watching television, or in a shopping mall, if you are especially brave. This game requires students to identify rhetorical devices that are used for marketing purposes on billboards and advertisements.

You will need:
- A dry erase board and marker (or a pen and paper) for each player
- A car and driver
- One or more players

Step 1: Set the Board

Make a list of rhetorical devices that you want to study in action. On paper or a dry erase board, draw a square and divide it into nine squares. You will need enough rhetorical devices to list one in each square. Each player should write one term per square. As in Bingo, individual players' boards do not need to be identical. A sample board is below, showing devices that often appear in advertisements and on billboards.

Litotes	Metonymy	Simile
Synecdoche	Alliteration	Assonance
Rhyme	Parallelism	Metaphor

Step 2: Begin Play

As in the alphabet game, players watch the sides of the road (and passing trucks!) carefully for examples of rhetorical devices. When one player sees a message that uses one of the rhetorical devices on the board, he must be the first to point it out. He can then mark that square off on his board.

Examples:
Coca-Cola® | "Open Happiness"—metonymy

The cola company shows you a picture of opening a bottle of their beverage, but they substitute the name of the object (a Coca-Cola) with an abstract idea (happiness) that they hope you will believe is associated with it closely enough as to be interchangeable.

"I Can't Believe It's Not Butter®"—litotes
Instead of saying simply, "You'll believe it's butter," the margarine company predicts consumers' disbelief by using a double negative, a device known as litotes.

Step 3: Exceptions and Challenges

Players may use the same billboard multiple times if it uses multiple rhetorical devices, but they may not use the same slogan for alliteration that another player identified three miles earlier. Players may challenge one another if they believe a rhetorical device has been misidentified.

Step 4: Victory

The first player to mark off three squares in a row (either vertically, horizontally, or diagonally) wins. For a greater challenge, draw a larger board (4x4 or 5x5), or play on the same board, using different colored markers to keep track of your squares, and try to block the other players from completing a row, as in Connect Four™ or Tic-Tac-Toe.

CANTERBURY CLUB

© 2015, Andrew Kern
This description of the Canterbury Club game is a simplification of a storytelling game being developed by the Kern family. It is used with their permission.

This game is a fun way for a group to enter the process of storytelling. Taking turns, each person adds to the story until it is complete.

You will need:
- A timer or stopwatch

- Your imagination
- At least three people (this is an excellent game for a large group)

Step 1: Identify the Characters

To begin, sit in a circle. One person at a time, go down the following list of characters and choose a character for each role. The first person will name a protagonist, the second person will name the sidekick, etc.
- The protagonist
- The protagonist's sidekick
- The antagonist
- Any other character (you can add more characters if you like)

You may choose actual people (Mom, Dad, Grandpa), fictional characters (Donald Duck, Hamlet, Cinderella, Atticus Finch), or inanimate objects (your 1994 Ford Aerostar). Not all characters have to come from the same source story or world: Hamlet may be accompanied by Donald Duck rather than Horatio.

Step 2: Choose the Settings
- Location 1
- Location 2

The story can be set somewhere on earth, in outer space, or in a different time, such as inside Noah's Ark. Get creative, and be as specific as possible about time and place.

Step 3: Identify the Problem

For example, your protagonist might need $5,000 to pay a debt collector. He might be stuck on an island with a hurricane on the way. He might be facing an irate dragon that stands between him and his long-lost love. Use your imagination and let the fun begin!

Step 4: Tell the Story

Taking turns, each person talks for one minute. When the timer goes off, that person must stop immediately, whether they are in the middle of a sentence or in the middle of a cliffhanger. The next person picks up the story exactly where the last person ended, but they may change the direction as extensively as they wish. By the end of round one (one full trip around the circle), all the characters must have made an appearance, and one location must have been identified. The second location must enter the story by the end of round two. Play continues as long as the story goes on, or you may set a predetermined amount of time in which the story must conclude. You may also opt to choose a moral for the story, which must be woven into the story as it develops.

SPEECH THIEF

Speech Thief is loosely based on a BBC Radio 4 comedy called "Just a Minute." This variation was developed by Matt Bianco for use in his Classical Conversations® Challenge IV class.

This game involves thinking on your feet and practicing good rhetorical skills in a friendly but competitive environment.

You will need:
- At least two people
- A book or other source of topics

Step 1: Choose a Topic
The first person (person A) reads a passage from a book. This can be any book. If you don't have a book handy, you can just pick a topic.

Step 2: Talk Away
The second person (person B) has to then talk for one minute about that passage or topic.

Step 3: Go for the Steal
Person B must stay on topic and do none of the following: repeat himself, pause, say "um," or say "like" unless it is being used to form a comparison. If he does any of these things, person A may challenge him. If the challenge is successful (the speaker did say "um," for example), person A has the opportunity to finish out the time remaining on the minute.

Step 4: Award the Points
If person B (the original speaker) completes the whole minute without being challenged, he receives three points. If person A (the thief) finishes the

minute successfully, he receives one point, and person B (the original speaker) receives only one point. The next round begins with the roles reversed.

Playing with more than two people works the same way. The only difference is that whoever stops the speaker gets to complete the minute. Any one speech can be "stolen" as many times as there are mistakes. Even if the last person says only one word, they still get the point for completing the minute.

After the student finishes speaking, other students can point out factual inaccuracies. If they can identify an actual inaccuracy and provide the correct information, they get one point. As many points can be earned as there are factual inaccuracies in the speech.

SCHEMES AND TROPES

This game involves correctly identifying schemes and tropes.

You will need:
- At least three people
- A few poems or speeches at hand
- Some knowledge of schemes and tropes (see appendix 2)

Step 1: Collect Your Bounty

To prepare, write all the schemes and tropes that everyone knows on a board or large piece of paper—the more, the better. If everyone doesn't know the same schemes and tropes, you can also write up a brief example or explanation of each.

Step 2: Play Begins

To begin, one person reads a poem or speech. The listeners raise their hand when they hear a scheme or trope that they recognize. The first person to correctly identify a scheme or trope gets that device. Just write their name next to the device on the board. Once someone has claimed a device in this way, they are the only person who can point out that particular device. Continue playing in the same way, moving to new poems or speeches as needed.

Step 3: Go for the Steal

If someone raises his hand and incorrectly identifies a device, all his previous devices become "unprotected." This means those devices can now be stolen. Underline that person's name on the board next to every device he owns so that everyone knows these devices are unprotected. The game continues normally, except that now the other players can guess these unprotected devices. If someone other than the original owner correctly identifies one of these devices in the following rounds, the device becomes his or hers. If the owner correctly identifies the device, it becomes protected again. He must "save" each of them from being stolen one at a time. In other words, one correct guess will not restore all of them at once. Exception: If three people in a row guess the wrong device, all of the devices owned by every player become unprotected.

Step 4: Winning the Game

The game ends when one player owns all the devices, or when a pre-determined time is up, at which point the person with the most devices wins.

ARISTOTELIAN RHETORIC

This game practices Aristotle's three ways of convincing an audience: *logos*, *ethos*, and *pathos*.

You will need:
- Two boxes, bowls, hats, or other containers
- At least three people
- A timer or stopwatch
- A set of notecards numbered 1–5 for each player OR enough erasable surfaces for each player to score the other speakers.

Step 1: Set the Stage

In the first container, place slips of paper each saying, "emotion" (*pathos*), "reason/logic" (*logos*), and "authority" (*ethos*). In the second container, place slips of paper saying ridiculous things, which the speaker will have to try to convince the audience are true. Some examples are: "All trees can walk at night," "Time travel has secretly brought dinosaurs to our time, and they will soon take over," and "If you run fast enough you can fly."

Step 2: Persuade, Persuade, Persuade

To play, one person selects a piece of paper from each container. The first will tell him how he has to convince his audience: either by appealing to the audience's emotions, their reason, or his own qualifications as a trusted authority. From the second container, the person will select his topic. He then has two minutes to attempt to convince his audience.

Step 3: Rate the Effort

After the two-minute speech is over, each member of the audience will rate how convincing the speech was on a scale of 1–5. You may combine the points or take an average for the speaker's total score. Then, it is the next person's turn to speak and the game continues. Compare the scores after each player has had a chance to speak.

APPENDIX TWO
COMMON RHETORICAL DEVICES

"Friends, Romans, countrymen—lend me your ears!"

In ancient Rome many great orators walked the Roman Forum. To stand out, an orator had to acquire and employ an extensive toolkit of tropes, schemes, and devices that he used to appeal not only to his audience's ears but also to the audience's minds and memories. Rhetoric was, to the Romans, a particular art form and a prerequisite for being a persuasive, influential leader. During the Renaissance, European nobles admired the structure and order of Greek and Roman civilization and sought to recreate it, so they tried to mimic some elements of ancient education and art, including rhetorical study. As a result, classical rhetoric saw a revival among the courts of France, Spain, England, and other nations of Western Europe.

Although classical rhetoric and its toolkit are no longer a required course of study for most aspiring leaders and intellectuals, writers and speakers today use many of the same classical techniques once prominent in ancient Rome. Think of Martin Luther King, Jr.'s famous "I Have a Dream" speech. His refrain, "I have a dream," is an example of **anaphora**. He uses **litotes** when he says, "I am not unmindful that some of you have come here out of great trials and tribulations." He also uses **parallelism**, **polysyndeton**, **metaphors**, and **personification**, terms that this appendix will help you to recognize.

Learning to see these devices in the writing of others will not only make you a better reader; it will also prepare you to become a stronger, more persuasive writer and speaker. You will have new access to ancient techniques that appeal to the eyes, the ears, the mind, and ultimately, the heart. Broadly speaking, most classical rhetorical techniques can be divided into two categories:

Schemes (S)—writing devices that deal with form, sounds, or word order and appeal to the senses.

Tropes (T)—writing devices that deal with images, ideas, or word meanings and appeal to the mind (memory or imagination).

This selection of rhetorical devices, although not comprehensive, will introduce you to some of the most commonly used techniques in classical rhetoric. Each term is defined, followed by an example. When you finish reading, you should begin to notice these devices in other books you read.

Keep in mind, this appendix will not provide an exhaustive catalog of every literary trope or scheme used in every work of literature you will ever study; rather, it will help you cultivate the practice of recognizing and naming these devices. Your eyes should pause, and you should begin to ask yourself the questions, "Why is this here? What purpose does it serve? How does it enhance or detract from this (book/poem/piece of writing)?" When you can do that consistently, you will have added another valuable instrument to your reader's and writer's toolkit. See what happened there? That's called a metaphor. To find out more, keep reading.

TERMS & DEFINITIONS

Alliteration—Latin, *ad-* (to) + *littera* (letter)
Repetition of initial consonant sounds or vowel sounds in close proximity. This technique was used instead of or alongside rhyming in Old and Middle English poetry. (S)
- *When the winter winds blew white snow across the water, we went west.*

Allusion—Latin, *ad-* (to) + *ludere* (to play)
An indirect reference to another literary work or to a historical figure or event. Sometimes the reference is to a character; other times it refers to a famous line or quotation. (T)
- *Give me liberty, or—well, really, just give me liberty. I dislike the alternative.*

Anaphora—Greek, *ana-* (back) + *pherein* (to bear)
Repetition of a word or a phrase at the beginning of subsequent clauses, lines, or sentences. (S)
- <u>We call beauty</u> strange. <u>We call beauty</u> irrational. <u>We call beauty</u> unapproachable.

Antithesis—Greek, *anti-* (against) + *tithenai* (to place)
Statement of a proposition and its opposite in close proximity. (S)
- <u>It was the hottest summer</u> she had ever seen, and at the same time <u>it was the coldest</u>.

Apostrophe—Greek, *apo-* (from) + *strephein* (to turn)
A form of address directed to an invisible being, an abstract concept, or an absent or nonexistent person. Apostrophe is often used in invocations. (T)
- <u>Oh, Time</u>! If only I had more time.

Assonance—Latin, *ad-* (to) + *sonare* (to sound)
Repetition of vowel sounds or patterns of vowel sounds in the final stressed syllable of a line. Assonance is not true rhyme because the associated consonants differ. (S)
- She walked to the <u>win</u>dow / where the birds came to <u>sing</u>.

Asyndeton—Greek, *a-* (not) + *syndein* (to bind together)
A series of clauses, typically joined by coordinating conjunctions, in which the conjunctions are removed to create a condensed, emphatic sentence. Asyndeton refers to a lack of connection within the sentence. (T)
- We bought candy, we sailed boats, we played on swing sets. We did everything.

Chiasmus—Greek, *khiazein* (to mark with an "x")
From the Greek letter chi (X), a group of words or sounds presented and then repeated in reverse. Chiasmus may refer to a combination of sounds, the order of a sentence's parts of speech, or a combination of words. (S)
- My son's <u>face rested on</u> my <u>mind</u> as my <u>hand rested</u> on the little boy's <u>face</u>.

Consonance—Latin, *con-* (with) + *sonare* (to sound)

Repetition of final consonant sounds, typically at the end of a line of verse. Consonance differs from rhyme in that the preceding vowel sounds are not the same. (S)

- *A hu__sh__ fell over the room as the po__sh__ knight announced his wi__sh__.*

Epistrophe—Greek, *epi-* (upon) + *strophe* (a turning)

Repetition of words or phrases at the end of successive stanzas, clauses, lines, or sentences. (S)

- *He walked into <u>the garden</u>. He bent to dig in <u>the garden</u>. He rested in <u>the garden</u>.*

Hyperbole—Greek, *hyper-* (beyond) + *bole* (a throwing)

Exaggeration for literary effect, either humor or emphasis. (T)

- *The green box in front of them was the biggest one in the whole world!*

Imagery—Latin, *imago* (copy, picture)

Use of vivid, specific, and descriptive language that evokes a strong image or appeals to the senses. Imagery often uses familiar comparisons to give shape to a new or unfamiliar concept. (T)

- *She gripped the rough bars of her cell and watched through the iron fence as a bird took flight through the damp mist.*

Litotes—Greek, *litos* (smooth, plain)

A form of understatement that consists of negating the idea's opposite. (T)

- *Trust me, I am <u>not unaware</u> of your plight.*

Metaphor—Greek, *meta-* (across) + *pherein* (to carry)

An implicit comparison between two unlike things, or between a character or event and a broader theme, concept, or idea. (T)

- *The wind <u>carved a serrated path</u> through the snow.* (Implied: wind = knife)

Metonymy—Greek, *meta-* (change) + *onoma* (name)
Use of an object closely associated with an idea to represent the idea itself. Metonymy is distinct from synecdoche because the word used to represent the idea is not necessarily part of what it references. (T)
- *The soldiers knew the threat he posed to the Crown.* (Implied: crown = kingdom)

Onomatopoeia—Greek, *onoma* (name) + *poiein* (to make)
A word created to represent a specific sound. The word is pronounced in such a way that it mimics the meaning of the word. More generally, onomatopoeia can refer to the way the overall sound of a poem reflects its meaning. (T)
- *The bees buzzed angrily around the honeysuckle.*

Parallelism—Greek, *para-* (beside) + *allos* (other)
An arrangement in which two or more elements of equal importance are arranged using similar phrasing or sentence structure. Parallelism may apply to verb forms, clauses, or entire sentences. (S)
- *She walked to the parking lot, drove to the airport, and then ran to the terminal.*

Personification—Latin, *persona* (person) + *facere* (to make)
Attribution of human characteristics to an inanimate object or non-human entity. (T)
- *The alarm clock yelled at her from across the darkened bedroom.*

Polysyndeton—Greek, *poly-* (many) + *syndein* (to bind together)
A series of clauses with coordinating conjunctions preceding each item, not just the final item in the series, as is typical. (S)
- *He stared at the crushed car, and the mangled trees, and the decimated house.*

Rhyme—Greek, *rhythmos* (measured time)
Two words with the same final consonant and/or vowel sound. Imperfect rhymes, also called near rhymes, may have the same vowel sound but a different final consonant (assonance), or the same concluding consonant but a different vowel sound (consonance). Rhymes can occur in the middle as well as at the end of a line. (S)
- *When the stars began to trace the sky / the bats began to fly.*

Simile—Latin, *simile* (a like thing)
An explicit comparison, signified by the words "like," "as," or "than." (T)
- *The book was rough and red like an oversized brick.*

Synecdoche—Greek, *syn-* (with) + *ek* (out) + *dekhesthai* (to receive)
Substitution of part of an object for the whole, or vice versa. Synecdoche is a more specific form of metonymy. (T)
- *Four hooves trotted by her hiding place, and she held her breath.* (Implied: hoof = horse)

Now that you have learned the names of some of the most common rhetorical techniques, go back and read the introduction to this appendix again. See how many rhetorical devices you can find and identify. You'll be amazed at what your eyes ignored before you knew where to look.

APPENDIX THREE
RESOURCES

ALSO FROM LEIGH BORTINS

—. *Echo in Celebration: A Call to Home-Centered Education.* 2nd ed. West End, NC: Classical Conversations MultiMedia, 2008. Print.
—. *The Core: Teaching Your Child the Foundations of Classical Education.* New York: Palgrave Macmillan, 2010. Print.
—. *The Question: Teaching Your Child the Essentials of Classical Education.* West End, NC: Classical Conversations MultiMedia, 2013. Print.

CHAPTER 1: CONFIDENT PARENTS

Bauer, S. Wise. *The Well-Educated Mind: A Guide to the Classical Education You Never Had.* New York: W. W. Norton, 2003. Print.
Campbell, Janice. *Transcripts Made Easy: The Homeschoolers Guide to High School Paperwork.* 3rd ed. Ashland, VA: Everyday Education, 2007. Print.
Copeland, Matt. *Socratic Circles.* Portland, ME: Stenhouse, 2005. Print.
Esolen, Anthony M. *Ten Ways to Destroy the Imagination of Your Child.* Wilmington, DE: ISI, 2010. Print.
Home School Legal Defense Association. Purcellville, VA. Web. http://hslda.org/.
Paul, Ron. *Liberty Defined: 50 Essential Issues That Affect Our Freedom.* New York: Grand Central Pub, 2011. Print.
Sande, Ken. *The Peacemaker: A Biblical Guide to Resolving Personal Conflict.* Grand Rapids, MI: Baker Books, 2004. Print.
Swope, Cheryl. *Simply Classical: A Beautiful Education for Any Child.* Louisville, KY: Memoria, 2013. Print.

Vogelgesang, Barb. "Providing Diversity for Homeschooled Students." Bright Hub Education, July 12, 2012. Web. http://www.brighthubeducation.com/homeschooling-and-socialization/121780-how-to-provide-diversity-awareness-for-your-kids/.

Wilson, Douglas. *The Case for Classical Christian Education*. Wheaton, IL: Crossway, 2003. Print.

—. *Recovering the Lost Tools of Learning: An Approach to Distinctively Christian Education*. Wheaton, IL: Crossway, 1991.

—. *Repairing the Ruins: The Classical and Christian Challenge to Modern Education*. Moscow, ID: Canon, 1996. Print.

Government Sources on Home Education

"First Look: Parent and Family Involvement in Education, from the National Household Education Surveys Program of 2012." National Center for Education Statistics. U.S. Department of Education, August 2013. http://nces.ed.gov/pubs2013/2013028.pdf.

"Issue Brief: 1.5 Million Homeschooled Students in the United States." National Center for Education Statistics. U.S. Department of Education, December 2008. Web. http://nces.ed.gov/pubs2009/2009030.pdf.

"Statistical Analysis Report: Homeschooling in the United States: 2003." National Center for Education Statistics. National Household Education Surveys. U.S. Department of Education, February 2006. Web. http://nces.ed.gov/pubs2006/2006042.pdf.

CHAPTER 2: RHETORIC DEFINED

Aristotle. *Rhetoric* [c. 350 BC] Trans. W. Rhys Roberts. Internet Classics Archive. Boston: MIT, 2009. Web. http://classics.mit.edu/Aristotle/rhetoric.1.i.html.

Augustine. *On Christian Doctrine* [5th c.]. *A Select Library of the Nicene and Post-Nicene Fathers of the Christian Church*. Trans. J. F. Shaw. Mineola, NY: Dover Publications, 2009.

Corbett, Edward P. J. *Classical Rhetoric for the Modern Student*. New York: Oxford University Press, 1965. Print.

Crider, Scott. *The Office of Assertion*. Wilmington, DE: ISI Books, 2005. Print.

Dodson, Will, Katie Fennell, and Alan Benson. *Techne Rhetorike: Techniques of Discourse for Writers and Speakers*. 2nd ed. Southlake, TX: Fountainhead, 2010. Print.

Pearcey, Nancy. *Saving Leonardo: A Call to Resist the Secular Assault on Mind, Morals, & Meaning*. Nashville, TN: B&H Publishing, 2010. Print.
Quintilian. *The Institutio Oratoria of Quintilian*. Trans. H. E. Butler. Cambridge, MA: Harvard University Press. 1980. Print.
Sayers, Dorothy. "The Lost Tools of Learning." Lecture. Oxford University, 1947.
Wilson, Thomas. *The Arte of Rhetorique* [1560]. Ed. G. H. Mair. Oxford: Clarendon Press, 1909. *Renascence Editions*. Transcribed by Judy Boss. University of Oregon, 1998. Web. http://www.luminarium.org/renascence-editions/arte/.

CHAPTER 3: READING

Dickens, Charles. *A Christmas Carol*. New York: Dover Publications, 1991.
Donne, John. "Batter my heart, three person'd God; for you." *Holy Sonnets*. Web. www.poetryfoundation.org.
Edwards, Lee, and Matthew Spalding. *Reading the Right Books: A Guide for the Intelligent Conservative*. New York: Heritage Foundation, 2013. Print.
Hawthorne, Nathaniel. *The Scarlet Letter*. New York: Dover Publications, 1994. Print.
Sire, James W. *How to Read Slowly: Reading for Comprehension*. Colorado Springs: Waterbrook Press, 1978. Print.
Spalding, Romalda Bishop, and Mary E. North. *The Writing Road to Reading: The Spalding Method for Teaching Speech, Spelling, Writing, and Reading*. 5th rev. ed. New York: Quill, 2003. Print.

CHAPTER 4: SPEECH AND DEBATE

Aristotle. *Rhetoric* [c. 350 BC] Trans. W. Rhys Roberts. Internet Classics Archive. Boston: MIT, 2009. Web. http://classics.mit.edu/Aristotle/rhetoric.1.i.html.
Corbett, Edward P. J. *Classical Rhetoric for the Modern Student*. New York: Oxford University Press, 1965. Print.
Hawthorne, Nathaniel. *The Scarlet Letter*. New York: Dover Publications, 1994. Print.
King, Jr., Martin Luther. "I Have a Dream" [1963]. In *American Rhetoric: The Power of Oratory in the United States*. Intellectual Properties Management, n.d. Web. http://www.americanrhetoric.com/speeches/mlkihaveadream.htm.

Lincoln, Abraham. "The Gettysburg Address" [1863]. American History Central, 2015. Web. http://www.www.americanhistorycentral.com/entry.php?rec=563.

Shakespeare, William. *The Tragedy of Julius Caesar*. Edited by Barbara A. Mowat. New Folger's ed. New York: Washington Square, 1992. Print.

CHAPTER 5: WRITING

Aristotle. *Rhetoric* [c. 350 BC] Trans. W. Rhys Roberts. Internet Classics Archive. Boston: MIT, 2009. Web. http://classics.mit.edu/Aristotle/rhetoric.1.i.html.

Corbett, Edward P. J. *Classical Rhetoric for the Modern Student*. New York: Oxford University Press, 1965. Print.

Crider, Scott. *The Office of Assertion*. Wilmington, DE: ISI Books, 2005. Print.

Hicks, David V. *Norms & Nobility: A Treatise on Education*. New York: Praeger, 1981. Print.

Kern, Andrew. *The Lost Tools of Writing*, 5th edition. Concord, NC: The CiRCE Institute, 2015.

Nightingale, Florence, *Notes on Matters Affecting the Health, Efficiency, and Hospital Administration of the British Army. Founded Chiefly on the Experience of the Late War*. Presented by Request to the Secretary of State for War. Privately printed for Miss Nightingale, Harrison and Sons, 1858. Web. http://www.uh.edu/engines/epi1712.htm.

Rhodes, Suzanne U. *The Roar on the Other Side: A Guide for Student Poets*. Moscow, ID: Canon Press, 2000. Print.

Tolkien, J. R. R. *The Hobbit*. London: George Allen & Unwin, 1937.

Weaver, Richard M. *The Ethics of Rhetoric*. Chicago: OH. Regnery, 1953. Print.

CHAPTER 6: SCIENCE

Atalay, Bülent. *Math and the Mona Lisa: The Art and Science of Leonardo da Vinci*. New York: Smithsonian Books, 2006. Print.

Boorstin, Daniel J. *The Discoverers*. New York: Random House, 1983. Print.

Boyer, Peter J. "The Covenant." *Annals of Science. The New Yorker*. September 6, 2010. Web. http://www.newyorker.com/reporting/2010/09/06/100906fa_fact_boyer.

Carson, Ben. *Gifted Hands*. Grand Rapids, MI: Zondervan, 1990. Print.

—, with Cecil Murphey. *Think Big: Unleashing Your Potential for Excellence*. Grand Rapids, MI: Zondervan, 1992. Print.

Collins, Francis S. *The Language of God: A Scientist Presents Evidence for Belief*. New York: Free Press, 2006. Print.

Crowther, J. G. *Six Great Scientists: Albert Einstein, Copernicus, Charles Darwin, Galileo, Isaac Newton, Marie Curie*. New York: Barnes & Noble Books, 1995. Print.

Doherty, Peter. *The Beginner's Guide to Winning the Nobel Prize: A Life in Science*. New York: Columbia University Press, 2006. Print.

"Engage to Excel: Producing One Million Additional College Graduates with Degrees in Science, Technology, Engineering, and Mathematics." [Report]. President's Council of Advisors on Science & Technology. Washington, DC: Government Printing Office, 2012. Web. http://www.whitehouse.gov/sites/default/files/microsites/ostp/pcast-engage-to-excel-final_2-25-12.pdf.

Gifted Hands: The Ben Carson Story. [Film.] Dir. Thomas Carter. Perf. Cuba Gooding, Jr., Sony Pictures, 2009.

Haas, Harald. "Harald Haas: Wireless data from every light bulb." TED talk. July 2011. Web. http://www.ted.com/talks/asld_haas_wireless_data_from_every_light_bulb.html.

Jones, Charlotte. *Mistakes That Worked: 40 Familiar Inventions and How They Came to Be*. New York: Random House, 1994. Print.

Stewart, Jeff. *Simple Physics: Why Balloons Rise, Apples Fall, and Golf Balls Go Away*. New York: Reader's Digest, 2010. Print.

Swenson, Richard A. *More than Meets the Eye: Fascinating Glimpses of God's Power and Design*. Colorado Springs: NavPress, 2000. Print.

The Truman Show. [Film.] Dir. Peter Weir. Perf. Jim Carrey and Laura Linney. Universal Pictures, 1998.

Wulffson, Don L. *The Kid Who Invented the Popsicle: And Other Extraordinary Stories About Ordinary Things*. New York: Puffin Books, 1999. Print.

Science Opportunities for High Schoolers

4-H Youth Development Organization: http://www.4-h.org/
Alaska Summer Research Academy: http://www.uaf.edu/asra
Boy Scouts of America: http://www.scouting.org/
Girl Scouts: http://www.girlscouts.org/
National Flight Academy: http://www.nationalflightacademy.com
Outward Bound: http://www.outwardbound.org/

CHAPTER 7: MATH

Hardy, G. H., and C. P. Snow. *A Mathematician's Apology*. Canto ed. London: Cambridge University Press, 1992. Print.

Nickel, James. *Mathematics: Is God Silent?* Rev., 2nd ed. Vallecito, CA: Ross House, 2001. Print.

Saxon, John H. *Advanced Mathematics: An Incremental Development*. Norman, OK: Saxon, 1989. Print.

—. *Algebra 1/2: An Incremental Development*. 2nd ed. Norman, OK: Saxon, 1997. Print.

—. *Algebra 1: An Incremental Development*. Orlando, FL: Saxon, 2009. Print.

—. *Algebra 2: An Incremental Development*. 2nd ed. Norman, OK: Saxon, 1997. Print.

—, and Frank Wang. *Calculus with Trigonometry and Analytic Geometry*. Norman, OK: Saxon, 1988.

Thompson, Silvanus P., and Martin Gardner. *Calculus Made Easy: Being a Very-simplest Introduction to Those Beautiful Methods of Reckoning Which Are Generally Called by the Terrifying Names of the Differential Calculus and the Integral Calculus*. Rev. ed. New York: St. Martin's, 1998. Print.

CHAPTER 8: GOVERNMENT AND ECONOMICS

Hazlitt, Henry. *Economics in One Lesson*. [1946] Reprint edition. New York: Crown Business, 1988.

Hicks, David V. *Norms & Nobility: A Treatise on Education*. New York: Praeger, 1981.

Maybury, Rick. *Whatever Happened to Penny Candy? For Students, Business People, and Investors: A Fast, Clear, and Fun Explanation of the Economics You Need for Success in Your Career, Business, and Investments*. Edited by Jane A. Williams. 6th ed. Placerville, CA: Bluestocking, 2010. Print.

Miller, Arthur. *The Crucible: A Play in Four Acts*. New York: Viking, 1953. Print.

Shakespeare, William. *Much Ado About Nothing*. Edited by Barbara A. Mowat.New Folger's ed. New York: Washington Square, 1995. Print.

—. *The Tragedy of Hamlet, Prince of Denmark*. Edited by Barbara A. Mowat. New Folger's ed. New York: Washington Square, 2002. Print.

Stowe, Harriet Beecher. *Uncle Tom's Cabin*. Oxford: Oxford University Press, 1998. Print.

Williams, Jane A.. *A Bluestocking Guide: Economics*. Placerville, CA: Bluestocking, 2004. Print.

CHAPTER 9: HISTORY

Boorstin, Daniel J. *The Discoverers*. New York: Random House, 1983. Print.

Greenholt, Jennifer, ed. *Words Aptly Spoken: American Documents*. 2nd ed. West End, NC: Classical Conversations MultiMedia, 2011. Print.

Kreeft, Peter. *The Journey: A Spiritual Roadmap for Modern Pilgrims*. Downers Grove, Ill.: InterVarsity, 1996. Print.

"Resolutions of the Utah State Legislature and Governor, March 6, 1897." Records of the U.S. Senate, RG 46. The National Archives, 2015. Web. http://www.archives.gov/legislative/features/17th-amendment/utah.html.

Schweikart, Larry, and Michael Allen. *A Patriot's History of the United States: From Columbus's Great Discovery to the War on Terror*. New York: Sentinel, 2004. Print.

Simmons, Tracy Lee. *Climbing Parnassus: A New Apologia for Greek and Latin*. Wilmington, DE: ISI, 2002. Print.

Sproul, R. C. *The Consequences of Ideas: Understanding the Concepts that Shaped Our World*. Wheaton, IL: Crossway, 2000. Print.

CHAPTER 10: LATIN AND FOREIGN LANGUAGES

Clark, Kevin, and Ravi Jain. *The Liberal Arts Tradition: A Philosophy of Christian Classical Education*. Camp Hill, PA: Classical Academic Press, 2013. Print.

Henle, R. J. *Latin: First Year*. Chicago: Loyola University Press, 1958. Print.

—. *Latin: Second Year*. Chicago: Loyola University Press, 1958. Print.

—. *Latin: Third Year*. Chicago: Loyola University Press, 1959. Print.

—. *Latin: Fourth Year*. Chicago: Loyola University Press, 1959. Print.

Homer. *The Odyssey*. Translated by Robert Fagles. New York: Penguin, 1997. Print.

Simmons, Tracy Lee. *Climbing Parnassus: A New Apologia for Greek and Latin*. Wilmington, DE. ISI, 2002. Print.

Simpson, D. P. *Cassel's New Latin-English, English-Latin Dictionary*. 5th ed. London: Cassell, 1968. Print.

Virgil. *The Aeneid*. Translated by Robert Fitzgerald. New York: Random House, 1983. Print.

Visual Latin series. Nashville: Compass Cinema, 2011. Video.

CHAPTER 11: FINE ARTS

Fujimura, Makoto. "Art, Love and Beauty: Introduction." December 16, 2013. Web. http://www.makotofujimura.com/writings/art-love-and-beauty-introduction/.
Juster, Norton. *The Phantom Tollbooth*. New York: Epstein & Carroll, 1961. Print.
Pogue, David, and Scott Speck. *Classical Music for Dummies*. Foster City, CA: IDG Worldwide, 1997. Print.
PreScripts series. West End, NC: Classical Conversations MultiMedia, 2012–2015. Print.
   PreScripts Cursive Letters and Coloring (2 titles)
   PreScripts Cursive Words and Drawing (2 titles)
   PreScripts Cursive Sentences and Art Lessons (3 titles)
   PreScripts Cursive Passages and Illuminations (2 titles)
Skogen, Caleb. *Math in Motion: First Steps in Music Theory*. West End, NC: Classical Conversations MultiMedia, 2015. Print.
Smith, Jane Stuart, and Betty Carlson. *The Gift of Music: Great Composers and Their Influences*. Rev. ed. Westchester, IL: Crossway, 1987. Print.
Strickland, Carol, and John Boswell. *The Annotated Mona Lisa: A Crash Course in Art History from Prehistoric to Post-Modern*. Kansas City: Andrews and McMeel, 1992. Print.
Veith, Gene Edward. *State of the Arts: From Bezalel to Mapplethorpe*. Wheaton, IL: Crossway, 1991. Print.

CHAPTER 12: A GRADUATION CONVERSATION

AcademicRecords.net. West End, NC. Web. http://academicrecords.net/transcript.nsf/.
Campbell, Janice. *Transcripts Made Easy: The Homeschoolers Guide to High School Paperwork*. 3rd ed. Ashland, VA: Everyday Education, 2007. Print.
CC Connected. West End, NC. Web. https://www.classicalconversations.com/connected.
Challenge and Post Graduation Advisor. West End, NC. Web. https://www.classicalconversations.com/classical/academic-services/challenge-and-post-graduation-advisor.
Classical Conversations Plus. West End, NC. Web. https://www.classical-conversations.com/classical/academic-services/cc.
The College Board. New York. Web. https://www.collegeboard.org/.

Gallo, Carmine. "The #1 Skill College Grads Should Have Learned in the 5th Grade." *Forbes.* May 29, 2013. Web. http://www.forbes.com/sites/carminegallo/2013/05/29/the-1-skill-college-grads-should-have-learned-in-the-5th-grade/.

Home School Legal Defense Association. Purcellville, VA. Web. http://hslda.org/.

White, Martha C. "The Real Reason New College Grads Can't Get Hired." *Time.* November 10, 2013. Web. http://business.time.com/2013/11/10/the-real-reason-new-college-grads-cant-get-hired/.

APPENDIX FOUR
REAL PARENTS RESPOND

We asked the greater Classical Conversations community to respond to a Facebook poll about their experiences, concerns, and joys related to homeschooling through high school. Here's how they replied:

What are your top concerns about homeschooling through high school?

"I wonder about keeping up with them in classes I have never taken. I want to be a resource for them in something like Calculus but I will be learning right along with them. Which I know has benefits, showing them it is important enough that I am learning and that I don't expect something from them I won't do myself. I just feel a little more prepared for the younger years." —Chelle

"Yes! My husband was homeschooled twenty years ago and only received his GED. He never went to college but he started 'real world' education (apprenticeship) ASAP. It was all by the blessings of the Lord and his diligence but he has always been able to support us and now our family of six lives well on his one income. Having an 'alternative' high school education is what prepared him for making money in the business world." —Corrie

"Having graduated 5, some with full scholarships using the classical method, and another seemingly stuck in the dialectic stage and struggling in community college, my biggest concern in training my last child, going into Challenge A, is to nurture the transference from the dialectic to the rhetoric stage with greater purposefulness. Note, this is not an easy task if the student is unregenerate, as our dependence on the Holy Spirit to bring illumination and give the 'Aha's!' rests on his perfect plan... But just as we 'trust' the acquisition of knowledge we have invested in our students will bring fruit... so we must also trust God's plan for each student is perfect, and that his word will not return void. By the rhetoric stage, many students 'know' the 'right' answer and will give a dialectic response... 'Jesus'...but not be able to support the interconnectivity of how each academic subject points to and supports his attributes and is an outworking of his deity. I think this is a 'big rock' to use as a catalyst to do the 'hard thing' in mastery...but alas, again, it must be inspired by the Holy Spirit and we can only emulate that passion and trust in his perfect plan for each student without the assurance of genuine conversion. But like in the 'Case for Christ'... teaching the dynamics of rhetorical thinking as a pattern for right thinking will ultimately be used by God to dispel the fallacy of wrong thinking, and be an agent, used by God to facilitate ultimate truth...in Him." —Cheryl

"How do these kids realize that the things they 'miss out on' are not that important in the long run?" —Cyndi

"The fear of 'blowing' it for my student. That I will somehow fail them by not being master of all they need to conquer." —Kathryn

"Keeping track of credits. College readiness." —Kathy

"How to make it challenging academically for all four years. I've seen students who are [academically] focused for the first two years of high school and then add in work and other activities so that academics takes a lesser role." —Gretchen

"My goals for my children are simple. I'd love for them to have a good foundation of knowledge. More importantly, I want them to have a thirst for knowledge and a love for learning. I want to homeschool through high school to avoid having these goals snuffed out and discouraged. I am not as concerned with college or career readiness because so few wind up using their college degree or keep the same job their whole lives these days. If they have a love for learning and the basic skills to pursue knowledge, a diligent work ethic AND, more than anything else that I want for them, a joy in the Lord and compassion for others, then I'm pleased as pie."
—Jessica

"Finding [an] alternative to going straight to college. For some students college may not be the right fit at 18 or 19. I want to know what else is out there." —Tiki

"Will my children be prepared to earn a living and support their own families some day? Will they 'know enough' to study in fields that interest them? Will they be ready for college or an apprenticeship? Will I be able to help them have a direction in their life?" —Becki

For veteran families, what has been your greatest joy as a result of homeschooling through high school?

"Narrowing the many joys to the greatest joy is a tough task! Watching my children grapple and wrestle with the truth of God's word as they try to apply it to their real life struggles is most rewarding. I wanted my children to know in whom or what they believed, why they believed it and be able to explain it eloquently. I taught and wanted them to have saving trust and faith in God through Jesus Christ, but if they choose (chose) not to, I wanted them to recognize the truth they would turn away from and the untruth they would turn to—and explain it. They have stayed with the faith, and the relationship we developed as a result of home schooling through high school allows me to walk with them as WE now grow together in our individual relationships with the Lord... Sorry this response is so wordy!" —Donna

"Continued relationship, love-focused learning." —Kathleen

INDEX

Page numbers for definitions and chapter designations are bold.

Symbols

17th Amendment. *See* history: U. S. Constitution

A

AcademicRecords.net 31, 248
actio 66
adult education 2, 26
Advanced Placement (AP) tests 22, 210. *See also* standardized testing
Aeneid, The 180, 182, 184, 247
algebra 131–133. *See also* math: algebra
alliteration. *See* rhetorical devices: alliteration
allusion. *See* rhetorical devices: allusion
American government voting process 147–152
anaphora. *See* rhetorical devices: anaphora
Annotated Mona Lisa, The 194
answer key 131
antithesis. *See* rhetorical devices: antithesis
apostrophe. *See* rhetorical devices: apostrophe
apprenticeship(s) 1, 2, 5, 119
argument
  in literature 66
argumentation 86, 147, 150
Aristotelian Rhetoric (game) 233–234
Aristotle 3, 38, 47–49, 75, 82, 87, 88, 128, 215, 233
  canons of rhetoric, five 42, **86**–87
  common topics, five 113–114
  Rhetoric 33, 45, 75, 86, 242, 243
arithmetic. *See* math: arithmetic
arrangement **44–45**, 196. *See also* canons of rhetoric, five
  confirmatio 79, 84, 166
  divisio 78–79, 165
  exordium 77–78, 165
  in American government 148–149
  in economics 153
  in fine arts 192–193, 205
    music 199, 201–202
  in government and economics 158
  in history 165–166, 171
  in Latin and foreign languages 180–181, 188
  in math 132–133, 139, 143

in reading 61, 64
  poetry 69
  universal questions 66
in science 126
  practical application 119–120
  research paper 114
in speech and debate 90
  forensic 87
  political 76–80
in writing 108
  persuasive essay 102
  research paper 95–97
narratio **78**, 166
peroratio **79**
refutatio 166
Art of Rhetoric, The 37–38, 243
assonance. *See* rhetorical devices: assonance
astronomy 2, 28
asyndeton. *See* rhetorical devices: asyndeton
Atalay, Bülent
  Math and the Mona Lisa 124, 244
athletics 3, 12
Augustine, Saint 3, 23
  On Christian Doctrine 40
Austen, Jane 23
authority, parental 10–19, 27–28, 31–32

B

Balthasar, Hans Urs von 213
Bartlett, Jonathan
  "The Many Lessons of Chemistry in Classical Education" 111
Bauerlein, Mark
  The Dumbest Generation 4
Beginner's Guide to Winning the Nobel Prize, The 117

Bianco, Matt 36, 231
  "History, Culture, and the Latin Language" 177–178
Bible 37, 48, 54, 67, 148, 160, 162, 163, 165, 167, 169
biology 11, 23, 24, 56, 111, 119, 138
Boyer, Peter J.
  "The Covenant" 125, 244

C

Caesar, Julius 23, 36, 184
  Battle in Gaul 27
  Gallic Wars 39
Campbell, Janice
  Transcripts Made Easy 31, 241, 248
canons of rhetoric, five **42–47**, 218–219
  arrangement **44–45**. *See also* arrangement
  delivery **47**. *See also* delivery
  elocution (style) **45–46**. *See also* elocution (style)
  invention **43–44**. *See also* invention
  memory **46**. *See also* memory
Canterbury Club (game) 229–230
Carry On, Mr. Bowditch 103, 112
Carson, Ben
  Gifted Hands 113, 244, 245
Carver, George Washington 122
Challenge program 117, 156, 180, 221. *See also* Classical Conversations
character(s) 66
chemistry 13, 32, 34, 35, 92, 111–112, 119, 138. *See also* science: chemistry
  Periodic Table of Elements 34, 112

chiasmus. *See* rhetorical devices: chiasmus
Cicero 23, 73, 184, 215
circumstance. *See* common topics, five
Clark, Kevin
　The Liberal Arts Tradition 173, 247
Classical Conversations 13, 15, 22, 25, 28, 31, 74, 156, 213, 216, 221
　Challenge program 80, 112, 180, 221
classical music 199, 200, 201, 212. *See also* fine arts
Classical Music for Dummies 200, 248
Classical Rhetoric for the Modern Student 37, 77, 242, 243, 244
Climbing Parnassus 55, 247
college 1, 3, 14, 15, 24, 117, 127, 138, 162, 222
　admissions 25–27, 31–32, 207–208, 209–211, 215
　alternatives to 2
　and homeschool students 25–26, 208–209, 209–211
　applications 2
　value of 26–27, 212–215
Collins, Francis S. 123, 125, 244
Common Core State Standards 27, 155
common topics, five 114, 168, 179
　circumstance 114, 179, 195
　comparison 114, 179, 195
　definition 114, 179, 195
　relationship 114, 179, 195
　testimony 114, 179, 196
communication skills 74, 106, 142, 211
community service 208

commutative laws for addition and multiplication 140. *See also* laws: math
comparison. *See* common topics, five
computer. *See* technology
confidence 156, 218
　of parents 9–32, 18, 23
　of students 20, 32, 42, 47, 112
Consequences of Ideas, The 112, 161, 247
consonance. *See* rhetorical devices: consonance
content (educational) 10, 11, 19, 21, 22, 24, 27–32
conversation games 227–234
cooking 21
Copeland, Matt
　Socratic Circles 241
Corbett, Edward P. J.
　Classical Rhetoric for the Modern Student 37, 77, 242, 243, 244
Core, The 23, 33, 34, 151, 218, 241
Courtney, Jennifer 212
　"Spontaneous Integration: Jazz Music, Playwrights, and the Cold War" 154
creative writing 105, 150
credits 22, 31–32. *See also* college
Crider, Scott
　The Office of Assertion 43, 95, 96, 159, 242, 244
critical thinking 74
Crucible, The 155
curiosity 20, 119, 124, 125, 128. *See also* inquiry, spirit of
current events 147

D

Declaration of Independence 169

Deddens, Kate
   "There Is Intelligence There" 203–204
definition. *See* common topics, five
delivery **47**. *See also* canons of rhetoric, five
   in American government 151–152
   in economics 154
   in fine arts 194–195, 197–198, 205
      music 200–201, 202–203
   in government and economics 158
   in history 168, 171
   in Latin and foreign languages 184–185, 188
   in math 135–136, 141–142, 143
   in reading 62–63, 65
      poetry 71–72
      universal questions 67
   in science 126
      practical application 121–122
      research paper 116–117
   in speech and debate 90
      forensic 87–88
      political 81–82
   in writing 108
      persuasive essay 104
      research paper 100–101
dialectic (logic) 16, 148. *See also* education: classical: dialectic (logic)
   analysis 39, 109, 148–149, 179, 192
   stage **34**, 35, 39, 74, 113, 175
Dickens, Charles 23, 48, 146
   A Christmas Carol 63–65, 243
      Ebenezer Scrooge (fictional character) 63–65
dispositio. *See* arrangement

distributive law 140. *See also* laws: math
diversity 18–19, 242
Doherty, Peter
   The Beginner's Guide to Winning the Nobel Prize 117, 124–125
Donne, John
   "Batter My Heart, Three-Person'd God" 68–71
   Holy Sonnets 243
drawing. *See* fine arts: media
Dumbest Generation, The 4

E

Echo in Celebration 241
economics 24, 38, 39, 74, **152–154**, 156, 157
education 207
   classical **34–35**, 212, 214, 220–221
      and Latin 175–176
      dialectic (logic) 29, 30, **34**, 128, 156, 167, 174, 178
      grammar 24, 29, 30, **34**, 174, 178
         in foreign language 175
         in fine arts 204
         literature in 54
      rhetoric **35**, 178
   modern 29, 54, 212
Elements of Style, The 98
elocutio. *See* elocution (style)
elocution (style) **45–46**. *See also* canons of rhetoric, five
   in American government 149–150
   in economics 153
   in fine arts 193, 196–197, 205
      music 199, 202
   in government and economics 158
   in history 166, 171

in Latin and foreign languages
    181–183, 188
in math 133–134, 139–140, 143
in reading 61–62, 64
  poetry 70
  universal questions 66
in science 126
  practical application 120–121
  research paper 114–115
in speech and debate 90
  forensic 87
  political 80
in writing 108
  persuasive essay 102–103
  research paper 97–99
End of Education, The 207
epistrophe. *See* rhetorical devices: epistrophe
Esolen, Anthony
  Ten Ways to Destroy the Imagination of Your Child 21, 241
Ethics of Rhetoric, The 106
ethos **48–49**. *See* modes of persuasion: *ethos*
extracurricular activities 12

F

Facebook 215
FAFSA 210
fear
  of homeschooling 9–10, 22–23
  of public speaking 74, 81
Federal Reserve Act 164
Fibonacci sequence 156
fine arts **189–205**
  composition 192–193
  illustration of *The Phantom Tollbooth* 191–195
  media
    collage 193

    drawing 193
    splatter paint 193
  music
    Handel's *Water Music* 201–203
    performance 198–201
  musical expression 199
  rule of thirds 193
  studying a masterpiece 195–198
  visual hierarchy 193
five canons of rhetoric. *See* canons of rhetoric, five
five common topics. *See* common topics, five
foreign languages. *See also* Latin
  Chinese 177–178
  Māori 162–163
  reading aloud 183–184
  teaching myths 174
  translation of 178–185
Founding Fathers 77, 84
frustration 15, 110, 158, 180
Fujimura, Makoto
  "Art, Love and Beauty" 204
fundamentals 10, 174, 216

G

Galileo, Galilei 124
Gallo, Carmine
  Forbes, "The #1 Skill College Grads Should Have Learned in the 5th Grade" 211
games **227–233**
geometry 25, 137
gifted students 29–31
government 74, 137, 156
  American 24, **145–152**
    voting process 147–152
  in political speech 75
grades 27, 31
graduation **207–216**, 219–220

grammar 163, 167, 175, 221. *See also* education: classical: grammar
  stage **34**, 35, 39, 151, 174, 176, 180, 198
Greenholt, Jen 247
  "History Integrates with Language Studies" 162–163
  "Putting Literary Characters on Trial" 85–86
  "The Tough Skin of Words" 105

H

habits 11
  good 19–27
Handel, Georg Frederic
  Water Music 201–203
handwriting 70
hard work 4, 19, 122, 198, 210, 222
Hardy, G. H.
  A Mathematician's Apology 127
harmony 190, 196, 197, 218
Hawthorne, Nathaniel
  The Scarlet Letter 58–63, 243
Hicks, David
  Norms & Nobility 106, 148–149, 178, 244, 246
high school 1, 2, 40, 47, 73, 85, 91, 93, 110, 111, 127, 175, 176, 210, 217
  homeschooling through 1, 2, 3, 4, 5, 6, 9–32, 33, 80, 103, 105, 122, 129, 142, 173, 174, 208, 209, 215, 216, 217, 219, 223
history **159–171**
  17th Amendment 164–168
  Federal Reserve Act 164
  significance of 168–170
Holy Sonnets 68–72, 243

Home Educated and Now Adults 13, 26
Homer
  The Iliad 62, 99, 182
  The Odyssey 247
homeschool
  through high school 16
Home School Legal Defense Association (HSLDA) 31, 241
humanities 93
hyperbole. *See* rhetorical devices: hyperbole

I

identity law (math) 133, 134. *See also* laws: math
Iliad, The 62, 99, 182
illiteracy 55
imagery. *See* rhetorical devices: imagery
imagination 33, 105, 110, 119, 191, 192, 195, 222
inquiry, spirit of 111. *See also* curiosity
Internet 94, 113, 192, 196. *See also* technology
inventio. See invention
invention **43–44**. *See also* canons of rhetoric, five
  in American government 147–148
  in economics 153
  in fine arts 191–192, 195–196, 205
    music 199, 201
  in government and economics 158
  in history 164–165, 171
  in Latin and foreign languages 179–180, 188
  in math 131–132, 138–139, 143
  in reading 60, 63–64

poetry 69
universal questions 65–66
in science 126
practical application 118–119
research paper 113–114
in speech and debate 90
forensic speech 86
political 76
in writing 108
persuasive essay 101
research paper 93–94
Island of the World 219

J

Jain, Ravi
The Liberal Arts Tradition 173, 247
Jefferson, Thomas 23, 146, 215
Juster, Norton
The Phantom Tollbooth 191–195, 248
justice 19, 35, 48, 88, 169, 208, 213

K

Keats, John
"Ode on a Grecian Urn" 189, 190, 195
Kern, Andrew 229
The Lost Tools of Writing 101
King, Martin Luther, Jr.
"I Have a Dream" 47, 78, 80, 235
knowledge 35, 55, 72, 74, 75, 90, 93, 99, 101, 108, 109, 115, 118, 120, 121, 122, 123, 124, 125, 126, 133, 135, 143, 150, 162, 170, 177, 179, 194, 200, 212, 215, 221
with understanding and wisdom 39–42, 49, 178

L

Latham, Jean Lee
Carry On, Mr. Bowditch 112
Latin and foreign languages **173–188**
as part of classical education 175–176
college acceptance of 175
translation 178–185
Western civilization 176–177
Why study Latin 175–178, 185–187
laws
in government 153, 156
in science 112, 115, 185
math 142
commutative 140
distributive 140
identity 133, 134
The Law of Christ 157
leadership 86, 118, 122, 128, 163, 221, 222
Lee, Harper
Atticus Finch (fictional character) 230
To Kill a Mockingbird 62
Tom Robinson (fictional character) 62
Leonardo da Vinci 100, 124, 195, 197
The Last Supper 196
Lewis, C. S.
Out of the Silent Planet 55–57
The Abolition of Man 212
The Lion, the Witch and the Wardrobe 56
Till We Have Faces 91
liberal arts 30, 74
Liberal Arts Tradition, The 173

Lincoln, Abraham
  "The Gettysburg Address" 77, 243
listening 71, 77, 82, 183, 190, 201, 210
literacy 48, 54, 55, 112, 125
literature
  children's 23, 58
  fairy tales 53, 54, 176
  short stories 23, 58, 92
litotes. *See* rhetorical devices: litotes
logos. *See* modes of persuasion: *logos*
"Lost Tools of Learning, The" 48
Lost Tools of Writing, The 101

M

Mandala Fellowship 116, 213
master teacher 29
math **127–143**
  algebra 13, 31, 131–132, 136, 140, 141, 142, 212, 221
  arithmetic 12, 130, 142
  higher 142–143
  practical application 130–136
Mathematician's Apology, A 127
Mathematics: Is God Silent? 137, 246
memoria. *See* memory
memory **46**. *See also* canons of rhetoric, five
  in American government 150–151
  in economics 153–154
  in fine arts 194, 197, 205
    music 200, 202
  in government and economics 158
  in history 167–168, 171
  in Latin and foreign languages 183–184, 188
  in math 135, 140–141, 143
  in reading 62, 64–65
    poetry 70–71
    universal questions 66
  in science 126
    practical application 121
    research paper 115
  in speech and debate 90
    forensic 87
    political 80–81
  in writing 108
    persuasive essay 104
    research paper 99–100
mentors 4, 5, 11, 28, 35, 89, 113, 118, 121, 174
metaphor. *See* rhetorical devices: metaphor
metonymy. *See* rhetorical devices: metonymy
Michelangelo 197
  David 40
middle school 33, 110, 174
military
  academies 26
Miller, Arthur
  The Crucible 155
Milton, John
  Paradise Lost 58, 98
missions
  serving in 27
mock trial 47, 136. *See also* speech and debate: mock trial
modes of persuasion 47–49
  ethos 47, **48–49**
    in history 160
    in science 99, 113
    in speech and debate 75, 86
    in writing 101, 102
  logos **47–48**
    in history 159–160
    in science 113
    in speech and debate 75, 86
    in writing 102

pathos 47–**48**
   in fine arts 193, 196
   in history 161
   in science 113
   in speech and debate 75, 86
   in writing 97, 102
music. *See* fine arts: music
myth of neutrality 160

N

Nickel, James
   Mathematics: Is God Silent? 137, 246
   Norms & Nobility 106, 148–149, 178, 244, 246

O

O'Brien, Michael
   Island of the World 219
Odyssey, The 247
Office of Assertion, The 43, 95, 96, 159, 242, 244
online course 22
onomatopoeia. *See* rhetorical devices: onomatopoeia
oratory
   ceremonial 88–90
   forensic 82–88
   political 75–82
Our Mother Tongue 24

P

Paradise Lost 58, 98
parallelism. *See* rhetorical devices: parallelism
parenting 9–32, 207–216, 217–223
Pasteur, Louis 91–93
pathos. *See* modes of persuasion: pathos

Patriot's History of the United States, A 160, 247
Pearcey, Nancy
   Saving Leonardo 41
peroratio 85
personification. *See* rhetorical devices: personification
persuasive essay 101–105
Phantom Tollbooth, The 191–195, 248
phonics 54
physics 2, 3, 22, 39, 111, 114, 116, 119, 122, 123, 127, 138, 185, 212, 221
Plato 128, 160
plot(s) 66
poetry 40, 45, 53, 67, 68–71
   alliteration in 70
   antithesis in 70
   asyndeton in 70
   canons of rhetoric 68–71
   forms of 199
   John Donne 68–71
   rhyme scheme 69
polysyndeton 235. *See also* rhetorical devices: polysyndeton
Postman, Neil
   The End of Education 207
pronuntiatio. *See* delivery
public speaking 35, 36, 47, 71, 74, 81, 85, 108
Pythagoras 128

Q

Question, The 33, 34, 43, 94, 129, 147, 148, 218, 241
Quintilian 41, 73, 85

R

Ray, Brian
  Home Educated and Now Adults 13, 26
  National Home Education Research Center 208
reading **53–72**
  character(s) 58–60
  conflict 60–61
relationship. *See* common topics, five
Renaissance 37, 40, 196, 197, 235
repetition
  as an aid to memory 46, 104, 167, 200, 205
  in alliteration 236
  in anaphora 237
  in assonance 237
  in classical education 203
  in consonance 238
  in elocution 80
  in epistrophe 238
  in invention 94
research paper 93–101, 112–117
rhetoric. **33–49** *See also* education: classical: rhetoric
Rhetoric. See Aristotle
rhetorical devices 45, 98–99, 166, 227. *See also* appendix 2
  alliteration 70, 98, 100, **236**
  allusion **236**
  anaphora 80, 235, **237**
  antithesis 70, **237**
  apostrophe **237**
  assonance **237**
  asyndeton 70, **237**
  chiasmus **237**
  consonance **238**
  epistrophe **238**
  hyperbole **238**
  imagery **238**
  litotes 235, **238**
  metaphor 45, 66, 98, 102, 105, 161, 191, 202, 235, **238**
  metonymy **239**
  onomatopoeia **239**
  parallelism 45, 235, **239**
  personification 235, **239**
  polysyndeton 235, **239**
  rhyme **240**
  simile 45, 98, 191, 202, **240**
  synedoche **240**
RhetoriGo (game) 227–229
Rhodes, Suzanne
  The Roar on the Other Side 106
rhyme. *See* rhetorical devices: rhyme
Roar on the Other Side, The 106

S

Sanford, Courtney
  "Going Deeper into *Out of the Silent Planet*" 55
  "What If the Art Teacher Taught Math?" 136–138
SAT 21, 23, 175, 209, 220
Saving Leonardo 41
Sayers, Dorothy
  "The Lost Tools of Learning" 48
Scarlet Letter, The 58–63, 243
schemes 166, **236**. *See also* appendix 2
Schemes and Tropes (game) 232–233
Schweikart, Larry
  A Patriot's History of the United States 160, 247
science **109–126**
  chemistry 111–112, 119
  practical application 117–122
  research paper 112–117
self-control 19, 27, 99, 222

INDEX

sentence structure 98, 142, 174, 239
Shakespeare, William 3, 13, 54, 67, 80, 112, 154, 176
  Hamlet 85, 155
  Much Ado About Nothing 157, 246
  The Tragedy of Julius Caesar 36–37, 89, 244
simile. *See* rhetorical devices: simile
Simmons, Tracy Lee
  Climbing Parnassus 55, 247
Simply Classical 31
skills
  versus subject content 21
socialization 12, 14, 242
social media 13, 97
Socratic Circles 241
Solomon (Bible) 40
sound bites 36
sources
  authority of 79, 99
  government, on home education 242
  Internet 94
  types of 113, 126
Spalding, Romalda Bishop
  The Writing Road to Reading 24, 243
special-needs students 18, 29, 29–31
speech and debate **73–90**
  Lincoln-Douglas debate 75
  mock trial 73, 75, 79, 81, 82–85, 87
  policy debate 71, 75
  types of oratory
    ceremonial 88–90
    forensic 82–88
    political 75–82
Speech Thief (game) 231–232
sports

  for homeschool families 12, 19, 208
  rugby 2, 3, 32
  Ultimate Frisbee 4
Sproul, R. C.
  The Consequences of Ideas 112, 161, 247
standardized testing 31, 210
statistics
  about homeschool families 242
  on homeschool performance 13, 208–209
STEM (science, technology, engineering, and math) 27, 74, 110, 124, 127
stick in the sand 124
Stowe, Harriet Beecher
  Uncle Tom's Cabin 48, 147, 246
Strickland, Carol
  The Annotated Mona Lisa 194
Strunk, William, and E. B. White
  The Elements of Style 98
style (elocution). *See* elocution (style)
Swenson, Richard A.
  Margin 123
  More Than Meets the Eye 123, 245
  The Overload Syndrome 123
Swope, Cheryl
  Simply Classical 31
syllogism(s) 60, 63
symmetry
  in nature 137
synedoche. *See* rhetorical devices: synedoche

T

technology 43, 94, 201
  Internet 94, 113, 192, 196
TeenPact 152

Ten Ways to Destroy the Imagination of Your Child 21, 241
testimony. *See* common topics, five
testing. *See also* SAT
  ACT 209
  Advanced Placement (AP) 210
  required 31
  SAT 209
  standardized 31, 210
textbooks 24, 124
theme(s)
  in reading 66
thesis 84, 89, 102, 114, 153
To Kill a Mockingbird 62
Tolkien, J. R. R.
  Bilbo Baggins (fictional character) 4, 101
  The Hobbit 101
topics. *See* common topics, five
topic wheel 55–57
Tragedy of Julius Caesar, The 36, 89, 244
transcripts 31–32
Transcripts Made Easy 241, 248
travel 3, 13, 16, 19, 21, 24, 56, 216, 234
Trivium
  arts 174
tropes 100, 166, **236**. *See also* appendix 2
truth, goodness, and beauty 4, 37, 105, 106, 146, 147, 185–186, 208, 213, 215

U

Uncle Tom's Cabin 48, 147, 246

understanding 3, 17, 24, 26, 29, 38, 39, 40, 42, 44, 49, 61, 63, 66, 69, 70, 94, 110, 111, 117, 121, 125, 128, 146, 149, 150, 152, 154, 155, 156, 157, 161, 162, 165, 166, 167, 170, 174, 176, 178, 181, 184, 201
unschooling 20
U.S. Constitution 39, 146, 148, 149, 169, 215
  17th Amendment 164–168

V

Veith, Gene Edward
  State of the Arts 248
virtue(s) 27, 28, 38, 55, 61, 62, 89, 102, 151, 168, 170, 171, 207, 208, 212, 213, 214
  per Aristotle 88
  per Bible 89
vocabulary 3, 21, 24, 26, 29, 34, 35, 39, 45, 98, 136, 174, 175, 178, 179, 180, 185, 187, 188, 190, 194, 201, 202

W

Washington, George 150
Weaver, Richard
  The Ethics of Rhetoric 106
Western civilization 173, 176–177
White, Martha C.
  Time, "The Real Reason New College Grads Can't Get Hired" 211
Wilson, Nancy
  Our Mother Tongue 24
Wilson, Thomas
  The Art of Rhetoric 37–38

wisdom 12, 14, 17, 28, 29, 38, 39, 40, 42, 49, 55, 57, 62, 67, 71, 89, 93, 94, 137, 151, 163, 168, 170, 171, 178, 192, 214
Words Aptly Spoken: American Documents 247
writing **91–108**
   academic 97
   determining audience 93
   outline(s) 95, 96
   persuasive essay 101–104
   research paper 93–101
Writing Road to Reading, The 24, 243

Y

young adult(s) 10, 14, 29
YouTube 30